Lily Dale

The Town That Talks to the Dead

CHRISTINE WICKER

HarperSanFrancisco
A Division of HarperCollins*Publishers*

HarperCollins books may be purchased for educational, business, or sales promotional use. For information please write: Special Markets Department, HarperCollins Publishers, 10 East 53rd Street, New York, NY 10022.

HarperCollins Web site: http://www.harpercollins.com

FIRST HARPERCOLLINS PAPERBACK EDITION PUBLISHED IN 2004

Designed by Kris Tobiassen

Library of Congress Cataloging-in-Publication Data is available.

ISBN-13: 978–0–06–115374–7
ISBN-10: 0–06–115374–5

07 08 09 10 RRD(H) 10 9 8 7 6 5 4 3 2

To Philip, my own blithe spirit

Lily Dale: How It Began

Lily Dale is sixty miles south of Buffalo, tucked off the side road of a side road to Interstate 90. It's easy to miss. Little Victorian houses sitting at the edge of a lake. A settlement of a few hundred people clinging to a religion that once had millions of believers and now has only a remnant. American flags flapping from screened porches. Fountains splashing in shady little pocket parks. Big-bellied cats strolling across streets as though they own them. So many cats sun themselves about town that squirrels are said to be fearful of touching ground.

Women set the tone in this lakeside community where houses are painted in pastels. During the height of the summer season, when twenty thousand visitors come to consult the town's mediums, it resembles nothing so much as a sorority sleepover for aging sisters. They laze about in the hotel parlor and fan themselves in white rockers that line the veranda. They sweep down the streets in flowing dresses. Tinsel stars and crystals hang in windows. Christmas lights twinkle from porches all year long. Stone angels stand sentry on walkways, and plaster elves march across lawns.

I was a religion reporter for the *Dallas Morning News* when I first drove a rental car past the filigree sign that proclaims Lily Dale to be the world's largest community of Spiritualists. The entrance shack where attendants take seven dollars from visitors during what the community calls camp season is white with bright blue trim and the walls and roof seem slightly out of plumb. Many things in Lily Dale are not quite square. For more than a hundred years, people of the Dale have believed they can talk with the dead. They think anybody can. Call them demented, sneer at their gullibility, suspect them of trickery—catch them in it even, lots of people have—but they won't give up what they believe.

I first read about Lily Dale in the *New York Times* in a little story that told everything except what I wanted to know. The reporter mentioned Lily Dale's 1879 founding, which makes it the oldest Spiritualist community in America and probably the world. He described the community's beginning as a summer camp for well-to-do freethinkers and Spiritualists, and he related stories its residents had told him. His skepticism was not quite hidden between carefully noncommittal lines, and that is a fine way for a reporter to behave in the face of such absurdity as Lily Dale presents—the only way really. He wrote like a good fact-based reporter living in a scientific age in which provable facts are the only allowable reality. He had no reason to write anything more and all the reason in the world not to. But I wanted more. I wanted to know why this strange little outpost clings to such absurd ideas. I wanted to know who these people are and what makes them tick.

When they remember that *New York Times* reporter in Lily Dale, they mention how much the community's tatty look dismayed him and what he said to Hilda Wilkinson after she fed him tea and lunch. According to the story, he told Hilda, who first came to the Dale seventy-five years ago, he didn't believe a thing he'd heard. He said he didn't know how anyone could believe such nonsense. And Hilda said, "Well, young man, you just hold on to your beliefs." She paused.

"You just hold on, young man. Until you wake up."

I put the story in a file where it sat for a year. In June, when Dallas temperatures were climbing toward 100 and every reporter in Texas was looking for a story in a cool climate, I showed it to my editors. Within two weeks, I was on a flight to Buffalo.

Covering the God beat, I've met lots of people who believe strange things. I've talked with a voodoo priestess in Cuba who communed with the Virgin Mary. I've interviewed a man walking across America pulling a big wooden cross because Jesus told him to. I've spent all night in Garland, Texas, with a Taiwanese cult waiting for God to come on television and announce the end of the world. They lived in Garland because their leader thought "Garland" was "God-land."

Weird never puts me off. I like it, and usually I understand it. In Lily Dale, some people were nervous about talking to me, but I told them straight out that I had not come to ridicule.

"You're afraid I'm going to write something that will make you seem crazy. Don't worry about that," I told them. "Everybody thinks you're nuts already. So there's no story there."

With regard to talking dead people, I considered myself ambivalent. Compared to most people in Lily Dale, I was a raging skeptic. Compared to most of my colleagues, I was a soft-headed sap. I didn't believe Lily Dale's people could chat with the dead, but I was willing to concede that I didn't know much about cosmic workings. I might be wrong.

And more to the point for a reporter, the Spiritualists were making the biggest brag in modern-day religion. Desperate for civic respectability in the face of science, most religions have pushed far away from the miracles on which they were founded. Not Spiritualism. Believers in this faith hold tight to their miracles, which they don't even think of as miracles actually, but as ordinary, accessible experience. I admired their pluck.

My first night was spent in a room above the old Assembly Hall. The ground floor is a dusty, wood-planked meeting room lined with grim-faced portraits of important Spiritualists from the 1800s and early 1900s. A private bedroom upstairs, with a shared bath, cost twenty-five dollars. Because it was the opening week of Lily Dale's summer season, every other available room was rented.

Lily Dale clings to its founding tradition as a summer camp by opening its hotels and restaurants each July and August for the summer season. The community's population swells to 450 as summer residents, many of them registered mediums, return to Lily Dale. Tourists come to consult the mediums and to attend workshops on topics such as heart healing and understanding out-of-body experiences.

When Lily Dale's unofficial town manager, Sue Glasier, showed me upstairs, I asked what made her a believer. She told me that years ago a medium said her father was coming through. The woman described him as a man with a terrible weight on his chest.

"My father died when a car he was working under fell on him," said Sue.

I couldn't sleep that first night. My legs were restless, and then my arms wanted to move. It was hot. Lily Dale has no air conditioning, and the little window in my room was catching no breeze. I twisted about under the thin sheet. At three in the morning I gave up on sleep and went to the terrace that looks over Cleveland Avenue. This is the community's main road, but, like all the streets in Lily Dale, it was built for horses and buggies, and it looked as though it hadn't been resurfaced since the horses left.

I could see the old Maplewood Hotel, where a sign in the lobby requests, NO READINGS, HEALINGS, CIRCLES, OR SÉANCES IN THIS AREA, PLEASE. Its high-ceilinged parlor is decorated with portraits that the Spiritualists swear were painted by spirits and with a tapestry sewn by a woman who was in a trance and didn't eat for nine years, according to a plaque near her work. Behind the Assembly Hall, cottages crouch close to the streets, their yards crowded with snowball bushes and hostas. Elms, maples, and firs wave overhead. I was in a place lost to time, buried in drifts of flowers. A faint breeze stirred my nightgown. A dog barked, a tree creaked. Otherwise, there was no sound. Lily Dale is a long way from anywhere, a bad place to be wakeful.

Maybe I could sleep if I stayed outside. I wrestled the limp mattress off the bed and dragged it to the porch. Within a few minutes I began to worry about being caught in my nightgown by the other guests. So again I fumbled into the hot, dark rooms, put on jeans and a shirt, returned to the mattress, and fell asleep. Within an hour, thunder woke me. Plops of rain splattered around me like June bugs falling from the sky. I groaned, got up, squeezed the mattress together so it would fit through the doorway, and walked it down the hall.

Many people can't sleep when they first come to Lily Dale. "It's the energy," I heard again and again. People say they can feel Lily Dale's power when they enter the gates. It calms some people and revs others up. One resident told me that her first summer in town she ran outside every morning to walk barefoot in the grass. "I needed to feel grounded," she said. Several Lily Dale houses are said to contain energy vortexes, and a spot in the woods is supposed to be so charged that the hair on your arms will stand up. Some people say fairies live in the woods. Others say brooding spirits called elementals live among the trees deep in the forest and take over after nightfall. Many people told me that the land Lily Dale sits on was once sacred to Native American tribes.

As dawn came, I lay in my bed, sore-eyed and dry-mouthed. The score was clearly 0–1, Lily Dale leading. Now that I know Lily Dale so much better, I wonder if I ever caught up. Maybe Lily Dale has always been ahead.

What would later be called Spiritualism started in 1848 when a Hydesville, New York, farm family heard knocks they thought were coming from the cellar of their house. According to the story, the knocks continued for months. One night the youngest daughter, nine-year-old Kate Fox, called out, "Here, Mr. Split-foot, do as I do." Split-foot was a jocular name for the devil.

She rubbed her finger against her thumb as though snapping her fingers but without any sound. One rap sounded for each motion of her fingers. "Only look, Mother," she exclaimed. "It can see as well as hear."

The family began asking questions and soon set up a system of taps for yes and no. They invited neighbors in, and the knocks continued. The answers to their questions eventually convinced them that the rapper was the spirit of a peddler and, further, that he had been murdered and buried in the cellar. It made a grand ghost story, although no one had ever been convicted of such a crime.

Kate and her sister Margaret began appearing before large audiences. Author James Fenimore Cooper, poet William Cullen Bryant, and New York newspaper publisher Horace Greeley were among those who attended their presentations. The Fox sisters were tested by many critics. They were bound, raised off the ground, and even strip-searched. No one ever found any devices.

Years later, Margaret confessed that the sisters made the noises themselves by clicking their knee and toe joints. She demonstrated her ability before a large audience. Kate confirmed her sister's account. The sisters meant only to trick their mother, who was easily frightened, but the joke got out of hand, they said. Before they died, both recanted their confessions.

By the early part of the twentieth century, so many mediums had been exposed as frauds that many of Spiritualism's faithful were wavering. Spiritualism might have died out then, but along came World War I and the flu of 1918. Millions died, and grieving family members turned to the mediums once again seeking otherworldly comfort. Along the way, the basement of the house in Hydesville was dug up. Human bones were found behind a wall, according to Spiritualist history. The Lily Dale museum has a peddler's box believed to have belonged to the murdered man. The Fox cottage itself was moved to Lily Dale in 1916, an acquisition that added to the town's mystique. It burned in 1955.

The area of New York State where Spiritualism started was a region known during the 1800s for mighty works of spirit. It came to be called the "burned-over district" because the "fires" of Christian revivals swept through again and again. In 1823 a New York farmboy named Joseph Smith said he received a set of golden plates from the angel Moroni. The translation of those plates became the Book of Mormon. In the 1830s a New York farmer and Baptist preacher named William Miller began telling rural New Yorkers that the world was going to end. As many as one million people attended his camp meetings, and by October 22, 1844, supposedly the last day, almost one hundred thousand people had sold their belongings and were awaiting judgment. The Shakers, who believed as Spiritualists did that spirits visit humans, established their Holy Sanctuary of the New World in New York. Quakers also had congregations in the area, and some of them were among Spiritualism's earliest and staunchest converts.

It's hard to know how many people were practicing Spiritualism at the religion's height because these believers have always resisted formal memberships and organization. Mediumship was so popular a profession by the 1850s that Ralph Waldo Emerson listed it in his journal as a new occupation, along with railroad man and landscape gardener. Estimates of the number of Spiritualists by journalists and historians in the decades around the turn of the century varied wildly. Some said the number of people rocking tables and summoning ghosts was only a few hundred thousand, while others estimated that 11 million folks communed with the spirits.

In the United States, the faith is now confined to about four hundred mostly tiny churches around the country, but inside those churches, and in Lily Dale, the spirits still speak as forcefully as ever. People of the Dale believe they have "proof" that the soul lives on. "There is no death and there are no dead," they like to say. If they're right, it's the biggest news since Jesus brought Lazarus back from the dead.

But how to prove it? Religion reporters learn pretty quickly that the usual reportorial methods don't yield the most important stories. We might expose a little grab and tickle under the choir robes, some tricky accounting with the church funds, but investigating the questions at the heart of religion, the ones that change people's lives, keep them on their knees, or give them a reason to get up, are mostly off-limits because nobody can interview the Source. Sister Jones heard God's voice. Preacher Smith knows God's will. Brother Hernando saw the Blessed Virgin's face in a tortilla. They can't prove it happened, but you can't prove it didn't. It's all hearsay and perception and a matter of faith.

Long before I read the books of William James, who was among America's greatest psychologists and philosophers, I agreed with his idea that religious accounts are worth listening to, no matter how farfetched they seem, and that a good way to judge a religion's validity is by the effect it has on people's lives. My first question is, do they really believe it? The second question is, how does it affect their lives? That's the story.

Sometimes there's a third question hovering behind the others. This one is just for me, not for the newspaper. I want to know how such belief would change me.

This curiosity is almost certainly a holdover from childhood. I was born again at nine, which was the right age for Southern Baptist children of my generation. I went down the aisle of the church as the congregation crooned choruses of "I Surrender All," answered yes when asked whether I would accept Jesus as my personal savior, and put my childish scrawl, smudged because I was left-handed, on the bottom of a pledge that I would never drink alcoholic beverages. The result was a feeling of elation and goodness that lasted for weeks and a feeling of having set myself apart from the unsaved that lasted about ten years. I rededicated my life at almost every revival and gave a Bible to my uncle inscribed with the hope that God would save his soul as God had saved mine.

I was educated out of faith. College so amazed me that I swallowed almost everything my professors said, and all of them seemed to be saying that the personal savior has no place in the life of smart people. Since then I have indulged in many alcoholic beverages and done other un-Baptist things with little remorse. Even so, those Big God ideas, the childlike longings that some people put away with their dolls or toy trucks, still live muffled within me. As a result, I often find myself uncommonly open to religious people's beliefs, no matter how bizarre their practices may seem.

I first noticed it on a Hare Krishna story. I goaded a devotee by saying, "You put out food for statues. You dance around in dresses. And you think people are going to be affected by what you say?"

He looked across the table and didn't say anything for a minute. Then he said, "I think I'll have an effect on you."

I grinned and shrugged. I thought not.

But he was right. He enchanted me somehow with the idea that odd-looking folks making a nuisance and a spectacle of themselves are calling God down, bringing him among us. The devotee said they chant and dance because God's presence blesses everyone, even the scoffers, who may need it most. The idea that ritual could lasso God and pull him down like some big soft cloud was an idea that the stripped-down literalism of my youth had not included. But it did change me, a little.

The stakes are high in religion, and nowhere are they higher than in Lily Dale. If the mediums are getting some special knowledge of other people's lives, whether they are getting it from spirits or God or the collective consciousness, if they are getting otherworldly information, life isn't what most of us think it is. If they are telling the truth, there might be a purpose, a plan, a future beyond the slow slouch toward death that life seems. If Lily Dale stands on something real, I wanted to know about it. Who wouldn't?

What began as a quick story turned into something bigger. I would spend three years of my life plumbing the mysteries of Lily Dale. I never intended for any of it to change me. But it did.

Note to the Reader: A Partial Cast of Characters can be found on page 275.

1

Lynn Mahaffey rides up and down the hills of Lily Dale on a rusty black Schwinn with a wire basket strapped to the back wheel by a plastic rope. She often wears light blue. It matches her eyes, faded to a soft sapphire now that she's close to eighty, but beautiful still. She rides her bike slowly, past tourists in shorts and sandals, past gingerbread cottages that advertise the services of mediums, past the mediums themselves as they hustle with skirts flying toward Forest Temple.

She bikes five miles every day, for her heart and for the world. She prays as she rides. She holds the earth in her mind, the whole globe, lapis and emerald spinning through space. She prays for everything on it, rich and poor, good and evil, human and otherwise. Upon it all she calls down blessing.

Lynn was in her early twenties in the 1940s when she first visited Lily Dale. Responding to an urge she couldn't explain, she took off her shoes before getting out of the car. "I knew I was on holy ground," she said.

Every day she pedals around the cafeteria with its big screened porch and stained cement floor. She skirts muddy puddles in the community's pitted roads. She passes Leolyn Woods, an old-growth forest bisected by a gravel path. The woods' path goes by the pet cemetery and leads to Lily Dale's holiest spot, Inspiration Stump, where the mediums gather to call up departed loved ones. Turn over any rock in Leolyn Woods and you're likely to find some Spiritualist's ashes moldering. The people of Lily Dale so often ask to be scattered in the woods that there's a name for the practice. "Walking them out" it's called.

Lynn's tires would bog down in the path's gravel, so she turns on the road and passes the wide field where Margaret Mary and Bob Hefner stand every month, counting Hail Marys on their rosaries and scanning the sky for the Virgin Mother, who has repeatedly assured Margaret Mary that she will appear. Lynn passes the Lily Dale Spiritualist Church, the little white church where people gather summer mornings hoping to be healed, and Assembly Hall, a two-story meetinghouse where students practice bending spoons and making tables rise. She coasts around men who carry passports to Orion in their wallets and women who give lessons in how to tell an angel from a human being. She wheels around widows hoping to talk with their late husbands, skirts lovestruck girls anxious to find out if their boyfriends are cheating, steers clear of divorcees yearning to know whether passion will ever visit them again.

If you came to Lily Dale a thousand times and passed Lynn on the street every day, you might never notice her. She's short and wears big glasses that sometimes slip down so that she has to take one hand off the handlebar and push them up by stabbing her forefinger into the nosepiece. A grandmother with fluffy gray hair, she is shy, humble, slightly hard of hearing, and soft-spoken. She has no standing in the world, no title, no lofty degrees, no certification.

In the years I visited this 123-year-old village to study the quick and the dead, I came to think of Lynn as a living version of the spirits said to be flitting about, whispering secrets in the mediums' ears, appearing in dreams, rising up in hazy wavering visions, applauding, encouraging, running things in a way that helps human happiness. If you don't have eyes to see, you'd never spot her. If you don't have ears to hear, you'd never listen. It takes some faith to heed an old woman who arrives each summer high in the passenger seat of a big RV, her husband, John, gripping the wheel, her bicycle strapped to the back of the car they're pulling. Just as it takes some faith to believe in spirits even if you see and hear them yourself.

It was Lynn who finally showed me that Lily Dale can be completely silly, banal, and simpleminded, but that nevertheless the people there are engaged in something vital and true. That understanding didn't come, however, until more than a year after I met her. Eventually her words would free me; in between, just about every piece of spiritual wisdom she gave shocked and dismayed me.

The woman who helped her change me was her friend and protégé, Shelley Takei. Shelley, who spends summers in a big lavender house on the hill near the entrance to Lily Dale, draws women like the Pied Piper draws children. And, like the Piper, she leads them right over the cliffs, out of what she likes to call consensus reality into free fall, a blissful new reality where all things feminine are all right. Shelley told me everything I needed to know about Lily Dale the first day I met her. She laid it out, but the more she talked the more she confused me. Like a Zen riddle, she is simple to describe but hard to understand.

Most people who visit Lily Dale probably go away unchanged. They find what they expect. Many are already dancing on the cosmic fringe, and Lily Dale affirms them. Skeptics, who like to call the place Silly Dale or Spooksville, also generally find Lily Dale to be the nonsense they expect it to be. But the majority of Lily Dale visitors are neither converts nor scoffers. They believe a little and doubt a little and don't make a religion of it. They come to play in Lily Dale, to flirt with mysteries, to entertain intriguing notions that can be pulled out at will and put away without regret. For them, Lily Dale is fun, pure and simple.

None of these visitors interested me much. I wanted to meet people with focused hopes, seekers who needed what the Dale offers and were changed by what they received. I wanted to talk to people who needed Lily Dale's promises so desperately that anyone who encountered them would ache at hearing of their pain and want to strike out at Lily Dale if it deceived them.

I found what I was looking for in a bereaved mother named Pat Naulty and a widow named Carol Lucas. Carol was in fresh grief, still dazed, as though her husband's death had been a cudgel blow to her head. She was apt to weep at anything. More than anything in life, Carol wanted her husband back.

Pat Naulty came to Lily Dale expecting nothing. The worst of her grief was long over. Her guilt was another matter. She had endured that and expected that she always would. Guilt had so numbed parts of her psyche that she didn't even long for succor.

I almost missed my third story. The day I first met her, Marian Boswell was a too-skinny little brunette talking compulsively about her troubles. I backed away as fast as I could, but I wasn't fast enough. Before I got free of her, she told me a story of Lily Dale power that I couldn't forget. So I contacted her again and listened some more. Hers was a tale of unearthly doings, of prophesized disaster, and of the indomitable human ability to find meaning and hope in the oddest ways.

2

"Just pop my brain out, put it in a computer, and I'd be perfectly happy," Dr. Pat Naulty said. "I'm all intellect." When people described the community college English professor as spiritual, she invariably thought, *What a crock.*

Pat came to Lily Dale for a rest. Her friend Shelley Takei invited her during the short break the professor allowed herself each summer. Pat, who was from Virginia Beach, knew only a little about the Dale. She imagined it as a sort of refuge for psychics, like the towns where circus people go for the winter, a sanctuary for misfits.

She wasn't thinking of her son John as she spotted the little road sign that sits on Highway 60 with the words LILY DALE and an arrow pointing west. She was thinking that after a hundred miles of state highways, too much coffee, and no restrooms, she needed a pit stop pretty bad.

Pat once thought about nothing but John. Fifteen years had passed, however, and even the worst grief has to shift its grip sometime. Pat had left her two sons and their dad to go to college. Some people said she abandoned them, but that wasn't true. Most people didn't understand. Pat would have died if she'd stayed in Indiana. She thought so then, and she thinks so now.

John, who was ten when she left, cried, begged her not to get divorced, promised he would be good if she stayed. When he was twelve, he told her he was going to live as though she didn't exist. "If you send me letters, I won't open them. If you send me presents, I will return them," he said. And for a year he did just that.

She kept writing and sending presents, and they all came back. When she called, he wouldn't come to the phone. But, one day, he opened a notebook of poems she had written to him when he was small, and they broke through. He remembered that she loved him.

As the years went by, it was John, and sometimes only John, who cheered her on. He was the same bighearted little boy who had always saved a piece of his candy to share with her. Their phone conversations never went long before he stopped talking about himself and said, "Now, tell me how you are."

She knew John was troubled during the fall of his sixteenth year. There'd been minor run-ins with the police, nothing serious, just silly kid tricks. She could hear the blue mood in his voice, but he agreed that she couldn't come see him until exams were over. He told her not to. She began writing him a letter, but she was so busy. It lay on the desk for days waiting for her to finish.

On the day John and two friends gathered in Vincennes, Indiana, with a gun, one bullet, and the idea that a game of Russian roulette might be fun, Pat was sleeping two thousand miles away. John's friends each took a turn, and twice the gun hammer clicked on empty. As John lifted the handgun to his temple his mother began to dream. She was at a party, and she had lost something important. An ache grew within her as she searched more and more frantically. What was it? Where was it?

She awoke. Her mouth was dry. Her tongue was thick and rasped against her palette. Her lips were pulled back over her teeth and so parched that they stuck there. For a moment she lay limp, not yet free of the dream's longing and sorrow. Then she pushed herself out of bed and went to the bathroom to splash water on her face and into her mouth. As she looked into the mirror, she tried to remember. What had she lost?

When the phone rang, Pat knew the voice. Years of love had taught her to hear so much in her ex-husband's hello that she could jump across that single word into all that might be coming. Years of anger and fear had sharpened that ability. He identified himself anyway.

And Pat said, "John's dead, isn't he?"

She heard what her voice said. Her mind didn't yet know it. Only her body understood. It was as if someone had taken a sledgehammer, aimed it at her breastbone, and let fly. Air gushed from her nose and mouth as her chest crushed into her body. Five years would pass before she could touch the bones near her heart without wincing at the pain.

As Pat passed the awnings of Lazaroni's restaurant and rounded the curve of Dale Drive as it skirts the edge of Cassadaga Lake, she forgot her need of a toilet. A powerful feeling of homecoming, so intense it was almost delirious, swept over her. This was something she had never felt.

"It was as though I was returning to a place I'd left a long time ago. I felt such delight. I laughed aloud," she said.

Scientists would say that Pat's feeling was a glitch in memory caused by the way the brain stores experience. At some time in her life she had been to a similar place, and now her brain was confused. It had lost the specifics of that particular memory and stored only the general feeling and look of the place. She mistook this faulty connection for homecoming and happiness. If Pat had only known more science, she would have reasoned that delight away. She never would have felt all woozy with wonder as she passed through the gates that separate Lily Dale from the world.

3

Sinclair Lewis was shocked by the poor deluded and bereaved souls he met in Lily Dale when he visited in 1917.

"No one could be flippant over the great tears, the broken voices, with which the old people greet the 'message,'" he wrote, characterizing the Dale's visitors as people who lived in the past. "No few of them are absolutely alone—parents, husband or wife, brothers, sisters, uncles, even children gone."

In one séance, as squeaky spirit voices spoke from within a curtained-off area known as the spirit cabinet, a woman sobbed and called to her dead husband, "Oh, my dear, my dear, it's so wonderful. Oh, my dear, I am so lonely for you. Is Charley with you? Oh, my dear!" Another woman moaned hysterically and finally fainted.

Lewis left the room with relief, writing that the cheerful music of the Saturday evening dance was decidedly "preferable to the spirit fog we had been swathed in."

Most of the spirit fog has now been banished from Lily Dale. Today's mediums practice in well-lighted parlors and do not use crystal balls, spirit cabinets, or Ouija boards. Trances are out of favor. Mediums speak in their own normal voices and rarely even shut their eyes. Spirits don't generally appear to the physical eye or make noises that the physical ear can hear. These days few people expect them to. People usually come to Lily Dale to talk about manifestations that only the mediums perceive.

What hasn't changed is Lily Dale's attraction for the bereaved. Sometimes their grief is so fresh it oozes. Sometimes it's ancient, calcified about them, a carapace that has grown between them and other living things. Some want a door that will let them into the past. Others want release. They all want a sign, a vision, a word that will give them surcease from the terrible gone of death. They seek forgiveness for wrongs they don't dare name. They have one last message that they must deliver.

And always the question is, are the Spiritualists good people helping or cold-hearted deceivers gulling the weak? It is here that Spiritualism's critics catch fire, sickened by what they see. Perhaps the saddest of the bereaved are parents who've recently lost a child. They huddle into one another, their heads tucked like wet sparrows, or they sit planted on the seats, separate, hardly looking at each other, their eyes wide, their feet flat on the ground, their faces as stiff as statues in a wax museum.

One blond woman came to Lily Dale hoping desperately for contact with her dead son. At an outdoor message service, where crowds gather hoping for a few free words from spirit, the medium picked her right away. "Do you have a son in spirit?" she asked.

The mother nodded.

"He's here," said the medium. "He wants you to know that. Are you into computers?"

The mother shook her head slowly.

"You're not. Well, you will be. I see you working with computers and being very successful."

The mother's face was wooden. She shook her head again.

"Yes. That's what the spirits are telling me," the medium said. "That's what they say."

The woman went to medium Lauren Thibodeau after the outdoor service and was near tears as she told Lauren what happened.

"She was right about my son," she said. "So she did know that, but if he was there, why didn't she give me a message? Why did she keep talking about computers? I hate computers. I don't work with them. I'm not going to work with them. All I wanted was a message from my son."

"Sometimes mediums get mixed up," Lauren said. "Sometimes they have an off day.

"Your son is here now, and he does have things to tell you," she said. The boy's spirit had come in with his mother, Lauren told me later. "Parents who have children in spirit almost always bring them," she said.

Carol Lucas was a widow of three months. Unlike those pitiable souls who so upset Lewis, she was not alone. A childhood friend had come with her for her visit to Lily Dale, and they stayed at the house of Carol's former philosophy professor, Frank Takei, Shelley's husband. Carol was not poor, she was not old, and no one would ever have said she could be easily deluded. She was a hardheaded, practical woman. Too perfectionist, she admitted, but responsible, dependable. Students in her high school English classes nicknamed her Mother Lucas after she wagged her finger at one of them during class and said, "You can't fool Mother Lucas."

At fifty-nine, she wore well-pressed, carefully chosen clothes. When she stood, her posture was invariably erect, and she did not shy away from using the fine vocabulary and precise expression that are an English teacher's natural way. Carol was the kind of person who white-knuckles every plane flight, certain that if she were at the controls, everyone would be safer. Never mind that she knew nothing about flying. She knew nothing about leukemia either.

When her husband, Noel, was diagnosed with chronic lymphocytic leukemia, she cried. Then she started looking for a cure. She spent hours on the Internet, whole days at the computer, working late into the night. Sometimes even that wouldn't be enough. She would awaken at 3:00 or 4:00 A.M. and go back, chasing one more link that might save her husband.

She bound stacks of printouts into three-ring notebooks. When she decided that Johns Hopkins was the best hospital for treatment, she and Noel left South Carolina, where they had retired to their dream house on a golf course, and went to Baltimore. Carol had done such a good research job that Johns Hopkins sponsored a workshop she helped put together for patients with chronic lymphocytic leukemia and their families. She and Noel were in Baltimore for the workshop when Noel's heart arrested. The doctors revived him, but his lungs filled with blood.

For the last six hours of Noel's life, Carol and their younger daughter sat by his side. The breathing tube in his throat didn't allow him to speak, and he didn't appear to be conscious, but Carol talked and talked. She told stories of good times she and Noel had shared since their first date when he was seventeen and she was fifteen and they were both just learning what love was about.

"I lost my best friend, the person who had been the center of my existence for forty-four years," she said.

In a sense, Carol's trip to Lily Dale was a bid to get a little leverage back. She had done everything she could to save him, but she had failed. Now, if the universe could be jiggled, the veil torn, the wall between this life and the next cracked, Carol was going to do it.

"I only see three choices," she said. "I can wither. I can become a recluse. Or I can use this for growth." Lily Dale was the path to growth.

On Friday night, the first evening of Carol's visit, she was sitting with Frank and Shelley on the long, screened back porch of the Takeis' house. They'd just been to a little outdoor amphitheater called Forest Temple for an outdoor message service. Each day during camp season the Dale hosts three outdoor services—one at Forest Temple and two at Inspiration Stump, a squat concrete pillar that is said to encase a tree stump. Mediums once stood on the Stump during message services. That ended when one of them had a heart attack in midproclamation. Lily Dale leaders decided that Stump energy might be a bit too strong.

Spiritualist religious practice includes giving messages from the dearly departed, which is called "serving spirit." These services contain no offering and no sermon, only spirit messages. They begin with a prayer asking that only the "highest and best" spirits be present. Mediums, who often say they must turn off the spirit voices or go crazy from all the chatter in their heads, want to make sure that not just any errant spirit comes beaming in when they open the channel.

Typically mediums stand before the group, scanning the crowd. Then they pick someone and ask permission to give a message.

Most often they ask, "May I come to you?" Some mediums prefer more flamboyant phraseology: "May I step into your vibrations?" or "May I touch in with you, my friend?"

That opening query is one of the few questions mediums in the Dale's public services are supposed to ask because the community wants to guard against what critics call "cold reading"—basing messages on bits of information mediums have cleverly elicited from their clients.

During my first summer in the Dale many spirits named John had died of something in the chest area. Many grandmotherly vibrations brought roses, peace, and love. Many female tourists heard the spirits say they were doing too much for others and not enough for themselves. Many men heard that they were misunderstood.

Could I have guessed that? I'd ask myself after a message. Often the answer was yes.

Mediums who are really "on" give their messages as fast as they can talk. Their words come out in a rush of images, advice, and predictions. It's as if they can't keep up with all that's coming through. Student mediums sit in the audience watching and sometimes get up to give their own messages. It's easy to see who knows the drill and who doesn't by how well they use the jargon.

"Let me say I want to bring you a female vibration," mediums are apt to say. When tourists shake their heads or deny that the messages make any sense, the mediums say, "Take it with you. It will mean something later."

Some mediums hear spirit voices, and some see visions or get feelings that they translate into messages. They sometimes spot spirits hovering over the crowd or standing behind their relatives. Some mediums describe spirit figures as looking like a piece of film projected onto a wall, slightly out of focus and wavery. Others say the figures look perfectly solid. Some see them as translucent images. Some say they appear to be behind wax paper. They may appear as shadowy figures flitting about at the outer edges of vision. They may signal their arrival with sparks of light glimpsed out of the corner of the eye.

At public services, "people with pushy relatives get the most messages," says medium Gretchen Clark Lazarony.

My dead relatives must be a genteel lot because I didn't get many messages. A medium at the Stump did once bring through a spirit in my family who hated wearing her false teeth. Lots of old people may hate wearing their dentures, but I never heard another medium give that message. The fact was I did have an elderly relative whose teeth hurt her mouth so much that she wore them only when she had to. She would put them on for company or a meal and then pull them out and forget where she left them. Every time we went somewhere the shout went up, "Find the teeth." We'd shake out pillows and flip bedcovers, check cups left on the counters, run our hands behind the sofa cushions. Finding those teeth was an event in our family. If that was a guess, it was a good one.

Sometimes the mediums laugh at private jokes when listening to spirit or say something into the air such as, "All right. All right. I'll tell them." When they describe someone's death, they often touch their chest or stomach, whichever part of themselves would be affected by the fatal illness that took the spirit, and grimace as though they are feeling pain. Maybe it is real, maybe it isn't, but it is good theater.

The crowd loves mediums who are loud and funny and fast. If they aren't, the tourists yawn and blink and look up at the trees. The medium Patricia Price calls these performances "doing standup" and says mediums have to be "comediums" to win the crowd. It doesn't matter a bit that poor old dead Mom has dropped in with her first words in fifty years. If she doesn't have anything snappy to say, she might as well float on off because nobody is interested in hearing her dither around.

The evening Carol Lucas attended her first service, Martie Hughes was one of the mediums. Martie, formerly in advertising, lives in Buffalo. She has creamy skin, dark blue eyes, and silvery hair that she wears short with soft bangs falling over her forehead. Her voice is gentle enough to lull a baby to sleep.

Like many mediums, Martie is middle-aged, unmarried, and of somewhat larger size than other people—physically and in personality. The tendency to bulk up often goes with mediumistic talent, I was told. That propensity is so evident in Lily Dale that one visitor threatened to sneak about town some night, go to every house with a sign that reads MEDIUM, and change it to LARGE. One sensitive told me she gained fifty pounds when she gave in to her gifts.

Some explain the weight gain by saying mediums need extra padding to protect their overly sensitive psyches. Medium Patricia Bell pooh-poohs that idea. Since they use their spleen to transmit messages, the sugar in their blood is depleted and they crave sweets, she says. Nonsense, says another local authority. It's because they get so caught up in spiritual worlds that they don't tend to mundane matters such as exercise and controlled eating.

I like to think that spirit connections give the mediums license to take up space. Maybe their bodies expand with their consciousness. Or maybe they need all the heft they can gather to stay grounded.

Alcoholism is also a common affliction among mediums, a fact that Patricia cites as backup for her sugar deprivation theory. John Slater, known as the dean of American Spiritualists in the 1920s, often disappeared for multiple-day binges with his secretary, forcing Lily Dale authorities to pacify his fans with concocted stories of illness and emergency.

"His liking for liquor was common talk about the camp, though in whispers," according to George Lawton, a psychology student who visited the Dale in the 1920s. "What is interesting is that I have never seen Mr. Slater so chastened and purified, in a spiritual sense," as he was when he returned.

Patricia Bell, who lives in the big pink and yellow house on Cleveland Avenue and does not drink alcohol, once found herself waking up with a strong taste of gin in her mouth. Puzzled, she mentioned the odd occurrence to another medium, who answered, "Oh, that was Billy Turner's drink of choice. He must still be around."

Billy Turner, who died about twenty years ago, started as a wildly popular child medium. Billy's mother wanted him to become a lawyer and to marry, but Billy was gay, and he also had the gift. So he stayed in medium work, but the work never made him happy and he drank. When Billy went on a bender, he didn't hide out, as Slater had. He liked singing to the tourists as they sat over coffee and cake in the cafeteria. "Yes, Jesus loves you. Yes, Jesus loves you," he would warble sweetly and then break off abruptly to tell the crowd, "That's a lie."

Skeptics often say mediums get their messages by picking up nonverbal cues and unconscious hints. I don't think so. Many mediums are so sweetly vague that I have wondered how they find their way home. Some of the Dale's best sensitives are awkward in one-on-one conversations. Trying to talk with them can be like George Burns talking to Gracie Allen. You're always the straight man faced with a wacky kind of wisdom you can never quite grasp. If it is your turn to speak—and it usually isn't—the medium's eyes start to waver and a distracted look comes over her face. Mediums treat conversational cues like gnats, ignoring them or swatting them away. If you have something to say, talk fast, because whatever the medium is paying attention to, it isn't you. Otherworldly input is many mediums' best hope.

Martie is fairly tuned in to the world around her. She makes eye contact, seems to hear living voices even when they aren't talking about her, and responds in a fairly earthbound way. Occasionally, she will get a preoccupied look and make a pronouncement that's a little more personal or a bit more philosophical than anything we "insensitives" are saying. She reattaches pretty quickly, often with the words, "I don't know why I said that," which I have taken to mean that whatever she just said was of a cosmic nature.

That evening Martie sat down, took a glass of water from Frank, and apologized to Carol.

"I would have called on you," she said, "but I really needed to talk with that woman in the hat."

During the daily free message services, each medium is allowed to give messages to three different people, and then another medium comes forward. The free events are Lily Dale's way of helping humanity, but they also give student mediums practice, and established mediums can pick up new business. Martie's third message went to a woman wearing a baseball cap over what looked to be a bald head—obviously a woman in cancer treatment.

"She thought she was going to die soon," Martie told Carol, "and I saw that she wasn't going to die until November. I needed to tell her to start enjoying the time she has left."

Carol received this bit of information with a murmur. Perfectly understandable. Of course. Did she want Martie to give her the message that came to her at Forest Temple?

She did. Of course. Believing Noel still existed was Carol's only solace. If she knew that her darling was happy, she could bear the dark stretch of lifeless time before her, but if Martie said something trivial or obviously false, if she turned out to be a faker thinking she could lead grief-addled widows astray with fanciful tales, that would kill all hope.

Carol took the chance. "Can you give me the message?"

Martie could, and so she began.

"Your husband was an avid golfer," she said.

That could have been a guess. Carol knew that. She is white, middle-class, middle-aged. Someone might have told Martie that she lived in South Carolina, where golfing is a year-round activity. But it was true that Noel had been a passionate golfer. They both were. They had done almost everything together. They worked in the same high school where he taught chemistry. They rode to and from work together. They sometimes lunched together. And they golfed together, although Noel was much better than Carol.

So yes, he was a golfer. Determined that she would give away as little as possible, Carol nodded.

"Yes."

"Well, he wants you to know that he has made a couple of holes-in-one since he passed over."

Is she being flip? Carol thought. *Why would he say that?* Carol hadn't spent much time imagining heaven, but holes-in-one were never part of what she did imagine.

Martie wasn't laughing. She put her hands out in front of her body, palms down.

"It's as though he is sitting at a table," the medium said, "and he's working his hands on the table, moving them. He says for me to tell you that you still aren't placing your feet correctly. He moves his hands to show you how to place your feet.

"If you don't, he says, you're going to . . ." Martie stopped and flicked her eyes up as though she were thinking. "If you don't . . ."

She pantomimed holding a golf club in front of her body, and she swung to the side in a way that would have made the ball slice.

Carol began to cry. Martie looked at her with the saddest, most tender expression.

"He's telling me that he likes it better when you are laughing."

When Carol's sobs subsided enough for her to speak, she said, "He always said that I was never going to make my shots unless I placed my feet differently, and he always used his hands, not his feet, to demonstrate. I used to get angry, and he would say, 'Fine, you stand the way you want to stand, but this is what's going to happen.'" And then he would slice through the air in the same kind of pantomime that Martie had used.

No one else could have known those things, Carol said. "It was something that Noel and Noel only would say." Her tears were coming from relief. "Martie was confirming what I had so much wanted to believe. I felt a sense of peace that couldn't have been more palpable if someone dropped a sheet over me."

The medium wasn't finished.

"You spent a lot of time delving into and trying to discover information about your husband's illness, didn't you? You became obsessive about it."

Carol laughed. "I'm sure there are people who would call me obsessive."

"I see piles of notes."

"You need to look again because I have those notes in three-ring binders."

"I feel, and your husband feels, that you need to put that behind you. When you go home, I would like you to wrap those binders as nicely as you want to, and I see a big red bow. And then I want you to put them in a box and put them away."

Carol knew that Martie was right. "A big part of me still anguishes because in spite of everything, I came up short. I had to let that go."

Everything the medium said comforted and amazed Carol. But Martie wasn't entirely accurate. "Your husband passed away months ago," she said.

"Well, it's been a few months," Carol replied. Their conversation was taking place in early July and Noel had died on April 8.

But Martie shook her head. "No," she said. "That's not what I'm getting. I'm getting that he died six to eight months ago."

When Carol told me her story, she stopped at that point and said, "Hold that in abeyance. Keep it in mind until I tell you what happened the next day."

4

Picnic tables scattered around the grass near the Good Vibrations Cafe were filled with visitors eating sandwiches. It was her first visit to Lily Dale, and Marian Boswell had come from a service at the Healing Temple. Every day during the summer season Lily Dale hosts two services for hands-on healing. Healers don't promise that the blind will see or the lame will walk, but they say it could happen. They're channeling divine healing energy, they say, and it will at least make you feel better.

Energy is an all-purpose word in Lily Dale. "I don't like her energy," someone would say with a shrug if she disliked a neighbor. It was so handy and neat a piece of jargon that I soon picked it up myself.

"Bad energy," I'd say regretfully when someone rubbed me wrong. Listeners would nod thoughtfully, taking a moment to consider all that meant.

The healers channel energy in order to readjust energy. The mediums raise their own energy to meet spirit energy. They also read energy. More than once when I protested that something a medium told me about myself wasn't true, she would reply, "I'm getting this from you energetically," as though that settled the matter and would shut me up for sure.

The spirits themselves are often energy. Mediums might tell a tourist, "I'm getting a male energy," and be answered with a too-eager guess: "Is it my father?"

"No, it's a younger energy. Perhaps from your father's side."

Healers channel energy while standing at the front of church. Little benches sit before them. When the benches are empty, the healers stare straight ahead with their hands folded. Anyone who wants healing sits on the bench, facing away from the healer, who then starts moving his or her hands over the supplicant. The healers start at the head and shoulders and move down the body, without touching the central body because mediums say that's illegal in New York unless you have a license. Some use a kind of sweeping motion. One healer told me she could feel the tangles of blocked energy as she smoothed them.

After the healers finish, they often hug the people who've been sitting before them, and sometimes they whisper something. Healers flick their hands when they finish, as though they're flinging water drops off their fingers. That's to release the pain and illness they have absorbed. Bad energy. Some say they can feel it in their own bodies, especially their hands. Finally, the healers go to a basin at the side of the church, rinse their hands, dry them, and return to their benches.

All the while, sweet music is playing. Being there is restful if you don't pay attention to how some people act. Certain healers have bigger reputations than others. So some people wait for those benches to be clear. Generally people take turns, but I once saw a woman in a pink suit practically knock an old lady over to get to the healer she wanted.

Marian meditated while her mother and their friend Mary Ellen went up front. As often happens when she meditates, her mind filled with vivid colors, she said. They swirled with such energy that she sometimes felt as if a cool breeze were being stirred up, but unlike previous times, when Marian opened her eyes, the colors didn't go away. They were everywhere, she said. Because this was her first visit to Lily Dale, Marian thought everyone saw them.

"What's with the colors?" she asked Mary Ellen.

As they walked toward the Good Vibrations Cafe, passing men eyed Marian, as they always did. With long brown hair, blue eyes, and plenty of curve, Marian had attracted male attention for so long she didn't know any other reality. She didn't look back. Marian had the man she wanted. She had the perfect husband. Everyone acknowledged that. Her mind was on spiritual matters.

Mary Ellen explained that she'd never seen the colors, and she didn't know anyone who had. As they settled at a picnic bench, Mary Ellen spotted a woman she knew, a surgeon from Cleveland, and motioned her over. The woman's husband had cancer, and, although she was not a medium, she often came to Lily Dale to take classes. They were chatting in a casual, companionable way when the woman abruptly leaned toward Marian and began talking in a stern voice, like a teacher lecturing a poor pupil. Her timbre was low, as though she had suddenly developed a cold or gotten a shot of testosterone.

"You're going to have to give up everything you know," she said, her eyes boring into Marian's. "You're going to have to jump into the void. It's not going to be easy. What you've done before has worked, but it's not going to work anymore."

Ominous words? Not to Marian. She was thrilled.

"I thought she was telling me that the wonderful life I was living would lead me into a new spiritual richness. I thought I'd already begun," Marian told me.

The next day she went home—to her lovely house that so many people envied, and she told her husband, whom so many women admired. She bragged almost. He listened sympathetically, as he always did. Everything she said interested him, her perfect husband, so handsome, so successful, so thoughtful.

Marian and Jack had met at work. Both were high-powered, ambitious, and successful. They fell in love. Both were married to other people, but that hadn't mattered. Although Marian's husband took the divorce hard, he was a good guy, and they'd been able to stay friends. Anyone could see how much happier Marian was.

She and Jack were a Barbie and Ken couple, in love with power and money and their own wonderful lives. Jack's divorce took years. He told Marian that his wife accused him of things, things Marian thought were absurd, like hiding money. But eventually they won their freedom and everything was perfect, until one day when Marian was in a business meeting and a ringing began in her ears.

"Do you hear that?" she asked the people next to her.

They didn't. It was a high-pitched piercing sound, something like what a dog whistle must sound like to a dog. Marian could hardly concentrate. When she left the meeting, the sound ceased. But the next day, when she sat down at the conference table ready to deal, the ringing began again. Again no one else heard it.

Inexplicably, her interest in work began to flag. Once eager to start the day early, she now came in late. She began giving tasks to her assistant. She started missing meetings, closing the door to her office. Instead of working, she read magazines and listened to music.

She quit her job with Jack's support and began renovating a house for them. She painted and gardened, and her life became wonderful again. Once, when working on her house, she dropped a tool, and as she bent to pick it up she muttered, "Fuck it."

As she raised up, Marian felt the presence of her late grandmother so forcefully that she heard herself say, "I'm sorry. I know you hate that kind of language."

But of course no one was there, and she felt a little silly. All that time working alone calmed her but also made her more and more reflective.

Jack brought Marian flowers every day. He surprised her with gifts of jewelry. When he was away on business, he sent long e-mails and tender letters. Other women compared their husbands to him and always found them lacking.

At night when Jack fell asleep, Marian would think back over her day. She would count the blessings of her wonderful life, and she would pray. But as she was thanking God and feeling so blessed, a memory of the pain she had caused her ex-husband often pushed its way into the dark room and settled on her like an ache. Her prayer would shift then, and she would ask, "God, how can such a wonderful life have come from so much suffering? Help me understand."

Marian wasn't nearly as Catholic as she'd once been. "When we were growing up there was a priest at the end of our dinner table every Sunday," she remembered. "My father was determined we'd all go to heaven whether it killed us or not."

When her parents divorced, her dad stopped believing in the God of the Catholic Church, and her mother started believing in all sorts of gods. She moved the kids to Flint, Michigan, and joined the hippie revolution. Marian had dabbled in lots of kinds of faith, but now it was those old Catholic ideas that seemed to be reasserting themselves.

"Help me understand," she begged God every night.

And he did.

Three years later, she laughed as she told me about her first day in Lily Dale. She had been so innocent, so egotistical, and so wrong. The surgeon wasn't being cryptic at all. She meant exactly what she said. Marian's prayers set her on the path toward the truth about her husband and about herself. She was going to lose it all. Everything she had.

5

Before coming to Lily Dale, I had consulted only two mediums. The first was a middle-aged housewife in Texas who told me that a man with animals on his wall would soon become important in my life. I was single then and took the message to mean love was on the way. I did meet a man with animals on his wall, an ornithologist with the natural history museum. He was married and did not become important in my life.

The second medium was a teenage cheerleader prophetess who was visiting churches around Dallas giving messages. I interviewed her over the phone, and she told me she saw a blond little boy close to me. She also said I'd soon receive lots of money and acclaim and buy a black Mercedes. None of that was true. But she did mention that I was having trouble sleeping, which was true. She said God was trying to talk with me, and I was too busy during the day to listen. So he was waking me up. That night when I awoke at 2:00 A.M. I remembered her words.

"God, are you trying to talk with me?" I asked.

I was answered by a silence of such dark depth that my mind went utterly blank before it, and I fell asleep immediately.

Despite my lack of success with mediums, I decided to do my own test of Lily Dale's powers and made an appointment for a reading with Gretchen Clark Lazarony, a fifth-generation resident of Lily Dale. She is one of four sisters referred to in Lily Dale as the "Clark girls," after their maiden name. Three are mediums, and all look younger than their years. Three are blondes, and they all have pale, beautiful skin. Thirty years ago, Gretchen was one of Lily Dale's youngest mediums. Now middle-aged, she's still one of the most respected.

Her family spent summers at Lily Dale when she was a child. Her parents were not mediums, but they were believers. "When I would tell my mother there was a lady in the corner, she would say, 'What's she wearing? What's she have to say, and what's she want?'" Gretchen remembered. She and her elder sister, Sherry Lee Calkins, began developing their powers only after their mother died and came back to communicate.

Gretchen's house, one of the community's nicer abodes, sits high above the street with the usual screened porch fronting it. Sherry Lee lives across the street. I was later told that the sisters sit behind their drapery and count the number of customers the other has, but I didn't believe it. They would never resort to such plebian methods. Astral travel would be more their style.

Astral travel, which is the ability to move around without one's body, isn't part of official Spiritualism, but a lot of people in Lily Dale say they do it. I once repeated Sherry Lee's claim of astral travel to another Spiritualist, who sniffed disdainfully.

"You don't believe people can astral travel?" I asked, thinking I'd stumbled onto a rare critic within the ranks.

"Oh, I believe that," she said. "I just don't believe she can do it."

Lily Dale is a gossipy community. When someone in Lily Dale passes on a good quip, it's prudent to ask, "Was that person living or dead when he said that?" The word *dead* isn't used, of course. They call it "passing over," "going from the earth plane," or "leaving for Summerland," the Spiritualist version of heaven. Dead people are called "spirit loved ones" or the "dearly departed." Anyone who slips up and goes around talking about dead people, as I occasionally did, is firmly corrected, as I occasionally was.

People say you can whisper gossip on one end of Lily Dale and before you run the half-dozen streets to the other end of the community, people on that side will be ready to repeat it back to you. Because the community has far fewer men than women, some of the men do rather well on the romance front, according to local gossip. As one person put it, "This place is just one big honey pot for some of these guys."

The hottest controversies, however, aren't about such mundane matters as debauchery. They're about matters of the spirit. Lily Dale squabbles don't address spiritual possibility—which everyone agrees is unlimited—but skill, which plenty of people take grim pleasure in reporting to be in short supply. Behind closed doors, Lily Dale fiercely debates which of its mediumistic sisters and brothers are really tight with the Beyond and which ones couldn't find spirit if they were dead themselves.

To hang a shingle in Lily Dale, mediums must pass a test. They are required to give individual readings to three members of the Lily Dale board and then give a public reading to an audience made up of the entire board. Although as many as a dozen mediums take the test every year, only thirty-six mediums were registered and able to give readings in Lily Dale the first year I was there. The low number is a matter of great pride among some people in the Dale. They think it speaks to the community's high standards, a notion they pass on to outsiders. But a sizable portion of the community rejects that contention entirely. "Who gets in is political," I heard many people say, echoing the suspicions of small-town America everywhere. "Lots of good mediums don't pass. The people who pass the test are the ones favored by the board."

Gretchen is a member of the town's more conservative contingent. A reserved woman, she's pleasant in a cool way, with an edge that stays sheathed most of the time but not so much that people forget she has it. She looks away from people as she talks and often wears a sort of half-smile, as though she's hoping you'll say something interesting but she doubts it. She answered my questions, but she didn't volunteer much, and she made it pretty clear that she wouldn't bother trying to convince me of anything.

I was being my most friendly, nonthreatening self, but I slipped up once. "I've been told that normal people can do what you do? Is that true?"

"We *are* normal," she snapped, "and what we do is perfectly normal."

I then tried asking a few questions that might puff her up a bit. "Do you have to meditate for long periods of time to prepare yourself for the work?"

"No," she said. "I don't."

"Is the work exhausting?"

"No," she said. "Not for me."

I kept tempting her with the chance to make herself sound mysterious and powerful, but she wouldn't go for it. She didn't even remember what she told people during readings, she said. "I'm just the telephone that the spirits use to get through," she said. "Does the telephone remember what's said over it? Neither do I."

I knew whom I wanted to contact, but I didn't expect Gretchen could do it. My Uncle Johnny had died that May. We were especially close, and I was at the hospital when he went in for a heart bypass. The doctor told us this operation had a 1 percent fatality rate. My uncle was sixty-three. His heart was strong. Nothing to worry about, the doc told us. I expected to go home that afternoon and be back at work the next day.

Something went wrong.

All my life I've feared loss, but I've been uncommonly lucky. So far only two people I'm close to have died. My grandmother and then my uncle. Both times, somewhat to my astonishment, I was sure that their spirits still lived. I can't say why. I just knew it. I looked at their bodies, and I knew that they had gone somewhere else. I can't prove it, of course, but I felt it so strongly that it was reality for me, like knowing you're in love or being sure the sun will come up. So when I went to Gretchen's house, I didn't doubt that life continued. What I doubted was that she could contact anyone who had gone to where that life went.

Gretchen ushered me into her reading room, a little parlor at the front of the house. It was a perfectly ordinary, well-lighted room. Gretchen told me she had once hoped to install red carpet and drapes as a way of warming the room up, but every time she stood in the reading room imagining how it would look, a little old lady with a terrible frown would appear in the corner. She'd purse her lips and shake her head. She didn't speak, and Gretchen didn't recognize her. So one day the medium asked the man who had sold her the house if he had any guesses about the woman's identity.

"That would be Mother," he said. "She hated red."

Gretchen and I sat facing one another. She said a few things that didn't mean anything to me. Then she said that she had a man. She put her hand to her chest, looked pained, and said, "Oh. He died of something with his lungs? No, his heart. Something with his heart.

"I'm getting the name John."

Now that might seem like a score, but to me it wasn't. His name was Johnny. No one ever called him John. My mother sometimes called him Brother John, but I never did. I'd heard about so many spirits named John since I'd come to Lily Dale that I figured, anybody would guess John, and what's the leading killer? Heart disease, right? Not a tough one to guess.

"Was there some kind of interruption at the funeral?" Gretchen asked, frowning as though she were trying to concentrate.

"No," I said.

"That's what I see. I see that the funeral was in two parts. What happened?"

"Nothing," I said.

"Are you sure? He's talking about the funeral being in two parts."

I didn't want to make the connection, but maybe there was one. My cousin and I argued before the funeral began. My uncle had believed she treated him badly. Maybe she had, maybe she hadn't. It was debatable, but I was far more angry and partisan once he was dead than I'd ever been when he was alive. The way I saw it, he couldn't take up for himself anymore but I could.

Sounds like some kind of Sicilian vendetta, I know. But I confronted her. The family took sides, and, just as the limo pulled up to take us to the funeral home, the whole clan broke into something pretty close to a street fight. My surviving sixty-something uncle was chasing my cousin's teenage son around the yard threatening to kick his butt. The widow was in the street crying. My mother and my cousin's husband were standing nose-to-nose. Finally an aunt yelled, "Let's go," and about half the family climbed into their cars and left in a screaming huff. The funeral wasn't in two parts exactly, but after the prefuneral fight the family was and still is.

The funeral was closed casket. A picture of my uncle sat on an easel beside it. None of us were crazy about that particular photograph. He was smiling, but in a kind of sad way, as though life were a little bitter to him. We'd all studied that photo enough to know how it made us feel. We'd been looking at it, crying beside it, for two days.

Now we filed into the church. My mother was beside me. My uncle's only daughter was down the row. As the organ played we sat facing the photo. But the smile looked different now. There seemed to be a kind of glint in his eyes, and he looked as though he were about to burst into laughter. I thought, *Get a grip, girl. You are imagining things.*

But his daughter, Andrea, was whispering to my mother. Then my mother was whispering to me, "Does that picture look different to you?

"Andrea thinks so, too. I didn't like that picture, but now he looks so pleased. Like he's really tickled. Something has happened."

We all three saw it. I'm not saying that picture really changed. It couldn't have. But it sure looked different to us.

And that brings me to the last part of Gretchen's message. I finally admitted that there'd been an argument right before the funeral—not an interruption, I said, not really, but half the family did go home.

"That's it, then," said Gretchen in the perky way that she has when she's settling something.

"He says to tell you that he was just real tickled about the whole thing."

A lot of people would have signed up as a believer right then, but if you don't have the faith, it doesn't matter what happens. You won't be convinced. You'll pass it off as something strange, and you'll let it go. Or if you're like me, you'll get stuck on something that doesn't fit and you won't be able to get past it.

For me, the problem was the name John. If Gretchen really had my uncle, why wouldn't he give the name that I knew him by? I was sure he would have. The interruption in the funeral? Well, the funeral hadn't really started, had it? What I couldn't explain away was that Gretchen had used the word *tickled*. At the funeral his picture had looked exactly like that, like he was tickled. And he would have been. He would have thought that ruckus was about the funniest dustup he'd ever seen.

6

I returned to Lily Dale on a cold March night. It was late. When I reserved the room, I told my hostess at the Lakeview guesthouse not to expect me until the next day, but once on the road I didn't want to stop. I pulled into the dirt-packed parking lot, fumbled through the darkness up the stairs of the veranda, and rang the bell. A tiny woman with so much dark red hair that I peered at it suspiciously, thinking it had to be a wig, answered the door.

"I had a feeling you would arrive tonight," said Jessie Furst, whose yard displayed a neat little sign that proclaimed her a medium.

I snickered somewhat gracelessly. Was she kidding?

No.

This time I planned to stay as long as it took to find out whether Lily Dale really had power. If it did, I wanted to know where that power came from. Were the mediums' messages guesswork? Chance? Telepathy? Fraud? Or was Lily Dale truly what so many of its residents believed it was? They call it a "thin place," one of those rare geographic locations where the barrier between human realities and spiritual verities is so thin that people can glimpse a universe beyond ordinary sight. The universe Lily Dale posits is far kinder than the one the rest of us live in. Everything that happens has a purpose, they say, and we all have a role.

I didn't believe any of that, but maybe I wanted to. Why else would I have come back?

A couple of signs sat in the foyer of Jessie's house. The first one irked me. It instructed visitors to take off their shoes and "borrow" a pair of slippers from a basket next to the sign. I didn't mind removing my shoes, and the slippers were a nice touch, but the quotes around borrow made me go all schoolmarmish. What did those quotes mean? That we weren't to borrow them but to take them with us? Or that we were to borrow them only and not steal them? Or did they mean nothing?

I was tired and peevish, I guess, because the next sign really made me roll my eyes. It said that Jessie did readings in person and over the phone. Over the phone? Maybe people could do readings in person, and maybe not. But over the phone? *No way,* I thought.

This was not a good start.

I'd been back in Lily Dale less than ten minutes, and I was already quibbling over quotes that were merely an attempt to be gracious and making a big deal over something most of Lily Dale thought of as nothing. Many mediums in Lily Dale do readings over the phone. I was starting way too early with the eye rolling. I didn't know yet about pets that come back with messages for their masters or the Andalusian stallion that invites people to a party. No one had yet talked about Vikings who march in the woods or living people whose faces are transfigured into those of famous dead people. I had a long way to go, and it wasn't going to be easy if I fought it every step of the way.

Lily Dale didn't look the same at the end of winter. The summer's sunlit charm was gone. Without the flowers, it was easy to see the village's cracks. Pastel hues that looked festive on a warm bright day washed out and blended into winter's gray. Ice floated on Cassadaga Lake. The tourists had disappeared as completely as the robins. Most of the mediums were gone too. Many winter in Florida. Those left were predominantly working folk—carpenters, carpet layers, truck drivers eking out a living in a region where jobs are scarce.

Cars, wearing coats of chalky grime, were the only signs of life. They stuck out around the community's parks like spiked collars, nudged next to curbs, sinking into muddy driveways. At night the blue light of television flickered from occupied houses, and the windows of Lily Dale's many vacant houses turned blind gray stares toward cold streets. If ghosts walk in Lily Dale, they have plenty of room during the off-season.

With the frippery that drapes and softens the community in the summer gone, all that was left was exactly what I wanted to know about—Spiritualist life outside the spotlight of tourists' expectations. One of my first stops was to see Betty Schultz, a tough old gal who didn't worry about choosing her words carefully.

I half-expected that the mediums would revert to normal after the tourists went home. If they did, these middle-aged and older women, most of them without a man and all of them without any money worth bragging over, would be exactly what society told them to be—drab, passed by, unimportant, a little pitiful really with their pretensions and lies. If they did revert to such a life, they wouldn't be the real thing, and I'd leave without wasting more of their time or my own.

But Lily Dale doesn't do what society expects. When the tourists go home, when the mediums shut their doors to the outside world, they don't quiet down. They up the amps.

Betty said she'd see me at two o'clock. "Two o'clock sharp," she said. "Be on time."

Betty Schultz is one of the grande dames of Lily Dale mediumship, a woman who speaks her mind and gets her way.

I'd heard about her during my first trip, and she was every bit as formidable as I had imagined. She had a kind of Bette Davis toughness that made you know she might say anything. She's retired now. Some people would pay her whatever she asked for just one more reading, but she won't do it.

As I walked toward Betty's house on a brisk afternoon with five minutes to spare, the trees weren't even thinking green, which was good because Lily Dale had one more blizzard between it and spring no matter what the calendar said. I passed several houses that a more prosperous community would have torn down years ago. Even some of the better houses in Lily Dale look close to collapse, paint peeling, porches sagging. The community has been kept poor by the same rules that have kept it alive all these years.

Only Spiritualists can buy houses in the 167-acre compound, a stricture that can be enforced because the Lily Dale Assembly is a religious corporation made up of community residents. Lily Dale has a volunteer fire department, a post office, and a governing board of elected representatives. Its separation from the settlements around it makes Lily Dale feel like a town, but it is actually a gated membership community within the town of Pomfret.

The rule that residents must be Spiritualists keeps the client base for real estate small, but that's a minor problem compared to the fact that Lily Dale residents don't own the land their houses sit on. They lease the land from the Assembly. This ensures the Spiritualists will never lose control of Lily Dale, but it also keeps real estate prices depressed. Banks generally won't lend money for houses that sit on land owned by someone else. As a result, buying in Lily Dale takes several kinds of faith, and that suits board members just fine.

Some people are repelled by Lily Dale's rough edges. They suspect that anything not polished and slick, not varnished with money, can't be good. Even many Lily Dale residents can't resist contrasting the shabbiness of little Lily Dale with the Chautauqua Institution, twenty miles away and founded in 1874, only five years earlier than Lily Dale, as a Protestant summer camp. Also on a lake, the Institution is now a grand place, with magnificent meeting halls, condos that sell for hundreds of thousands of dollars, an elegant hotel, and 7,500 residents. It has a symphony, an opera, a conservatory theater, and a ballet.

Some residents of Lily Dale boast that their community has resisted temptations that would have led it away from its founding principles toward the riches and acclaim Chautauqua has. Others bemoan lost opportunities.

In the summer, when Lily Dale leaders try to get big-name New Agers for lectures, it's a tough sell. Not only is the Assembly too poor to pay good money, but celebrities don't like the accommodations. They want modern rooms with air conditioning. They want room service and fine restaurants, all of which Chautauqua has and Lily Dale does not. Some luminaries have come anyway. The author Deepak Chopra spoke in the Dale before he became so famous. Author Wayne Dyer visits every year. Mediums James Van Praagh and John Edward were there the summers I visited. Edward's appearance, before he began hosting his television program *Crossing Over,* was poorly publicized, and he didn't draw the crowd he should have. Van Praagh's sellout appearance was the talk of the season. At the annual meeting, Lily Dale's president bragged so much about the famous medium's prowess that he offended some of his constituents, who felt their own powers were being somehow undermined.

Lily Dale's tatty side gave me a certain ease. Small, cramped rooms, the moldy smell of old walls, weedy yards, and porches with broken furniture don't put me off. I spent much of my childhood in such places, and I like them. They're freer. People don't have to follow as many rules. To the people of Lily Dale, that's important and always has been.

Their beliefs once caused them to be considered freethinkers. Freethinking about religion, which included escape from Christian ideas about original sin and atonement, were important reasons for the original appeal of Spiritualism. Early Spiritualists supported the abolition of slavery, women's rights, and free love, which in the nineteenth century meant the right to divorce. Lily Dale was one of the first platforms to allow women to speak. Susan B. Anthony spoke at the community's annual Women's Day so often that she was known as Aunt Susan. She was not a Spiritualist, but once, when she sat for a reading, the medium said she was bringing through Susan B.'s aunt. Anthony was unimpressed.

"I didn't like her when she was alive, and I don't want to hear from her now," she snapped. "Why don't you bring someone interesting like Elizabeth Cady?"

Political crusading went out of fashion in Lily Dale long ago. The community's two churches rarely adjure members to go out and redress the wrongs of the world. The idea seems to be to get in touch with the spirits, and they will take it from there.

Betty's screen door rattled. The porch creaked and smelled faintly musty. When I knocked, I could hear her schnauzer barking inside. I was right on time.

Betty was wearing house slippers. She'd fallen not long before while walking her dog in the woods. She lay in the cold for quite some time, and it was close to dark before she was found. Betty reclined on the coach as we talked. I sat in a chair before her, facing an antique photo.

"That's my grandfather on the wall. He's the only one with money, so I put him on the wall."

An elaborately carved teak chair sat across the room. Betty invited me to sit in it. I did.

"Do you feel anything?" she asked.

No.

"How are your feet?"

Fine.

Betty looked disappointed.

"Once a lady sat there and said, 'I can't feel my legs. I can't feel my legs.' I said, 'You better get out. You're sitting on my father.' I knew he was in the chair. He had sugar. He'd had a foot amputated, and his legs were very bad."

My feet were fine, but I got up anyway. The dog was giving me a strange look.

"Dogs are very aware of spirits," Betty said. "Nobody has told them spirits don't exist."

She has four dogs in spirit and a dead friend who takes care of them. "Every once in a while he'll bring me a dog and I'll lose it," she said, looking mournful. "Show me people, but don't show me dogs. I love my dogs."

Nobody in Lily Dale seems to doubt that pets live on after death and visit their owners. One medium specializes in pets that have passed over. The best story I heard of that ilk was about a woman worried that her late dog was angry because she adopted a new puppy. When she consulted a medium, he told her, "Your dog doesn't mind the new dog, but he doesn't like the pup using his food bowl."

"What should I do?" the woman asked.

"Have a ceremony to retire the old bowl," the medium said, "and buy a new bowl for your new dog."

At one point in our interview Betty stared at the ceiling, cackled, and said, "Oh, you think so, do you?"

Looking my way again, she said, "Don't mind me. I'm talking to my spirit helpers. I call them 'the boys.'"

Betty isn't married now, but she once was.

"My husband thought I was a nutcase," she said.

Imagine that.

She took a drag off her cigarette and said, "I finally divorced him."

I laughed and glanced at Betty's face to see how that went over. It went over fine.

Betty didn't mind that I might think she was crazy, didn't mind at all.

Gertie Rowe, her mentor who could float seven trumpets in the air, taught Betty not to care what others thought. "They put her in a nuthouse more than once," Betty confided, "and her sister would have to go and bail her out."

Betty has seen it all.

When two young men disappeared and were suspected to have drowned in Cassadaga Lake right off Lily Dale's shores, their spirits appeared at Inspiration Stump, dripping water. Betty, saddened to see that they really had drowned and surprised because she had thought the missing boys were much younger, sighed and gave them the comfort they were seeking. "All right, boys," she said. "We'll find you." They did.

Once she had a lump in her breast. Her doctor asked, "What do the spooks say?"

"They say 'not cancerous,'" she told him.

"I don't think so either," he said, and that was that.

Betty's mediumship has helped people believe there is a God, she said. It has helped them believe in the afterlife, and that's its purpose. As for questions about this life and asking favors from spirit, "You don't ask unless you're desperate" she said. "You don't get piggish. You don't get the lottery, but I've always been taken care of."

Is her religion real?

"Take everything I have. Take my loved ones. Take my home. Leave my puppy dog alone, but take everything else I have. I will survive. But take my religion, and I won't. My belief in my God, my spirit loved ones, my understanding of natural laws, it's what's gotten me through it all. Bungled as I have, it's what's gotten me through."

One thing puzzled me. Why would she retire? Mediumship is a good way to pick up a buck. All it takes is sitting in a chair and talking. Why retire?

"It's hard on your body. It takes a lot of energy, and the right chemistry," she said. "Gertie Rowe always said, 'Have the good sense to know when to get out.'"

It isn't that Betty has lost her powers. If she's at the Stump listening as mediums work, she tunes in to check their accuracy. "Ninety percent accurate is real good," she said.

I left Betty's house in high spirits. By the time you get to her age, society has definitely cast you aside. You aren't in the movies. You aren't in the songs. You aren't even in the books because, if you were, they'd be so depressing no one would buy them. Betty was an old woman, living alone with nothing but an old dog to keep her company. And she wasn't pitiful.

She had enough powers left to check on the youngsters, and she had spirit men flitting about the house. Once, she sent them upstairs to look for a book and then excused herself after yelling into the air, "All right. If you can't find it, I'll help you." Another time, apparently tired of chatter only she could hear, she snapped, "Fellows, while you're not doing anything else see if you can get someone to come up here and take care of that tree before it falls and breaks the house. Please. Thank you."

She always says please and thank you.

I couldn't verify anything Betty said, not with facts and not in my own experience. Some might suspect she wasn't latched on too tight, but maybe Lily Tomlin's Trudy the Bag Lady was right. Reality is just a collective hunch.

I didn't think Betty was faking it. She was not some trumped-up gypsy pretender peering into a crystal ball. As far as I could tell, she was the real thing. What I wasn't sure of was what the real thing is.

7

I picked my way carefully across the wet ground at the back of the big Victorian that sits on a corner of Cleveland Avenue. Stone angels guard the steep walk at the front of the house owned by Shelley Takei and her sister, Danielle. A lighted star can be seen in the house's uppermost window. White Christmas lights are strung along the white banisters of the long veranda. As I opened the door to a screened back porch that ran the length of the house, I faced a poster of Dorothy and Toto from *The Wizard of Oz*. On the floor of the porch, sticking out of the wall as though the house has fallen on them, are two cylinders of striped material stuffed to look like skinny legs. On the feet is a pair of glittering ruby slippers. It's the Wicked Witch. On the poster is the quote, "Toto, I have a feeling we're not in Kansas anymore."

"That's for sure," I muttered.

When I knocked, Frank Takei, Shelley's husband, opened the door, invited me inside, and called his wife from somewhere in the depths of the house. I always think of Shelley as having come toward me with arms outstretched. I know she didn't. She also didn't say, "I'm so glad to see you, darling." She didn't know me, and Shelley disdains such "crunchy-granola" ways. But I remember it that way, probably because she often greeted me with those words later, and even that first day she acted as though seeing me was just the purest delight. She seemed to think I was so wonderful that I almost immediately began to wonder whether maybe I was. This is not a greeting reporters often get. People are more likely to back away like I'm a rabid weasel.

I felt pretty lost and lonely those first months in Lily Dale as I wandered among aroma therapists, Reiki practitioners, and people who study irises looking for disease, folks who, when asked what they do for a living, are likely to say, "I'm a healer." Before Lily Dale, I'd never heard anybody but Jesus called a healer, and I'm not sure even he touted himself that way. I'm not saying I doubted they were healers. I just didn't understand what they meant, and asking didn't get me anywhere. The community was full of happy-hearted, perky people, believers in humanity's essential goodness, the kind of people who said, "God is love," and addressed the deity as "Mother/Father God," the kind of people whose outlook contrasted so drastically with my own that they depressed me.

I would eventually find that Shelley wasn't all that different in terms of optimism, but, with a Ph.D. in transpersonal psychology and plenty of skepticism about what she saw, she at least spoke a language I sometimes understood. Her claim to Lily Dale fame is that she has spent summers in the Dale for more than twenty years, has taken practically every course offered, has spent untold hours practicing mediumship, and has never been able to conjure so much as a good "boo!" She calls herself a "remedial reader" and formed a club for the likewise impaired called the Lower Archy of the Pink Sisterhood of the Metafuzzies and Blissninnies. "Lower Archy because we're not the hierarchy, and Pink Sisterhood because we're not the White Brotherhood," she always explains. She claims to have twenty members, but with no dues, no meetings, and no rules, membership is hard to track. The club motto is, "We don't know jack shit, but we care."

Shelley likes to say she analyzes everything in Lily Dale with Occam's razor, meaning that she shaves off all that can be explained in a rational, normal way and then looks at what is left. Often there isn't much.

"I listen to everything the skeptics say, and I usually agree with them," she said.

I'd heard that Lily Dale is full of energy vortexes. Shelley is a human version. Reporters are experts at instant intimacy, but Shelley had me beat. Talking with her was such a quick connection that it was close to eerie.

She was delighted that I was a reporter. Nothing about my intentions scared her. She never even asked what they were.

"I know lots of people," she said. "I'll introduce you to them all."

I hadn't been more than an hour in Shelley's purple-carpeted living room, sitting under the golden gaze of the life-size papier-mâché angel at the end of the room, listening to stories of the women who came through her house all summer, before I realized a fact that many women before me had noted and been similarly mesmerized by. Shelley is free. She isn't bound in the same way that I am and have been all my life.

She has cropped brown hair, short stature, medium build. She dresses with a little more style than most middle-aged women at an upstate New York summer community—Capri pants, soft flowing shirts, and sandals. At fifty-five, she moves like the dancer she once was, light on her feet and quick. Whether she is lying on one of the room's two white sofas or sitting in the overstuffed old chair, she always seems to have draped herself—a little like Cleopatra, one friend said, queen of her domain, perfectly comfortable with herself and everything around her. She dislikes freeways and constricting underwear. Pretty normal.

Except. She never wears a watch and says she is always on time. She stays up late every night and sleeps until ten in the morning no matter who is in the house. She rarely goes to church even though belonging to a Spiritualist church is a requirement for buying a house in the Dale, and she does not meditate. That is heresy in Lily Dale, where meditation is the way to the spirits and the way to wisdom. Shelley's refusal has ruffled folks so much that some have put their faces into hers and shouted, "You've got to meditate." But she doesn't.

"Most people who meditate are trying to deal with some problem I don't have," she said.

When I say she is free, I don't mean free in the ways people often mean when they say that about a woman. Shelley is married, has grown children, hopes for grandchildren. In fact, her life is ordinary in many outward ways. She married Frank, who was her philosophy professor, more than thirty years ago. She stayed home with her children, only going back to school for her Ph.D. when they were able to toddle after their own pursuits. She and her sister first came to Lily Dale out of curiosity. They stayed because the place charmed them.

Still, Shelley isn't like any adult I've ever met. She has a business card that identifies her as a licensed femologist and certified joyologist, titles she affirms by living them out. Frank told me that when their kids were little they would often clamor for attention as soon as she started talking on the phone. Shelley kept a box of cereal on the counter. Without interrupting her phone chat, she would sit on the counter and toss cereal about the room while the kids scrambled for it like puppies after treats.

When her son was a teenager, he composed a song about penises and mothers and things that might be done with both. Other mothers would have been horrified, and Shelley did hope he kept it from them. Meanwhile, she was his best audience.

"What else do sixteen-year-old boys think about but sex, and who do they most need to break away from but Mother? It made perfect sense," said Shelley, who can still sing parts of it. She supports anybody who is killing the demons they need to kill, and if they can be funny doing it, so much the better.

"Quinn would sing that song, and I'd fall off my chair laughing," she said.

She and a gray-haired former nun named Mary Ockuly often greet each other by bumping hips. Once when we were standing with medium Sherry Lee Calkins and her two grandchildren, the adults were discussing an upcoming musical performance. As Shelley stood to the side with the kids, I noticed all three swinging their arms, clapping in front of their bodies and then clapping in back, just idly swinging and clapping. Not saying a word, just entertaining themselves.

The nine-bedroom Victorian house had no rules as far as I could tell, except that you had to strip your bed of the sheets and pillowcases before you left and remake it with a set of sheets from the closet. At one time a sign on the back door outlawed any talk of negative things, but Shelley took the sign down when it wasn't needed anymore. Now a sign says, THIS HOUSE IS PROTECTED BY ANGELS.

Anybody can smoke cigarettes in Shelley's house, and most people do. Profanity is completely accepted. A favorite Takei story is of the time their older daughter returned from a school that teaches healing and mediumship and threw herself over the sofa, groaning.

Her brother Quinn asked, "What's wrong? Too spiritual?"

"Too much fucking love," she yelled.

The only word that ever ruffles Shelley in the least is *should*.

"There are no *shoulds* in Lily Dale," she told me, cigarette in hand, feet propped on the kitchen bar.

Shelley likes to think of her house as a salon where women come every summer to discuss ways their lives have been touched by the eternal. Women can say things there they've never said before, tell stories that would cause the rest of the world to call them insane, and talk as long as they want. That's all anyone does. They rarely clean house or cook. They rarely read and only occasionally watch television. They talk for hours, for days, for weeks, and nobody ever runs out of things to talk about.

In any given week, the house may contain women telling any number of strange stories. Mary Ann Spears, a therapist who sees dead relatives of her grieving clients, might be in town, or C. J., who was color-blind until she came to Lily Dale.

"Would you like to talk with C. J.?" Shelley asked. "The last I heard she was outside the gift shop. She saw the color blue and started following it. I'll have to see if I can find her."

I talked to C. J., who confirmed the story. She now sees color whenever she comes to Lily Dale. The ability lasts for some time after she leaves the community and then gradually fades away.

Lorie might also be in town. She's a therapist for autistic children and perhaps the most spiritual person Shelley knows, Shelley told me. One of the first questions Lorie asked Shelley about Lily Dale was, "Why do they have artificial flowers?"

Lots of yards have tattered plastic flowers stuck into weathered old vases, and Lorie couldn't understand why a place that claims so much spirit power wouldn't be able to conjure up enough real blooms to go around. A quiet, often solemn, woman who has never had much money and has never seemed to care, Lorie told me that one morning well before dawn she was walking down the hill after milking the cow her family owned when she saw a blazing light coming from the window of her toddler son's upstairs room.

Thinking the house was on fire, she dropped the milk pails and began running toward the house. Streaks of white light continued shooting out of her son's room. It looked like lightning, but the sky was clear. When she entered the bedroom, her son was standing in his crib, jumping up and down, yelling, "Light. Light." But the room was perfectly safe and normal and dark, no fire, no light, and no evidence of anything like that.

Emmie Chetkin, reputedly the richest woman in Lily Dale and certainly the most powerful personality, is also a friend of Shelley's. Emmie's family is Spiritualist backwards and forwards. The Lily Dale museum has a newspaper photo of her trance-medium grandmother at a table, eyes closed, slack-jawed, floating a trumpet in front of two stunned witnesses. Some of Emmie's grown children live in Lily Dale with their children. Her family runs a fancy restaurant called Lazaroni's, about a mile away on Dale Drive. Chetkin family arguments spill out into the community occasionally as Emmie, who does everything at top speed, roars about in her SUV, braking if she sees a friend so she can hang out the window and talk about the latest fracas. "She's got all the money in the world and just as many troubles," one Lily Dale dame said.

Several people said Emmie was buying up houses so she could take over the town. The idea that rich people, gamblers, and greedy developers covet the community's lakeside acres and plot to wrest them from Spiritualist control is a common worry.

Emmie laughed at her neighbors' suspicions. "Why would I want to do that?" she asked, rolling her eyes, throwing out her hands. She had a point. Nobody in the Dale can stand against the force of her will as it is.

She travels all over the world looking for psychics and healers. The best ones seem to come from Brazil, she told me. She once brought back a guy named Mauricio Panasset, who was also championed by Shirley MacLaine. He did healings on Emmie's friends, who said balls of light came out of his hands. The room was so bright that you could see the light through solid walls, they said.

"What stories!" Emmie said, hooting at the thought. "You couldn't see light through walls.

"People will say anything," she said, as she went on to tell about the time she saw a South American healer stick a huge butcher knife in someone's back. "There wasn't a bit of blood."

The women rarely bring their husbands or their children. Shelley's husband, Frank, comes to Lily Dale every June and usually leaves at the end of the month when the community starts its summer season and, as he put it, the estrogen gets too high.

There was much talk about the rise of the feminine and how the way women relate to each other is the new paradigm for spirituality. The idea that women have suppressed their innate knowledge and wisdom is a central theme of a book Shelley is writing. What kind of knowledge and wisdom?

"What are women always talking about?" Shelley asked.

Men. Relatives. Relationships.

"Relationships," she said triumphantly. "Why? Because they are the most important thing in the world, and women know it. Men don't."

Not that Shelley embraces every woman who manages to get through the gate. At the cafeteria, when we found ourselves seated with wacky pilgrims full of mysterious hints about their cosmic connections and eager willingness to tell us about their pain, Shelley would fall unusually silent.

"Fake orphans are all over the place," she once said after we left.

"What's a fake orphan?" I asked.

"The ones in the cafeteria," she said, "sitting there with their wounds hanging out."

Shelley knows all the community's best stories. She remembers when the Assembly went to court to evict Christian Spiritualists who wanted to start a church of their own. People had big, crudely lettered signs on their houses, some condemning the Christians and some condemning the Assembly for trying to evict them. She remembers the year the Assembly president was kicked out of the annual meeting because he'd forgotten to pay his dues. They shut the doors behind him, but he wouldn't leave. Instead, he lay outside the door, flat on the ground, prostrating himself in supplication and repentance. When Emmie Chetkin shamed the Assembly into letting him return, he crawled up the aisle. It was some kind of Native American rite of humility, I was told.

Shelley knows which medium brings through dead pets, which one sings as she comes forward to give messages, and which one is likely to berate visitors for their failings. After lunch one day, she introduced me to a future member of the Assembly board, who stuck out his hand and said, "You're fine. How am I?" She pointed out the guy who calls himself a citizen of the Pleiades, the medium who is rumored to stand on her roof at night looking for aliens, and the blonde who once flicked her hair back declaring, "My hair is very spiritual."

It isn't exactly true that Shelley has seen nothing in the way of spirit power herself. That's the way she tells it, but if she were of a different temperament, she might be proclaiming herself quite the sensitive. She and a friend once saw the hazy figure of a woman in an upstairs bedroom of the house.

"Is she wearing an apron?" Shelley whispered to her friend because she thought she saw an apron. The friend whispered back, "That's what it looks like."

One night when the upstairs was totally empty, she and friends heard the stairs creak, one at a time in descending order, as though someone were walking down. Once when medium Patricia Price was giving messages in the auditorium, Shelley saw a figure in the air behind her. He was short and fat, wearing a peaked hat that looked like something from the Prussian army. Shelley's friend Julia was sitting next to her, and she saw him too, hat and all. Then Patricia gave a message that included a description of the man they saw.

Another time she and friends made a midnight visit to the Stump. Shelley felt something nudge her right shoulder. She looked behind her. Nothing there. She felt the nudge again. This time it was harder.

In her head she heard the words, "Tell her."

Shelley looked across the circle at a woman named Mary Anne. She knew she was supposed to tell Mary Anne that Annie was present. She didn't hear the words. She simply knew what she was supposed to do. So she did.

Mary Anne began to sob. Annie was her aunt.

An image of a string of pearls appeared in Shelley's mind.

"She's bringing you a string of pearls," Shelley said.

Among Annie's most valued possessions was a string of pearls.

Another time, after days of having one medium after another walk into her house, gaze into the air, and say, "My, this is a busy place," Shelley wailed to medium Greg Kehn that she was sick of everyone seeing spirits in her house while she saw nothing. Greg said, "You can see them. If you want to."

"How?" Shelley asked plaintively.

"Turn all the lights out except this lamp," he said, pointing to a lava lamp in the display case of the living room. "Sit in that chair," he said, pointing to the overstuffed easy chair that's been with the house since before Shelley and her sister bought it.

"Be patient. You'll see something."

She did as she was told, and at about midnight she saw a mottled red and purple color rising just outside the pool of light. It formed itself into what looked like a body.

"I blinked my eyes. I thought, *I'm imagining it.* But it stayed," she said. "It wouldn't go away. It was like, 'Here, sucker. You wanted it, you got it.' "

Another time Greg told Shelley that she would have plumbing problems in the next year. "When they want to dig up the yard to replace the pipe, tell them no," he said. "You won't be able to snake it. You'll have to use something that bites or grabs."

Within the year, everything he said happened. The plumbers wanted to dig up the yard. She told them to get a tool that could grasp and cut whatever was clogging the pipes, and pull it out. They did. It worked.

One July, Shelley was at a Forest Temple message service when a medium she didn't much like said, "Are you aware that you're involved in a legal dispute?"

"I thought, *Like hell, I am,*" she said.

Eight months later a lawyer called to say a letter from Shelley was being entered as evidence in a harassment suit. He read the letter.

"I had never written such a letter," Shelley said. A former client had forged her signature.

It was dated July of the previous summer, the very month the medium had given her the message.

Did any of these things convince her that spirit power exists? No.

"Because if this is real, why can't I do it?" she asked. "Why can't I be a medium? Because I can't. I've tried and I can't.

"It's like I'm always saying about the mediums, 'Either they're crazy or I'm stupid.' I've never figured out which."

She thinks most Lily Dale experiences could be exaggeration, delusion, or wishful thinking. "People are making it up all the time." And yet, she said, "it's still the closest thing to the Temple of Eleusis that we have. There are things you can't reject no matter how discerning you are."

The Temple of Eleusis was where ancient Greeks explored the Mysteries and celebrated the rites of spring in honor of Demeter, the goddess of agriculture, fertility, and marriage.

She and Frank teach classes for Virginia Beach's Association for Research and Enlightenment (ARE), which grew around Edgar

Cayce's channeling. "I've seen people arrive at ARE exhausted after driving all night, with everything they own packed in their cars, because God told them to come there," she said. "What they're looking for is Lily Dale, but they don't know it exists."

By this time nodding in response to statements that make no sense came easy. So I nodded, then asked my next question.

How did you get this way?

Never coy, she didn't demur as though wondering what I meant. She knew. I meant, how did she get so free.

"I found out I was right."

About what?

"About everything."

How did you find that out?

"Lynnie," she said. "My Lynnie. She taught me."

She meant Lynn of the bicycle and the prayers. I nodded.

8

The mediums are nice people, and they believe what they say, but some of them could be getting carried away with their own imaginations," Hilda Wilkinson said.

I was surprised to hear anyone in Lily Dale admit it.

Ron Robertson, Lily Dale's Assembly president, introduced me to Hilda, which was a smart move. Letting a reporter know that not everybody in Lily Dale accepted any claim was smart, and Hilda had great credentials. She'd never been a medium, and she didn't entirely approve of making money off spirit communication. She was also ninety-five. If she was faking, she'd been faking for a very long time.

Hilda was an example of one of Lily Dale's proudest boasts, which is that people don't age as fast in their community as elsewhere. "I don't color my hair, and I have my own teeth," she told me. Her hair had only a grizzle of gray. Her face was sweet behind big glasses. Under five foot and about ninety pounds, she cut her own lawn in the summer and blew snow off her own driveway when hard winters came raging across Lake Erie.

Hilda converted to Spiritualism early. She was six years old, had just crawled out of bed, and was washing up while her eight-year-old sister, Julia, lingered under the covers. From behind her, Hilda heard a guttural voice. She turned to see Julia sitting bolt upright, her face wooden, her body stiff. Words were coming from Julia's mouth, but they were not her own. Hilda ran from the room, screaming, "Julia's talking with the voice of a man."

Hilda laughed at that part of the story. She didn't remember her mother being particularly upset. Their family attended a Christian church, but New York State was full of Spiritualists.

"My mother understood," Hilda said as we sat over cups of hot tea at the dining room table of her little white frame house. "My sister was a born medium. She never took money for it. The voice told her that it wanted to speak through her, and she would be taken care of."

Hilda asked whether I wanted to see her chalk slates. I did. Lily Dale is full of relics said to demonstrate the miracles of spirit aptitude. Lots of people have their grandmother's trumpets—tin, megaphone-like cones that supposedly floated about rooms while spirits talked out of them. Hilda's trophies were chalk slates filled with writing. Early Spiritualist mediums would put a piece of chalk between two blank slates and bind them together with twine. Hilda said she held one end of the slates and the medium held the other. She could hear the chalk scraping as spirits wrote the messages, she told me.

This was the very trick exposed by Hereward Carrington, once one of the country's most famous psychic investigators.

In 1907, the most powerful and popular medium in Lily Dale was an ill-tempered man named Pierre L. O. A. Keeler. Carrington, who called Keeler the best slate-writing medium in the country, had reams of letters from highly placed professional men attesting to Keeler's veracity and otherworldly talents. But Carrington, an investigator for the American Society for Psychical Research, was no ordinary customer. He was a keen observer and the author of a book detailing fifty-three different ways in which slate writers tricked the unwary.

The Lily Dale he visited was far more flamboyant than the community today. Mediums so disliked light that they nailed planks over the windows of their séance rooms. "One would pass such cottages at night, and hear issuing from them, anything but melodious sounds—the house itself dark, shadowy, and closely boarded up," he wrote in his report to the society. The mediums further improved their chances by constructing so-called spirit cabinets—curtained-off portions of the rooms from which spirits emerged once all lights were extinguished. Spirits demanded such conditions, the mediums said.

Mediums induced spirits to appear as lights, produce various thumps and noises, even touch the living. Spirit photographers made spirits appear in photographs. Without touching a paintbrush, mediums who worked with spirit painters made full portraits appear. Pressure to produce such sights and sounds was intense because people believed it could be done, and they came in droves to witness such feats. Forbidding them could have dire commercial results. When the Onset, Massachusetts, camp outlawed physical mediumship, it found itself with so few Spiritualist tourists that it was forced to become merely a summer resort, according to Carrington.

In the summer of 1907, Carrington picked Lily Dale as a site for his two-week investigation, not because he suspected it of fraud, but because it was the "best and most aristocratic camp in the States—and the best known." It was so popular that up to four thousand people would show up for a lecture. The community once had a bowling alley and a ballroom where orchestras played and elegant dances were held. The smart set of American Spiritualism came for picnics in the early years and then stayed to build summer houses. Eventually some started living there all year. If anyone could do physical manifestations, it was likely to be someone in Lily Dale. And in Lily Dale it was likely to be Keeler.

"[I] entered his house with high hopes that here, at last, I should meet with physical phenomena that were genuine, or at least such as I could not readily explain," Carrington wrote.

Keeler, he noted, was a touchy man who had to be approached with caution and humility, "otherwise one finds oneself turned out of doors with short ceremony." The medium had reason to be cranky. The University of Pennsylvania's Seybert Commission on Spiritualism had already exposed him as a fraud. He had also been outed in a book titled *The Spirit World Unmasked.*

Carrington called himself Charles Henderson and wore a pair of smoked eyeglasses to make it seem that his eyesight was defective. Keeler worked in daylight, using a table covered with a cloth that fell six to eight inches below the edges except on the side where the medium sat. On that side, the cloth hung about a foot.

In the first session, Carrington could not detect even one trick. Keeler had earned his title as the best slate medium in the country. Carrington was positive that fraud had taken place, but he couldn't prove it.

In the second session, Carrington gave Keeler four questions written on paper that crackled as it was folded into little pellets. The pellets were placed in the center of the table. The medium then gave his client five slates and asked him to clean them. As he did so, Carrington saw Keeler exchange two pellets, one after the other.

"These pellets he held in the palm of his right hand, which he then dropped carelessly into his lap," the investigator wrote. As he busily cleaned the slates, Carrington could hear the faint crackle of his paper being unfolded and then the soft scratching of a slate pencil writing on a board in the medium's lap.

Before he gave the medium two of the cleaned slates, Carrington pressed his thumbnail in the soft wood of the slates' frames. The slates were then bound together with the pencil in between.

First they were held by both men over the table, and then Keeler pulled the slates toward him and slipped them under the table, bidding Carrington to grasp them there. In the instant when Keeler put the slates under the table, he dropped them onto his lap and picked up the finished slates, which he had written answers on. When returned to the tabletop, neither slate had the mark made by the investigator's thumbnail.

As the two men held the bound slates between them, Carrington heard what seemed to be the sound of a pencil writing. This was supposed to be evidence of spirits at work, but watching the medium's wrist, Carrington saw the slight twitching of a muscle produced as Keeler's finger scratched against the underside of the slates. "[H]is wrists are well covered with fatty-tissue, it is very difficult to detect this movement; but, by watching intently, I clearly saw it—corresponding to the [sound of] scratches on the slate."

When the slates were unbound, Carrington also observed that the pencil between the two slates was perfectly sharp and unused. In addition, some of the more inane and nonspecific writing that could have applied to any customer was written in red and yellow pencil. The pencil between the slates was black.

Keeler was tossed out of Lily Dale after Carrington's report became public, but by the 1920s he was back, and Hilda gave him three dollars to reach spirit through his slates. Even then, Lily Dale answered its critics as it always has: it admits everything. There used to be a shocking amount of fraud, perpetrated by bad mediums, and there's still some of it around, the mediums say. It blackens the names of good, honest mediums, and it ought to be stopped. In the 1940s, Lily Dale outlawed all physical mediumship except in classes and private circles.

Today Lily Dale's finest mediums delight in telling of faked trumpet sessions they've exposed. They entertain their classes with stories of how the great frauds of old did their tricks—reading hotel registers, memorizing car tags so they could research records, keeping a secret book that contained names and details of known Spiritualists. One medium told me that concealed trapdoors had been found in houses. I was told that carpenters tearing walls apart had found clappers that could be used to make spirit rapping.

Alexander DeChard, the father of Lily Dale resident Ron DeChard, was one of the mediums suspected of cheating during the 1930s and 1940s when physical mediums were being pressured to leave Lily Dale. He was tested by community leaders, who strapped him to his chair wearing nothing but his underwear. Alexander passed the test, but more than fifty years later his son Ron is still bitter about the humiliation.

One evening medium Patricia Price showed a group of us how to fake billet reading. Billets are folded pieces of paper on which questions for the spirits have been written by members of an audience. The questions are placed in a basket, and the medium draws one. Without unfolding the paper, the medium holds the paper to her forehead, supposedly intuits the question, and answers it with the help of spirits.

The trick is achieved by having a plant in the audience, who has agreed to claim the first answer as his own. The medium picks a question from the basket. Without unfolding it, she gives the bogus answer. She then unfolds the paper, reads it to herself, and looks at the audience. But the question she speaks aloud is not the one on the paper. Instead, she substitutes a question that fits the bogus answer she just gave. Her confederate in the audience gasps in amazement and says the spirits must be present because that is the very question he asked and the answer he most hoped for.

Now the medium is in business. She knows one of the audience's questions, and that's all she needs. She picks another billet, holds it to her forehead and gives the answer to the question she read on the first piece of paper. And so it goes. Each time she simply answers the question printed on the last billet she read. The audience is astonished, and spirit help is entirely unnecessary.

Patricia had a great time showing that trick, and afterward she warned us, "Always be suspicious. Always use your common sense." And then she added, as the mediums invariably do, "But you know, you can't have a fake without having something real first."

What sounded like a self-serving rationalization was an observation made by William James, who helped found the American Society for Psychical Research in 1884.

> One swindler imitates a previous swindler, but the first swindler of that kind imitated someone who was honest. You can no more create an absolutely new trick than you can create a new word without any previous basis. You don't know how to go about it. Try, reader, yourself, to invent an unprecedented kind of "physical phenomenon of spiritualism." When *I* try, I find myself mentally turning over the regular medium-stock, and thinking how I might improve some item.

Well, maybe. But magicians might disagree. I bet none of them have seen a woman sawed in half, and they still do the trick. Some manifestations of spirit the early Spiritualists came up with were pretty strange. Ectoplasm, a jellylike white substance that oozed out of mediums' chests and formed itself into shapes, for instance. Nobody in Lily Dale said they'd seen such a thing, but it did happen in the old days, many people told me, and the museum has a newspaper photo of a woman with a hazy-looking white hand reaching out of her sternum.

James also agreed with another Lily Dale idea. Just because someone cheats sometimes doesn't mean they cheat all the time. Scientists lie too, James wrote, demonstrating with a story about the time he made a dead turtle's heart seem to beat because a fellow scientist needed the motion for a demonstration.

People of the Dale usually explain that physical mediumship is real but rare. It can't be produced at will. Old-time mediums, such as Keeler, were able to do the feats they claimed to do, but they weren't able to produce them on demand. And so they resorted to trickery sometimes. Hilda firmly believes her slates are legit. She has believed that for most of her life, and she'll die believing it.

I could barely read the scrawls on Hilda's black slates, but I could see that each slate had different handwriting.

Are these signatures of real people you knew?

"Of course," she said, looking puzzled, as if wondering whether I might be somewhat dim. I didn't take offense. People in Lily Dale often tell the most fantastic stories and then look at you as if you're the one who's odd.

You're left-handed," Hilda said. "That means you're from Atlantis."

I nodded as though that were good news. The truth was that I didn't know anything about Atlantis. I suspected that it had never existed, and if it did, what difference did it make that I'd lived there? I didn't ask.

Then Hilda told me I was an old soul.

That time I knew what she meant. An old soul is someone born many times before. I wasn't sure why Hilda thought such a thing, but I'd heard versions of it before. They hadn't always been compliments. Once when I was four, a mean-tempered uncle said something rude. I don't remember what I replied, but it made him furious. He glared down at me.

"You little adult," he snarled.

Some years later, a neighbor told my mother that I'd been born an old lady. "Old soul" sounds much nicer than "old lady." Maybe I was coming up in the world.

I waited patiently as Hilda told me all she wanted to tell. When she began to repeat herself, I posed the one question that really intrigued me. Why did she doubt the mediums? I had not asked earlier because I didn't want to scare her into thinking that I was in Lily Dale for only the dirt. I wasn't. The dirt hardly interested me at all. That was easy prey. I could catch the dirt anytime. No. I was interested in her doubts because none of Hilda's certainties convinced me.

That's always the case. When religious people tell me that they know, absolutely know the truth, I am never assured that they are telling the truth. They are showing me their public face. What convinces is the other face, the one that can only be glimpsed. When their eyes shift, when doubt widens their countenance into blank confusion and they fumble because words come hard, I know I've hit the right spot. This is what they worry about in the dead of night, when the sureties everyone believes seem far away and they are left with only their own thoughts. The questions they pose to themselves then, and how they answer them, are the heart of faith. When I see that look, I become very still and careful, as watchful as the voyeur standing outside the barn, peering between the slats.

During one interview, a medium smiled placidly as she told me about healing and love and the power of spirit. She said that she believed in what I was doing. I thought that was taking a big risk considering that nobody ever knows what a journalist is really doing. But I listened until she ran down, and then I figured, *If she says she trusts me, let's see how much.*

"Okay," I said, "so tell me the truth. What's going on here? What are you doing?"

She looked away, laughed a little, and then she looked back at me with a half-smile. "I don't know," she said. "I don't think anybody does. If you ever tell anybody I said that, I'll deny it."

Then she got up from her chair saying, "Let me show you something," and went to the back of her house. She returned with a letter. It was from a mother who had called the medium wanting information about her dead son. The mother sent a picture of a group with several males.

"Tell me what you can," she asked the medium.

"I was able to say which one was her son and how he died," said the medium. "I don't know how I knew. I told her that he was moving away from her because he needed to go on with his life on the other side, and she needed to go on with her life too.

"I was right. That was what she wanted to know, but she hadn't told me. She didn't feel his presence anymore, and she was frantic to know why."

The medium shook her head. "I don't understand it. I don't think anybody does. But you tell me. Is that real?"

Everything she told the mother might be coincidence and good guesses, but the medium's doubt made me think that whatever her gifts might be, she was groping in the dark like the rest of us.

I had misjudged Hilda, however. I didn't need to be cagey with her. She was old enough to say whatever she wanted, anytime she wanted, and she did. "I saw one of those mediums in church this morning. They pay her forty dollars an hour. I wouldn't give her fifteen cents," she said.

Her doubts about Lily Dale's present-day mediums stemmed partly from her sister Julia, whom she called a born medium. Julia didn't have to take lessons or be coached, as modern mediums are, Hilda said. She didn't have to fish around for information or come out with vague clues.

"These mediums today tell people they've got some spirit who's a little round woman with gray hair. What good is that? I want names," Hilda said. "Mediums like Jack Kelly gave names of spirits. You didn't have to guess who the spirit was. You knew."

Jack Kelly, who lived on Second Street in Lily Dale, was Mae West's favorite medium. A flashy little guy who drank a bit and sometimes chased women, his picture in the Assembly Hall shows him wearing an ascot and smiling in a roguish kind of way. Jack was quite the man. In those days mediums did elaborate performances during Spiritualist services. They called it platform work, and it drew big crowds.

Kelly would put himself into trance by thumping his head against the wall. His guide, the spirit that gives mediums information, could be heard as an unintelligible, high-pitched whining that would continue throughout Kelly's performance. Born in Wales and once a coal miner, Kelly told people he couldn't read and write as a boy and that spirit had taught him.

When he did billet reading, another Lily Dale medium, Ray Torrey, would tie a blindfold over Jack's eyes. Jack would always say, "Tie it tighter." Ray, a big man, would wrench it around until he thought Jack's head was going to burst, and Jack would say, "Tighter."

Kelly would often increase the drama by singling out members of the audience and saying, "Stop scratching your nose," or "Quit pulling your ear." After each answer, Kelly would crumple the billet into a wad and toss it into a wastebasket that assistants moved to different locations during his performance. He never missed.

During World War II, when a young girl asked whether her soldier cousin who was missing in action would be returning, the blindfolded medium strode to the back of the room, turned out the lights, and said in a thundering voice, "Gordon is home." Months later they received word that the soldier had died at the Battle of the Bulge.

Jack was so fond of blindfolds that he once drove from Buffalo to Lily Dale wearing one, claiming that the spirits would guide the car. The highway patrolman who stopped him was less than impressed and would have hauled Jack to jail, but the medium so astounded the cop with all he knew about the man's dead relatives that the officer let him go. Or so the story is told.

During his platform performances Jack stuck hatpins all over his forehead. He stuck them so far in that when he walked around the platform they would bob and wave before him. Burly farmers would try to pull them out, but nobody could. When Jack finally plucked the hatpins from his forehead, there wasn't a spot of blood on his face.

Stories of Jack's wonderful feats were always increasing. In the early fifties, a woman from Pittsford, New York, told the Dunkirk newspaper that he cured her of blindness.

Mae West, who depended on Jack for career guidance and who knows what else, once chased him all the way from California to Lily Dale. Mae's bodyguards were gorgeous, remembered Betty Schultz, who saw them. Jack often entertained Mae's friends at parties in Santa Monica while Mae sat to the side dressed in an elegant, floor-length gown. It was said that a five-carat diamond ring he wore was a gift from her. Jack died well before Mae did, but that didn't end their story.

In 1974, ten years after his death, Mae settled down to watch television in her Hollywood apartment one evening. While waiting for the television to warm up, she heard a deep voice. It was as though someone was trying to say something but couldn't get the words out, Mae told an interviewer. She looked toward the other end of the couch and saw two feet in men's shoes.

Then trousers appeared, and, finally, Jack Kelly, clad in full-dress white tie, looking about thirty years old. He was completely solid, she told the interviewer.

West yelled for her bodyguard, who was in the other room, and the apparition began to disappear. "He dissolved right before my eyes, down through the couch, and was gone," Mae told a reporter. The bodyguard, shouting, "What happened?" ran into the room, but only Mae was on the couch.

I asked Hilda, why aren't the mediums of today able to do what the old-timers did?

"It's the money," she said. "These mediums charge too much money, and that's why they don't have the power mediums once did." Hilda can remember when mediums left a basket by the door for donations and didn't name a fee. She can well remember when five dollars was considered plenty. Now mediums charge forty to seventy-five dollars for a half-hour of time.

I asked Hilda whether anybody in Lily Dale was a born medium.

"I don't want to say anything against any of them," she said. "They're good people."

But was there one whom she could absolutely vouch for?

"Anne Gehman," she said. "She's a born medium."

Then Hilda shook her head and looked worried. "I don't know for sure, because Anne's had several husbands, and you'd think that if she was a true medium she wouldn't have so much trouble. She also said that Gerald Ford was going to win another term, and he didn't."

But one of the husbands died. Anne couldn't be held accountable for that, and, as for the wrong predictions, nobody's right all the time. Even Hilda doesn't expect that. Anne, who lived in Washington, D.C., and was married to a Georgetown University professor, spent part of her summers in a big pink and white cottage that faces the lake. She helped catch serial killer Ted Bundy and had some of the most powerful people in Washington as her clients, Hilda said.

Before I left, the old lady gave me a piece of advice.

"Learn everything you can while you're on the earth plane," she said, "and remember this: you take your bundle with you. Everything you learn here goes into the next world for you to use."

I'm convinced that we believe certain things about religion because they seem right. Some people call that a knowing. Some people call it resonance. Some people call it God talking. Whatever it is, that feeling is what really communicates to us, and we find ourselves thinking, *That's right. I believe that.*

When Hilda said we take our bundle with us, I thought, *That's right. I believe that.* And her words shifted something in me. I quoted them many times to other people who never failed to nod and say, "Ummm," as though I'd just imparted some great notion. I didn't realize that Hilda's words weren't as magical to everyone as they were to me until I repeated them to one rather blunt friend, who nodded, said, "Ummm," and then demanded, "What does that mean?" Probably everyone else was thinking that also and was too nice to say so.

To me, Hilda's words meant I could stop thinking I was accomplishing too little too late. They relieved me of the terrible envy one feels when someone younger does something marvelous. They gave me a sense that my life made sense and counted for something. Were her words true? I don't know, but they helped me. I might have used that piece of wisdom as a pointer to indicate that Lily Dale had lessons of a spiritual nature to teach me, but I didn't. It took me a long time to take Lily Dale seriously enough to learn from it.

Even so, I liked Hilda's idea so well that I even quoted it to Betty Schultz.

Betty had a more casual attitude about how much knowledge a person needs. "You want to know enough to say, 'Oh, I'm dead. I want to go up,'" she said.

9

The main question I wanted answered—how do beliefs change lives?—would seem easy to answer. Since people of Lily Dale believe "there is no death and there are no dead," they ought to feel less grief than the rest of us. If death is just passing over to another life, they ought to have no fear of death themselves.

I saw little evidence that Spiritualists walked toward death any more happily than the rest of us. They'd had no suicide cults, no laced Kool-Aid parties. I heard of no great mediums who voluntarily passed over in order to use their ability on the other side for the benefit of humankind. Several did claim to feel great peace and to have no fear of death. Medium Sherry Lee Calkins mentioned that the angel of death is not the grim fellow most people imagine him to be. "I consider the angel of death to be a birthday boy or birthday girl as the case may be," she said. "He's a friend."

In Lily Dale the past is quite alive. Close enough to touch, they say. Lily Dale residents regularly report seeing wraiths strolling the streets dressed in Victorian-era clothes. Native American braves often pad single file by the edge of the lake with tomahawks in hand, according to more than one living resident. Relatives often cross from the other side to speak, to move things about, to show themselves in various locations.

Yes, folks in Lily Dale frequently see the dead and hear them, they say. But grief, well, that's a strong emotion, hard to conquer. Visions and voices are nice, considerable comfort, but they're not warm bodies.

Lily Dale resident Bonnie Mikula, as stout a believer as anyone I met, told me of grief so crushing that it almost drove her crazy. Every night her sobs were so loud that her daughter slept with the radio on to drown out the sounds. During the day Bonnie was so lost and angry that the two fought constantly. A little red-haired nurse and single mother who specialized in survival, Bonnie could not accept the injustice of losing her longtime lover, Chapman Clark.

Chapman, the only brother of Sherry Lee Calkins and Gretchen Clark Lazarony, was not a medium, as his sisters were. He was a healer. He had often healed Bonnie's headaches with a touch. And every night when they were apart, he dropped in for telepathic chats at 10:00 P.M., she told me. Bonnie knew he was terribly ill in the weeks before he died, but he promised that he would never leave her, and she believed him. She thought that man could do anything.

He was found one balmy April afternoon lying in the grass, his lawn mower beside him, his glasses folded next to him, his arms crossed over his chest. It was as though Chapman Clark, fifty-five, a healthy-looking, handsome bear of a man, decided one lovely afternoon that the time had come to quit mowing and die. So he made himself comfortable, arranged himself presentably, and did just that.

"Chapman was always in control," said his friend Shelley Takei, who told me that version of his death.

But in Lily Dale, where *dead* and *gone* are words never used together, that wasn't the end of the story. Soon after his demise, her brother assured her that he hadn't been preparing to die, said Sherry Lee. In fact, he hadn't felt a thing that day. He was dead before he hit the ground. He also told her that the lesion in his brain hadn't killed him. That was important to Sherry Lee, since she and Gretchen had done a healing on Chapman to shrink the tumor. They'd gone inside his brain and worked a bit of magic, according to Lily Dale lore.

Chapman had also come back to comfort Bonnie, she told me, but it hadn't helped. She shouted at him that he needed to stay away. His presence only made things worse. "There he was having a great time, and I was left behind," she said.

Bonnie and his sister weren't the only persons who testified that Chapman had returned. He hadn't been dead a week before he was tramping around Betty Schultz's house, exciting her dog, disrupting the old lady's rest, and causing the kind of commotion that Betty would never have tolerated from Chapman when he was alive. The next day Betty paid a visit to Sherry Lee.

"Chap showed up," she said in her customarily abrupt way. "What's this about a pig?" It seems Chapman was holding a ceramic pig when he appeared at Betty's house. It's well known in Lily Dale that spirits often bring some token to identify themselves in case the living don't believe they're who they claim to be. Of course, Betty had known Chap most of his life, did recognize him, and didn't doubt him for a minute. Nevertheless, the pig was a nice touch, Sherry Lee thought.

The sisters buried Chap in Mr. Piggy, an old, chipped, faded cookie jar that they had fought over as children. One of them had taken it for her own after their mother died, but Chap loved it, and since he was the first to go, they gave it to him. They cremated him. Burying a body six feet under might keep a spirit earthbound, according to some Spiritualist thinking, and Chap, a bachelor all his life, was a man who loved his freedom. So the sisters cast two-thirds of their only brother's ashes to the winds and buried the rest in the cookie jar.

At the funeral, Bonnie and the Clark sisters stood around the little hole in the ground with a bottle of Glenlivet—another nice touch, since Chapman had loved his scotch. The sisters poured a little scotch on the grave, and then each grieving woman took a swig herself. They handed the gravedigger the rest of the bottle. He tipped it up, swigged, and said, "Damn, that's good stuff."

Chapman appeared to Sherry Lee several times afterward. In her accounts of those visits, his behavior seemed decidedly strange to me, although it made perfect sense to his eldest sister. Once he came holding a buttercup under his chin. As he twirled it, he chanted, "Butter, butter, who doesn't like butter?" Sherry Lee called her daughter with the exciting news. The girl hoped to buy a farm near Buffalo but hadn't been able to afford anything she liked. Sherry Lee said Chapman was returning to let her know that she would find a house and it would have buttercups around it. Soon thereafter her daughter did indeed find such a house.

One longtime believer in spirit communication said of an aunt who had died two weeks earlier, "It's about time she checked in." Shortly thereafter the aunt did make contact, but not in the form anyone expected. She left her name on the caller ID of a telephone, according to the story. Spirit methods are infinitely varied, say Spiritualist accounts. They often flicker lights or appear as a smell associated with the loved one. Sometimes they manifest as nothing more than a feeling.

Kent Bentkowski's father contacted him via telephone. The two had not spoken for six years before the father's death. After his father's passing, Kent's telephone began to ring at all hours of the day and night. When he or his wife, Paula, answered, there was no sound on the line. The calls continued—sometimes five and six times a day, sometimes only once a day—for six months, until finally Paula said, "I know who it is. It's your father. So just say, 'What do you want?'"

Kent was too frightened by the thought to say anything during the next few calls, but finally he picked up the phone and said, "Hi, Dad. I know it's you. What do you want?"

A voice that Kent said sounded exactly like his father's said, "I'm sorry."

Kent said he then called the operator, explained what had happened, and asked where the call had come from. After checking, she replied, "Mr. Bentkowski, I don't know how to tell you this, but no one has called your line since yesterday."

One medium believed her late husband was in her hotel room after she rose in the middle of the night to go to the toilet. She sat on the commode, but the seat had been left up, and just as she dropped into the water she heard a loud laugh echoing off the tiled walls. It was her husband's inimitable guffaw. She would have known it anywhere.

Martie Hughes, like many mediums, sees spirits only in her mind's eye, and she's not eager for them to appear in any other way. "It would scare the poop out of me," she said. On occasions when she is alone and believes a spirit might be hovering around, she closes her eyes tightly. "I don't want to see them," she said. When I asked why, her answer was similar to those I received from many mediums as I probed for details on life with the spirits.

She embarked on a long explanation about the difference in vibrations. She feels different vibrations when working with a client than when receiving her own visions. The time an angel sat on the edge of her bed was a different vibration than the time she awoke at 4:30 A.M. knowing she had to go to another town to visit her friend who was at the moment thinking of suicide.

What exactly is a vibration?

"Energy. Energy is made up of vibrations," she said and began another long explanation. I interrupted her.

Why is it so hard to get Spiritualists to describe their reality in ways that nonmediumistic people can relate to?

"It's like asking someone from Sweden how it's different to speak Swedish," she replied.

Mary Ann Spears, the North Carolina psychotherapist who sees the dead relatives of her clients, said she doesn't even try explaining. "You need to talk with like-minded people," she said. "I'm not going to try to explain this to anybody who doesn't understand it."

Mary Ann's mediumistic specialty developed one day during an ordinary psychotherapy session. She was listening to a client who was ashen-faced with grief, weeping, bent over in his chair, hardly able to talk, when beside him appeared an apparition.

"There was his radiant daughter standing there, gesturing, saying, 'Tell him. Tell him I'm here,'" Mary Ann said.

His daughter had died three years earlier when a truck hit her in New York City. The driver was never found. The father could not stop blaming himself.

Mary Ann wondered, *Should I tell him? Would it be malfeasance? Would it help or hurt if I mentioned that I see his daughter?* She didn't know. So she asked him whether he believed in everlasting life. When he said he did, she told him that his daughter was standing beside him.

"I described her down to what she was wearing and her tiny beautiful face," Mary Ann said. "I never did know whether he believed me."

Since then, she said, lots of dead people have appeared next to her grieving clients. They always bring the same message: "Tell him (or her) I'm alive." They wave their arms, shout in exasperation, jump up and down. They bring objects and animals to prove who they are. It can be most distracting, she said.

The spirits don't return because they worry about the sorrow their relatives feel, said Mary Ann. "They don't think like that. They're spirit. They see there's a problem, and they know that the way to solve it is to let people know they aren't dead. So they do."

When living people tell Mary Ann they are afraid to be buried or fearful about being burned during cremation, she feels amazed, dismayed, and somewhat alienated, as though she were on the outside looking in. They completely misunderstand, she said.

"You're wearing a suit of clothes and you step out of them," she said. "You're still you. You just leave this suit of clothes behind. You're fully conscious, but the body doesn't mean anything to you anymore."

Spiritualists often talk of spirits who keep them company over many years. At the house with a little sign that reads, RAYMOND TORREY MEDIUM, an old man often sits in the front room that serves as his office and medium's parlor. Around his head white hair fans out in a glinting halo, lit by sun that shafts through the dusty window. Ray was once known throughout America's Spiritualist community as the singing medium because he always sang at services. Customers come less often now that he is in his nineties. That's all right in a way. Solitude gives him more time to talk with his baby daughter who died sixty years ago.

Ray has a son in his twenties, but it's still the long-gone daughter who comforts him most. He watched her grow up in the spirit world until she reached a pretty thirty-five years old, when, right in accordance with some Spiritualists' thought, she stopped aging. There's difference of opinion over what age spirit bodies assume after they pass over. Many Spiritualists say thirty-five is the perfect age when physical form and maturity come together most harmoniously, and so spirit entities take that age. Others say spirits become the age when they were happiest.

When spirits appear to their loved ones, however, they often manifest at the age when they died in order to be recognized, the mediums say. There seems to be agreement on the fact that babies who die do grow up. So Ray expected to see his daughter move through childhood into her adult years, and that is what he saw, he said.

Some days she's the only one who seems to understand him, he told me sadly.

Medium Greg Kehn once comforted a client by telling her that the loneliness so many people suffer from is an illusion. "If they could see what I see, they would know that they are never alone. Spirits are all around them," he said.

That idea causes some people to worry about privacy, a concern the mediums wave away. "The spirits aren't watching you do embarrassing things. They're on a different plane," they say. That may be, but when Martie Hughes smelled cherry pipe tobacco and received the impression that a sea captain who had gone to spirit was roaming about her house, she immediately laid down some rules.

The first was that he was not to appear before her physical eyes. "When I open my eyes, I do not want to see you standing there," she said. And the second rule was, "The bathroom is off limits."

"I did not want him to see me naked," she said.

Some of the mediums looked at me somberly and said, "This is going to be a spiritual journey for you." I was polite about that, but I didn't think so. They also told me that I had psychic ability. They tell a lot of people that.

"Haven't you had feelings about things that were going to happen?" the mediums asked.

"Not really," I'd reply. That wasn't exactly true. I do have premonitions. I think I'm going to die every time I get on a plane. If it's not me who is going to die, it's someone I love. Every time my relatives plan to visit, every time the phone rings after dark, I'm positive that the Old Reaper is rapping. I've been so sure I was going to die that I've left messages on my desk for my kinfolk to open once I'm gone. I used to buy all sorts of food before I went on a trip, as though produce waiting to be cooked would exert some protective force. On the way to the airport, I have reminded my husband more than once that he's to take care of my parents if I don't come back.

I do not tell people about my fears because "death by irony" is another one of them. In the newspaper business, you're always writing or reading some story about somebody who moved out of the city to be safe and got run over by a tractor or somebody who left a note on her desk about dying before she left on the trip that killed her. Those stories often say, "Ironically . . . ," and that's death by irony.

When the mediums tried to convince me that I had power, I said politely, "No. I don't sense things." That wasn't a lie, because I'm never right. Thank God. If I believed all the terrors I sense, I'd never leave the house.

I came to Lily Dale as an observer. Nothing more. But Lily Dale doesn't like that. It's an equal opportunity place. "Anybody can do what we do," the mediums said repeatedly. "You can do it too."

10

Pat Naulty, the English professor whose son died playing Russian roulette, was walking away from an afternoon message service at the Forest Temple when a man parking his car waved and called to her. At the service, a medium had given Pat a message that indicated Pat was confused and uncertain. It was the same message that the same medium had delivered to her the night before. Pat wasn't confused and she wasn't uncertain, but Lily Dale itself so entranced her that she was still fairly blissed out and open to almost anything. So she dutifully searched her consciousness to see whether perhaps the medium knew something that she ought to pay attention to. No. There was nothing.

The night before, Pat had slept at Shelley's house in the goddess room, a little upstairs bedroom decorated with paintings of women's faces amid swirling colors. An alcove in one wall had been turned into an altar bedecked with gold cloth and crystals. Like much of Shelley's decor, the altar was just overdone enough to go past reverence into playfulness. On the back of the bedroom door hung Shelley's version of goddess attire, a T-shirt decorated with the words, "You call me a bitch like that's a BAD thing."

Shelley delighted in warning guests about the goddess room. It has strong currents running through it, according to many of the sensitives who have slept there. Some women have reported that, as they fall into the darkness of dreams, powerful currents of cosmic energy toss and tumble them. Sometimes they awake in the night and hear a murmuring crowd of indistinct female voices.

As Pat walked back to Shelley's house her second day in Lily Dale, she eyed the pudgy little guy calling to her.

"My God, you have the most beautiful energy," he yelled across the street.

Pat did feel as though she were glowing with some strange new light, but still. The little man was apparently coming on to her, and she thought, *Oh, please!* New Age jargon was not the way to her heart.

"Thank you very much," she said in that bright voice women use for the brush-off. She kept walking. But he blocked her path.

He had a questioning look on his face. "Who's Gertrude?" he asked.

Pat stopped. He had her attention now.

"That was my mother."

"She's hugging you."

If she's hugging me, Pat wondered, *why can't I feel her?*

Pat was not particularly a believer in such messages, but neither was she unacquainted with psychic strangeness. In her twenties she had precognitive dreams. Only one had been of any value. That one came while she and her husband were traveling to visit his parents in Indiana. It was late, and Pat, pregnant with her older son, Willie, suddenly felt so sleepy that she couldn't keep her head up. So she laid it in her husband's lap as he drove. In her dream she saw their car cresting a hill, gathering speed as it traveled into the night. In the black road, sat a dark car, stalled, without lights and empty. As they crashed, Pat cried out and flung her arm into the dashboard.

She sat up and told her husband what she'd dreamed. A hill was ahead. "It looked like that hill," she said. Her husband eased off the accelerator, and, as they coasted down the incline, he braked right behind a dark car, stalled, without lights and empty.

Pat's other prophetic dreams had been confusing and useless. Days before her father died of a heart attack she dreamed that she was attending a funeral. But she hadn't known whose funeral it was. Even if she had known, what could she have done? Years later she dreamed of another graveyard. This one was at the edge of a river and had gravestones that lay flat on the earth. For two months, the dreams repeated themselves. When her sister called to say that their apparently healthy, forty-nine-year-old mother had collapsed with heart failure, Pat asked, "What hospital did they take her to?"

And her sister answered, "Patty, she's dead." They buried Gertrude in a cemetery with flat gravestones at the edge of a river—just like the one in the dream.

The dreams and forebodings ended when Pat was in her thirties. "I pretty much willed them to quit," she said, "and when they did I was relieved."

She hadn't thought about her psychic moments in a long time. They were no part of who she thought herself to be.

"Gertrude wants you to know that she approves of what you've done," the man said. "She's proud you got your degree and that you're teaching." How did he know she was teaching? How did he know these words she needed so much to hear?

Gertrude's death had been the reason Pat returned to college. Only Gertrude could have understood how desperate she had been. As a child, Pat often begged her mother to divorce her father, but Gertrude always replied that she had no education, no skills, and no way of supporting the family. When Pat's father died, her mother became young again, Pat said. For two years, she was vibrant and free and excited about life in a way her daughters had never seen. Then she died.

"I was determined that what happened to my mother wouldn't happen to me," Pat said. So she went to college. When her marriage began to rend under the pressure that decision helped create, she left the house, found a little place to live, and kept going to college. She was determined to get a Ph.D. and become a professor. "I felt like that was what I had to do, what I was born to do," she said.

She thought her sons would stay with their father until she was settled, and then they would live with her. When she was ready, however, their father wouldn't let them go, she said. Then her son John died, and Pat felt that she had killed him. She should have stayed with the boys, no matter what it cost her, she thought. But it was too late.

The man in the parking lot was looking at her with narrowed eyes. "There's also a teenage boy here," he said. "He's tall and gangly, and he's wearing a baseball cap." John was six-foot-two when he shot himself, so big for his age that everyone thought he was older. He had sandy hair and lopsided dimples.

"That's John," she said.

Pat doesn't remember the man's name, only that he was a visiting medium from Ohio. He was on his way to the Stump, where visiting mediums are allowed to give messages, but he talked so long with Pat that he missed the service.

Pat had been in Lily Dale one full day. The next day, she would get a reading from Lauren Thibodeau, a medium with a Ph.D. in counseling. That night Pat annoyed Shelley and the other guests by talking incessantly. She dominated conversations, talked about herself, asked too many questions. She couldn't shut up, and then she couldn't sleep. It was all too wonderful, like a completely different life. She had evidence that John's spirit was alive and still present. Tomorrow, maybe, she would hear words from him that she longed for but didn't dare hope to hear.

11

The June day I met Murry King was early in my research, before the summer season had actually started. I'd just had my ears boxed, figuratively speaking, by a medium named Rose Clifford. I wanted to talk with Rose because she was to teach a class on spoon bending. People said it couldn't be done anymore. But there was Rose, about to teach it. I wanted to ask this sweet-looking Englishwoman how she did it, but I never got the chance.

Before I could ask my first question, she peppered me with queries about my intentions, my background, my character, and my right to ask anybody anything. Everything I said she called lies. When I mentioned that she wasn't being very polite, she said, "I don't think you're even a journalist." Fearing she was about to tell me I wasn't married and probably not a woman either, I grabbed my notebook and fled.

At the end of the street, still dazed, I stumbled into Murry King, my first complete, totally committed skeptic. Murry's doubt about all of Lily Dale's supernatural claims caused me to think we were kindred souls. I was wrong about that. Like Shelley, Murry still thought Lily Dale might very well be a place of great spiritual wisdom, a notion that made no sense to me. What somebody says is true or not true. What somebody does is right or wrong. But not in the Dale. People there live enmeshed in worlds glimpsed between the facts, worlds in which I'm not an easy traveler.

Murry King was a handyman and friend to all stray cats, lost dogs, and little old ladies who needed a chore done and didn't want to pay. A big man with enough belly to be substantial, he had a ruff of gray hair that stood over a forehead expanded by his hair-line's retreat, and he talked softly, with calm deliberation.

Raised in a Catholic orphanage, Murry once hoped to be a monk but lost heart after a year during which he spent some time wandering in the forest trying to obey Teresa of Avila's injunction to make every deed a prayer. "I couldn't do it. So I gave it up," he said. He'd knocked around most of his life, married, divorced, been a Marine, gone to graduate school, and run a restaurant. He arrived in Lily Dale to help a friend renovate a house. Before they finished, he experienced heart trouble and needed a quadruple bypass. He stayed in the Dale to recuperate and hadn't got around to leaving.

Murry's tendency to sink into a funk every winter made Lily Dale, with its long gray winters, a dicey place for him to be. The previous winter he had refused to answer his door or telephone. Neighbors, convinced he'd died, called the emergency squad. People in uniforms were ready to break down the door when Murry answered, annoyed, almost comatose with depression, but completely alive. He went to a doctor, who asked whether he was hearing voices; Murry replied, "Doc, where I live, I'm the only one who doesn't."

Murry was not a believer, even though he bent a spoon or two in a class taught by Anne Gehman. My attention sharpened at hearing Anne's name because she was Hilda's example of a born medium. During Anne's class Murry held his spoons so the handles protruded from his fists. Spoon benders usually grasp the spoons at each end and apply a little pressure, but Murry wasn't interested in something so easily faked. He merely held his spoons with the handles protruding from his fists and then watched as the handles twisted into curlicues. I asked to see the spoons, but he had lost them.

This was the first spoon-bending story I heard, but not the last. I was told about whole classes of people who bent spoons while standing on the shore of the lake. Each time a piece of cutlery surrendered itself, the class cheered so loudly that all of Lily Dale could hear it. Anne herself displays a big bag of bent silverware, spoons turned to curlicues, forks with tines as wild as Einstein's hair.

Murry's bent spoons pushed him toward conviction, but only briefly. He tried to do it again and couldn't. "I don't know what bent the spoons. Hypnotism maybe," he said. But the way Murry sees it, if you can't do it again, it doesn't count. That's an idea that Murry shares with the scientific world, which has looked into the claims of Spiritualism thousands of times. Lots of researchers say they have found amazing things going on amid all the claims. Metal bending, object moving, ESP, conversations with the dead—they've all had their distinguished advocates, bearing evidence, but getting the phenomena to repeat themselves for other scientists has been the rub. It's hardly ever happened.

"I haven't seen anything in Lily Dale to convince me they are communicating with spirit," Murry said. "There's a lot of exaggeration, and I guess you would say hopeful enthusiasm."

If the spirits wanted to convert Murry, they had their chance fifty-five years ago. He was a first-grader when his mother placed him in the orphanage. She promised to come back. Instead, she died. Every night while the other children slept, Murry padded across the floor to the window. Looking into the cold, dark sky, he prayed that his mother would send some sign she was with him, but she never did. No voice. No vision. Not even a shooting star. Nothing.

Murry grew up, married, and moved to Georgia. One midnight he was looking toward the starry sky when a thought flashed across his mind.

My father is dead.

Murry and his father didn't communicate, didn't much like each other. Murray rarely thought of his father, which made this premonition so odd that he wrote down the date, September 1, 1976. Ten years later he had a conversation with his stepmother, who told him his father was dead.

"When did he die?" Murry asked.

"September 1, 1976," she answered. "He had a heart attack at midnight."

After telling me the story, Murry paused until he got the raised eyebrow he was waiting for, and then he asked, "Was he stopping in to say good-bye on his way out? And why would he?" What kind of pitiless universe would ignore the sobs of an orphaned child and then send a message to a man who didn't even care?

"I'm sixty-one years old now, and the only thing I know is that we don't know nothing, and even that's on shaky ground," he said.

Some days later I sat near Murry during a Sunday night message service at the Healing Temple, and I saw one secret of Lily Dale's power acted out. True to my usual response when enlightenment presents itself, I dismissed it.

One of the mediums that night looked at Murry.

"May I come to you?" she asked.

"Thank you," Murry said in polite assent.

"They're telling me that you've had a rough spring," said the sensitive, "but that new activity is ahead for you. You're feeling some strain about that."

Everybody knew that he had bid to take over the cafeteria for the summer season. Running the cafeteria was a big job, and it meant a lot to Lily Dale because tourists had only two choices for food, the Good Vibrations Cafe or the cafeteria. The responsibility of operating the cafeteria scared Murry, as everybody knew. The medium didn't need spirit help for that.

I looked to see how Murry, avowed skeptic, was taking what seemed to me to be an obvious bit of play-acting. He was nodding.

"They're saying that you will have some trials. Keep your chins up, and you will do fine," she said.

Good grief. Even I knew people worried that Murry might not have the grit to manage a staff.

What I could not understand was how that medium kept from laughing as she credited the spirits with ideas that I was certain were her own. Murry couldn't be buying this nonsense. I didn't see his face as the message continued. Afterward the medium came laughing toward Murry.

He grabbed her in a body hug and yelled, "I'll get you for that chins comment."

Everyone left the church. I didn't speak until we were in the yard.

"Come on, Murry. That wasn't a message. Anybody could have said that," I said.

Murry peered at me through his glasses and then looked over my head in a thoughtful way. Murry would soon get the chance he wanted, and it was going to be a bigger struggle than anyone knew. He was about to start a three-meal-a-day, seven-day-a-week cafeteria with two hundred dollars for food. During the opening night fish fry, he would run out of fish long before he ran out of customers because he could afford only a couple of dozen fillets. During the first weeks of the season, customers would look for jelly or mustard and find none because Murry had purchased only a little of each. Whenever the cafeteria ran out of supplies, he would raid the cash register and drive furiously to a nearby store. By summer's end, he would have scandalized the community by hiring what looked to be street people, whom he allowed to sleep above the cafeteria with companions and pets.

"When I need them, I know where they are," he defended himself.

But all that was in the future on the night Murry got his reading. The only thing present tense was his fear.

"I guess you're right," he said, acknowledging that anybody might have said the medium's words, "but I was grateful. I needed the support."

Okay. I got it. Murry was about to win the cafeteria contract because no one else wanted it. Now Lily Dale was going to back him, shore up his efforts, and make him a success. I liked it. Later I heard that one of his neighbors worked without pay to help him. *How sweet,* I thought. *How Mayberry of them.*

The town is full of star-gazing Aunt Beas and ghost-busting Barney Fifes. Dreamy and full of goodwill, the Dale embraces everybody, calls the spirit world down to help them, and then mixes it up. Lily Dale's charm is as much about being *believed in* as it is about believing.

That's partly why people who move there often think they've found a little paradise. Neighbors help one another. Old people are looked after and included in gatherings. When someone falls sick, everybody knows it and helps. Children can play outside at night. There's no crime to speak of. Volunteer firefighters are the town's heroes. Residents sit on front porches from which American flags wave. A silver tea opens the summer season.

The two churches are so democratic that they have no appointed ministers. Each week a friend or neighbor mounts the platform to talk about what's on his or her mind. Even the spirits themselves are bound by the Dale's fierce love for individual rights. In one town meeting Gretchen Clark Lazarony made the mistake of quoting her spirit guide as she was defending her own opinion. Resident Ron DeChard promptly got up and said his spirit guide came to him while he was on the toilet. After giving a nonsense message, Ron said, his guide instructed him, "Flush." The assembly laughed as though that were the richest joke ever, and Gretchen apologized.

12

The first time I tried to contact spirit was the night medium Patricia Price showed us how to fake reading billets. Faking was easy, she said, but so was doing the real thing. She had us pair off and write a question to spirit on a piece of paper. My partner and I sat with knees facing and exchanged our folded notes. My partner was a nice older woman who'd been a Spiritualist for forty years. None of her three children was a believer. Holding her note, I shut my eyes and waited. Nothing. My mind was completely blank.

"Keep trying," she said. "Something will come."

I saw a sheaf of pink roses. That was so lame. It's what local wags call the universal message: "I've got a grandmotherly spirit with roses and she's sending love." I didn't have the grandmother or the love. Just roses. How humiliating.

But that's all I saw, and so I said it. "I see roses." She smiled.

"Anything else? Be patient with yourself."

"Nooooo."

The Spiritualist lady looked disappointed. This was ridiculous. I felt silly and at the same time inadequate. It was as though I'd failed to make the in-crowd, been snubbed by the spirits. I was not the first to feel Lily Dale's peculiar pressures.

"One of the most curious facts about the Dale Spiritualists is the pique they exhibit when compelled to admit that they are not receiving any messages," wrote psychology student George Lawton after visiting Lily Dale in 1929. "A person returning to the hotel veranda from a meeting is apt to be met with the eagerly-put query: 'Did you get a message?'" If the answer was no for too many days, the Spiritualist was likely to begin responding with a "Spiritualist type of feeling of inferiority—a sense of hurt and shame arising from the belief that one of two things is true: either he is unloved by those in the beyond or, through some fault or even delinquent strain, he generates vibrations which repel all attempts at communication."

I opened the Spiritualist lady's note. On it was written, "How did you die? Was it really the car wreck that killed you?"

My partner didn't even smirk. "You did get something," she said gently.

Right. So what was spirit saying? He was pelted to death with roses?

I grimaced.

"That was his mother sending love," the Spiritualist lady said.

Nice try. This is all Lily Dale is, I thought. Nice, gullible, well-intentioned people coming together and convincing each other that they're special enough to talk with ghosties. That's what Murry's message seemed to be, and now here it was again. All these messages were information the mediums already knew or inanities that allowed the hearer to fill in the blanks. I went away discouraged. I'd begun to like the people in Lily Dale. I hated thinking that they were dupes.

William James noted that belief in psychic events has been recorded in every society in every age. He listened to and investigated such accounts, and the sheer number of them impressed him. Any one of the stories might not be enough to convince a cautious person, he reasoned. Each account is a mere twig that can be easily snapped, but put the accounts together and they make a sturdy bundle that does not yield easily.

"I find myself believing that there is 'something' in these never ending reports of physical phenomena, although I haven't yet the least possible notion of the something," he wrote in *The Final Impressions of a Psychical Researcher.* One of the bundles of sticks I encountered as I researched psychic events was the number of brilliant people who have believed that reality might include spirits, talking dead people, meaningful coincidences, or other strange events.

Thomas Edison was one of those who trusted spirit help and other strange forces. He once connected rubber tubes to his forehead, directed them toward a pendulum suspended on the wall of his laboratory, and attempted to move it with the force of his will. He recorded mind trips into the outer reaches of the cosmos, and when dealing with a problem he couldn't solve, he often napped as a way of accessing impressions from the universe at large. When he awoke, a new idea would lead him to the solution. His ideas and inventions didn't come from his own brain, he said. He was merely a receiving apparatus or recording plate.

He believed the universe consists of an infinite number of "monads," conscious centers of spiritual force or energy that are constant and immortal. Humans are made up of these bits of energy combined in different ways, he said. Late in life he worked on a spirit machine to detect and record the monads he believed were prowling through the ether of space.

He theorized that living people may communicate with the dead because personality is recorded in the brain's memory cells. When the physical body decomposes, memory cells may abandon the useless vessel and swarm free in space. These bits of energy are intelligences that carry the essence of the human personality they once were part of.

Carl G. Jung experienced a number of what seemed to be poltergeist experiences, and séances he attended for two years were the basis for his doctoral dissertation. He was not a Spiritualist, as the title of his dissertation—*On the Psychology and Psychopathology of So-called Occult Phenomena*—attests. But his experiences with séances caused him to wonder whether the unconscious mind receives strange and mysterious material that the conscious mind would never be able to accept. Later in life the psychiatrist followed his own inner voices into strange realms. Biblical, mythical, and historical figures arose in his mind. Salome appeared, and Elijah the prophet. In one of his dreams a winged figure came sailing across the sky. It was an old man with the horns of a bull, who became known to Jung as Philemon. Jung considered Philemon his *psychagogue,* the teacher who would instruct his soul on matters of the unconscious.

The old man Philemon was a fantasy and also a "force which was not of myself," Jung wrote. Philemon assured Jung that thoughts are like people in a room. Neither he nor any other thinker generates their own thoughts, Philemon said. So thought is not the thinker's responsibility.

Jung worried about his own mental stability, but the fact that he could step in and out of his visions reassured him. One day he found himself less in control. He felt a strange and almost unbearable tension. Even his children seemed to act oddly. He felt surrounded by outside voices, while his mind was filled with inner voices. Relief came only when he began to write.

For three nights, he wrote a document that he called *Seven Sermons of the Dead.* The dead he referred to were spokesmen for the realm beyond human understanding, he believed. The manuscript was written in old-fashioned language, and at the end Jung signed the manuscript with the name Basilides, an Alexandrian Gnostic who lived about 120 years after Christ. Jung wrote that the conversations helped him organize and explain his theories about collective consciousness, which he would spend much of his life exploring.

Jung seemed to be of two minds about the spirits communicating with him. "Spirits are complexes of the collective unconscious which appear when the individual loses his adaptation to reality or which seek to replace the inadequate attitude of a whole people by a new one. They are therefore either pathological fantasies or new but as yet unknown ideas," he wrote. Jung also said that Westerners use thinking and sensation as their dominant ways of experiencing the world. This separation from feeling and intuition cuts them off from whole realms of knowledge.

Freud didn't agree with Jung's mystical ideas and the psychiatrists' association ended over them. But even the father of psychoanalysis himself believed telepathy might be possible when he noticed that patients and analysts often seemed to be able to pick up each other's thought.

Commodore Cornelius Vanderbilt, once the richest man in America, credited the spirit world with having given him good health and financial success. Asked how he made such astute business decisions, he said, "Do as I do. Consult the spirits."

His mistress, Tennessee Claflin, and her sister, Victoria Woodhull, were well-known clairvoyants in the mid-1800s who advised the millionaire on investments and other matters. He was so grateful for their aid that he helped finance a brokerage firm the sisters started for female investors, the first such business ever.

Vanderbilt believed portraits enabled spirits to communicate and always carried a miniature of his late mother, Phebe, in his breast pocket. When Victoria attempted to conjure Phebe's spirit, she sat under the old lady's portrait in the parlor of the Vanderbilt mansion. During the sessions, Vanderbilt said he could smell soap and lavender, scents that reminded him of his mother. He trusted Victoria's talents implicitly, and she helped him in many ways. But she had her limits. When the millionaire wanted her to construct a spirit portrait of his late father, whose face Vanderbilt well recalled, she declined despite many offers of ample payment.

Vanderbilt once gave a Staten Island medium enough money to retire to Vermont after she rid him of two spirits who had haunted his dreams. One was a seven-year-old boy killed by Vanderbilt's carriage horses in Central Park, and another was a railroad worker mangled beneath the wheels of the Commodore's private railroad car, the *Flying Devil*.

Muckraker and Socialist Upton Sinclair was one of the most famous and respected journalists of the early twentieth century. He became a believer in psychic phenomena after his wife, Mary Craig, began experimenting with telepathy.

"I am the despair of my orthodox materialistic friends because I insist upon believing in the possibility of so many strange things," he wrote in his autobiography. "My materialistic friends know that these things are *a priori* impossible; whereas I assert that nothing is *a priori* impossible. It is a question of evidence, and I am willing to hear the evidence about anything whatever."

He detailed his and Mary Craig's experiments in a book titled *Mental Radio.* Sinclair wrote that he would sit at a desk in one room while his wife reclined in another room. He would draw a picture and take it to his wife. Without looking at it, she would put the picture face down on her solar plexus, get a mental impression, and draw it. The book, which records 210 successes, reproduces both his drawings and Mary Craig's.

When he couldn't find a publisher, Sinclair published the book himself. His friends objected vehemently, warning him that *Mental Radio* would ruin his credibility. One published an article titled "Sinclair Goes Spooky."

But not everyone was so frightened of the subject. A publisher did eventually pick up the book, and Albert Einstein wrote the preface for a German edition. He wrote that while telepathy might seem fantastic, it was inconceivable "that so conscientious an observer and writer as Upton Sinclair should attempt a deliberate deception of the reading world. His good faith and trustworthiness cannot be doubted."

The Sinclairs had many psychic experiences and sat in circles with a number of mediums. One of the most dramatic stories was of the weekend Mary Craig had a premonition that something terrible was going wrong for their friend Jack London. She and Upton debated driving to London's ranch but decided not to. Sinclair wrote that two days later they received news London had killed himself. (Other sources say London died of kidney disease, and some blame a morphine overdose.)

Poet William Blake was famous for believing in unearthly powers. In more recent times, so was poet James Merrill, who, with his companion David Jackson, spent twenty years consulting the Ouija board. Night after night in the cupola of their house in Stonington, Connecticut, they sat next to each other in lavender Victorian chairs, while the board sat on a round table topped with milk glass. They used the handle of an upside-down, blue-and-white willowware teacup as their pointer and propped a mirror on a chair facing the table so they could see each other and the spirits could see them. Merrill kept one hand on the cup and transcribed with the other.

Their main spirit guide was Ephraim, who identified himself as a Greek Jew and a favorite of the Emperor Tiberius. With Ephraim's help, they composed a three-part, 560-page epic poem called *The Changing Light at Sandover.* It was filled with gods, angels, demons, and ghosts. Some people think it was Merrill's masterpiece. Others have dealt with it less kindly.

In the early years of Merrill and Jackson's Ouija boarding, Ephraim dazzled the writers with his wit and connected them with dead friends. W. H. Auden and both men's parents supposedly made contact.

Their friend Alison Lurie wrote a book about their Ouija board experiences. In it she wrote that David's unconscious mind was the main impetus for the spirit messages and that James went along as a way of giving his lover, who was a failed novelist, an outlet for creativity. But the two men gave every evidence of truly believing that they were in contact with spirits. They told Lurie that their guide once directed David to put his hand flat on the board. Both men said they saw his hand become red and creased as though it had been stepped on, and he could not lift it from the board.

Commerce with spirits was so alluring, Lurie wrote, that her two friends withdrew from real life as it became "drab, faded, even unreal" in comparison. Eventually spirits began to assure Merrill and Jackson that they were more highly evolved spiritual beings than ordinary mortals. Ephraim encouraged the couple to take other lovers whenever they liked. They did, and Merrill died of complications from HIV infection.

Lily Dale doesn't have many celebrities these days. Anne Gehman, the medium said to have congressional clients, is fairly well known, and some of the others have wide followings, but the only medium who ever made big news was Neal Rzepkowski, a local physician who made national headlines during the 1990s when he was dismissed from the staff of a nearby hospital because he was HIV positive.

When Neal first came to Lily Dale, he was a Catholic teenager working at a nearby YMCA summer camp. A medium brought his dead uncle through and predicted that Neal was going to be a physician. Neal was so impressed with the medium's message that he decided he too would summon the spirits.

"I thought, *He's a human. So if he can do it, I can do it. If there's a trick to it, I'll learn it,*" Neal said. He began taking psychic development classes and sitting in circles. For more than a year he didn't get a thing.

"I thought, *What they're doing is weeding us out before they give us the real trick,*" he said.

Then one night during a service, Neal was called upon to give a message. His attention was drawn to a woman he did not know. In his mind's eye, he saw hovering over the woman's head an image of the U.S. Capitol and a young man in an army uniform.

"You must have a son who's stationed in Washington who is on your mind," he told her. And she said, "That's exactly right."

Neal thought, *Oh, my God. How did I do that?* He was so flustered that he lost the rest of the message. But that experience so encouraged him that he continued studying spirit communication, and a month after he got his medical degree he became a Spiritualist minister.

Often named as one of Lily Dale's best mediums, Neal doesn't believe intuitive gifts are as rare as others think they are. It isn't uncommon for seasoned physicians to walk into a room and know what ails a patient, he said. "They don't call it intuition," he said. "They call it experience." But in his opinion, the energy he taps into and the knowledge other doctors pick up come from the same source.

I asked Neal why spirit guides didn't warn him before he became infected with the HIV virus. He gave an answer that Spiritualists often give when explaining their misfortunes and failures. They are on earth to learn their own lessons, they say. Spirits aren't going to get in the way of that.

He now doctors others with the virus.

"HIV has been a gift for me and most of my patients," said Neal. "You live life totally differently. You enjoy it much more." I tried to understand that perspective. I questioned it until Neal began to look at me impatiently as if he suspected that English might not be a language I understood. But I never did get it. If he really feels that way—and why would he lie?—he has attained a level of spirituality I can't fathom, one that's almost as transcendent as the mediums' other claims.

13

The morning after newly widowed Carol Lucas saw Martie Hughes and received a celestial lesson in golf, she had her appointment with medium Sherry Lee Calkins, who lives in a big green house called the Divine Wisdom Retreat. Sherry Lee, sister to Gretchen, who gave me my first Lily Dale message, and also sister to the late Chapman, who returned from the Yonder Land twirling a buttercup, spends many nights astral traveling. She once managed a former husband's construction business in Latin America by whisking her astral body into his Colombian office each night and examining the books, she told me. She also said she used her astral abilities to tour sites for buildings the construction company bid on, allowing her husband to amaze his competitors by how much he knew.

She once battled an Amazonian witch doctor who opposed their building plans. She met him on the astral plane, she said. When she realized he was ready to turn the cosmic highway into a battlefield, she called in her long-dead father and grandfather and settled herself under a hair dryer, turned on high to disrupt the witch doctor's electrical impulses. Then she sent her noncorporeal self out to meet him. She won the battle, of course. She's one of the Dale's finest sensitives.

Angelic entities are a special interest of Sherry Lee's, and she looks a little like an angel herself. Blond curls frame her face. She has wide blue eyes behind gold-rimmed glasses and beautiful pale skin that doesn't show anything of her sixty-four years. She speaks briskly in a sweet-toned voice and is likely to address people as "dear heart." Angels are all around, said Sherry Lee, who teaches workshops on them. People often encounter them and think they're human. A good way to know the difference is to look at their feet. An angel's feet never touch the earth, she said.

When I began writing this book, Sherry Lee generously used her powers of clairvoyance to reassure me. "Don't worry about a thing," she said. "They've been working on this book a long time. They want this story out."

Clearly she wasn't talking about corporeal beings.

"They've got it all worked out," she said. "The book is written. You've been chosen as the way for it to get here."

Seeing something wary in my expression, she reassured me, "They've done the work, but you'll get the money and the credit."

Great, I thought. *Now if they'll just deliver, I can go home and wait for the bucks.*

She advised me to listen carefully to the tape I made of our interview because spirit voices are sometimes audible on such recordings. I followed her advice but couldn't hear them. She does not allow tape recording of her readings. Many mediums don't. They're afraid of having false predictions used against them, I was told by mediums who do allow recordings.

Instead, Sherry Lee draws symbolic pictures as she gives messages. Spirits guide her hand, she said. Her pictures always include a four-year timeline, two years back and two years forward. Clients keep the drawings, and she encourages people to bring them back at the next reading.

When Carol arrived in Sherry Lee's parlor hoping to hear more about Noel, the medium wasted no time. She started drawing furiously and talking fast in a singsong patter. She rarely hesitated. Her observations were asserted as flat facts. Even her questions often sounded like statements.

"Your husband has passed over, is that correct?

"I sense bad blood, not necessarily an operation where there was a lot of blood, but I'm thinking bad blood or tainted blood."

"Yes." This was good, really good. Carol felt hope rising.

Sherry could not have known those details. Frank and Shelley Takei, who were hosting Carol that weekend, had made the appointment with Sherry Lee, but they had said nothing to the medium about Carol, they assured her, and Carol trusted them completely. Could Sherry Lee have known from other sources that Frank and Shelley were expecting a recently widowed guest? Possibly, but not likely. Sherry Lee runs with Lily Dale's old guard and lives at the other end of the community. The Takeis fraternize with a less establishment group that rarely communicates with Sherry Lee. A widow in Lily Dale isn't rare enough to make good gossip.

Of course, if the mediums operate an organized, efficient conspiracy to check up on clients, Sherry could have gotten that information and a lot more. But even in my most paranoid moments I found that hard to believe. A community that can't fix the holes in its streets or install a septic system that won't overflow at the height of summer is hardly likely to run an underground information system that functions reliably. The mediums would be better off guessing.

"I want you to know that your husband is sitting on the arm of the sofa there." Sherry Lee nodded toward where Carol sat. "Did he make it a point to sit on the arm of the sofa rather than the seat?"

Carol shook her head. Not that she remembered.

"Your father has passed but not your mother, right?"

"Yes." After Martie's messages, Carol was being especially careful to reveal nothing. Her absolute belief that Martie had been in touch with Noel made Carol more cautious. She had what she came for, and now she was going to be even more picky about what she accepted. Her guard up, she kept her head lowered, writing down everything Sherry Lee said.

"Your father was right there to help your husband over."

Carol's dad had died in 1990. He and Noel adored each other. When Noel became ill, Carol often talked to her dad's spirit, asking him to help in any way he could.

"Your husband passed away several months ago, right?"

Carol's head snapped up.

"No. In April." First Martie made that mistake, and now Sherry Lee. Where was this idea coming from?

"That's not what I'm getting," said Sherry Lee. "Something was going on in November."

Carol shook her head. Both mediums challenged her as though she didn't know when her husband died. What made them so stubborn?

Sherry Lee frowned for a few seconds as though gathering her thoughts.

"Your husband's father also passed over, didn't he? Some time ago?"

"Oh, yes, in the seventies."

"I feel that his father came forward and gave him some strength, a tremendous amount of strength so that he lived longer."

All this was very well, but none of it amounted to much. Except for the first sentences, it could have been good guesses, and the rest didn't seem to apply.

"Your husband has a message for you. The gathering you held for him was everything he could have wanted. I'm reading that to mean the funeral," Sherry Lee said.

"No, I didn't have a funeral. I had a memorial in June before I came up here."

Noel didn't want people filing by to look at his body in a casket, and he didn't want a preacher saying words over him. Hearing that the memorial service pleased Noel meant so much to Carol that she felt tears well up.

"Oh," Sherry Lee said, "so you had him cremated." Not a question. A statement. Carol answered nevertheless.

"That's right."

"I was getting something about a hat and wearing his favorite hat. I thought if he had been buried, maybe it was in that hat. Now I think that he wants some of his ashes to be put with the hat. You haven't distributed the ashes yet, right?"

"Right. I haven't yet." But a hat? He wanted his ashes in a favorite hat? She didn't even know what his favorite hat was.

"Someone in your life is very dominant, whose name begins with G."

Carol shook her head, searching her mind. She couldn't think of anyone, and then she remembered. Her mother is called G. G. by the grandchildren. Of course.

"My mother," she said. Sherry Lee barely nodded.

"Your guardian angel is here," said Sherry Lee. "Yours happens to be wearing . . . I thought it was a sash, but it's a tire."

Carol laughed.

"Only my guardian angel would be tacky enough to wear a tire."

"You've had a near-fatal occasion that involved a tire."

Again Carol drew a blank. "No."

"Did you pull off the road to change a tire?"

"No."

"Well, that's what I'm getting," Sherry Lee said. She never retracts a thing.

"Were you a therapist?"

"No, a teacher."

"I see you working with children who were very troubled, on an individual basis."

That was true. Troubled kids had always come to Carol with their problems.

Now Sherry Lee moved to the future.

"I see you not necessarily with kids. I see you with a role, and I want to say therapist, but it might not be a therapist as we think of it. But I see you with a partnership. By August of next year I see you in a partnership, and I'm going to leave the door open to work as some kind of therapist." She marked the date on the time-line she was drawing.

Sherry Lee paused. "Here's something you are not going to want to hear."

Carol looked up. "If it's bad news, I don't want to hear it." She was too shaky.

"I would not give you bad news," Sherry Lee said, a little miffed. "I see this partnership starting as a business but evolving into marriage."

"That is not something I want to hear," Carol snapped. "I don't see myself ever becoming involved with someone else in a marriage."

The medium laughed. "I said it wasn't something you would want to hear."

The session satisfied Carol, but it had some misses. At least, that's how it seemed as she gave Sherry Lee her forty-five dollars and left.

At a quarter to six the next morning, Carol bolted upright in bed. "It couldn't have been more dramatic if the Mormon Tabernacle Choir had assembled in my bedroom. I knew what the tire meant."

When she and her younger daughter were driving back from Johns Hopkins with Noel's ashes, their car developed a shimmy.

They made it to Greenville, South Carolina, where Carol's older daughter lives. She asked David, her son-in-law, to take the car around the block and see whether he could tell her what the problem was. When he returned, he said, "Carol, you have a bad tire. You have a bad bulge in that tire. I'll take it in to be fixed."

At the service station the mechanic said, "Man, I hope nobody was driving on this tire because it is an accident waiting to happen."

When Carol returned home, she told her younger daughter about the reading.

"Don't you remember Dad coming to sit on the edge of the sofa?" her daughter asked. "He did that all the time. I have pictures of him sitting that way."

The idea of Noel's favorite hat was still a mystery to Carol, but that didn't bother her. The only true mistake Sherry Lee made was that strange mention of Noel having died several months ago. The same mistake Martie made.

Was it coincidence or did they both know something even Carol had forgotten? Martie's message had amazed Carol, but if that had been all there was, she might have eventually explained it away. She might have been able to believe that Martie had pulled that image from her subconscious memories. That would be an amazing feat, but it wouldn't mean that Noel's spirit was still alive.

If, however, two mediums independently came up with a fact that even Carol didn't know, she would be convinced they weren't getting their information from her and they weren't guessing. They were getting messages from somewhere else, from Noel, who still existed and now understood all that had gone on.

Sherry Lee said Noel had almost died in November. Carol had medical records of everything, of every day, every setback, every rally. So she pulled those heavy stacks of paper out and began a sad search through them. As she read, all the memories came back, harder now to relive because she knew the outcome. November.

There it was, just as Sherry Lee said it would be.

Noel's white count had risen astronomically high in November, high enough that he could have died. No one knew why. Then it dipped again. Drastically. He was out of danger. Still, no one knew why.

Had Noel stayed alive longer than he was supposed to? Martie and Sherry Lee thought so. Sherry Lee had the date right. Maybe?

All right, certainly. Carol believed it. "To have two of them in a twelve-hour period and to have some of the things they said reflect one another, it was overwhelming," she said, "and yet gratifying and edifying."

She was convinced. "What I'd hoped for was true." The realization soothed her like a warm hand. Noel was all right. Everything was going to be fine. The glimmer of hope she came to Lily Dale with was now a dancing flame. Carol would look toward that glow many times in the coming months.

14

When I heard that Patricia Price, the medium who had taught us how to fake billet reading, was having a yearly reunion of her students, I wrangled an invitation. We were to meet for dinner at a restaurant on the water. On the way over a nurse who gave me a ride spoke of having talked with the Archangel Michael. She never saw him, or heard a voice outside herself, she said. It was more like a voice in her head, like her own thoughts but also like someone else speaking.

I asked her what I always asked people when they said God talked to them.

How did you know it was him?

"He said so," she answered.

Eventually she asked the Archangel to go away because the conversations made her think she was crazy. When she first started talking to him, she told Michael, "You've got to help here. Give me something so I don't feel like I'm becoming psychotic."

He didn't say anything for several minutes after she made her request, she told me, and then . . . the nurse stopped talking and put her hand to her mouth.

"Oh," she caught her breath. "I'll probably break up telling this. I always do.

"He said, 'I love you.' I said, 'You love me? That's it? That's all you have to give me?' "

Here she paused again and steadied her breathing. Her voice was solemn as she said the words. "He said, 'Usually that's enough.' "

"That was the last you heard from him?" I asked.

"Yes. It was. I think of that answer all the time."

No one spoke. The mood in the car was somber, as if she had just said something so profound that it required a pause before other talk proceeded.

The most frequent gift Lily Dale spirits bring is love. For a long time, I resisted such messages as too easy. I thought, *Why can't the spirits say something more useful? What good is love?* I wasn't alone in that criticism. Lots of people noted that numbers for the lottery might be more appreciated.

But I've since changed my ideas. Love might be the most important thing any of us has to convey. September 11, 2001, convinced me. When the planes were being hijacked and the World Trade Center was about to collapse, people who called relatives for one last word said the same thing, "I love you." None said, "The lotto ticket is in the bureau," or "The will is in the top left desk drawer." They said, "I'm safe. I'm all right. And I love you." I don't say that means the mediums are really talking with spirits, but the content of the messages doesn't necessarily rule that out.

Listening to the Archangel Michael's nurse, I thought, *This is strange. She seems normal, as do most of the other people here who tell strange things, but if these experiences are so common, why have I never had one?* And then I remembered a memory so deeply imbedded in my interior reality that it seemed almost normal when it happened. It only seems strange when I put it into words.

After my husband and I bought our house in Wisconsin, we learned that the forty-eight-year-old woman who had lived there with her family had died of breast cancer a few months before. We had seen her photo over the mantel when we looked at the house. Pretty and blond, she was posing at a wedding with her husband. I didn't look closely at the photo, but I remember how lovely she looked.

She'd been diagnosed in October, we later learned, and died in March. We bought the house in July. Her cosmetics were still under the sink in the master bedroom vanity. We met her husband when we closed on the house. He had that dazed look of fresh grief, like a kid who'd just awakened from a deep sleep and doesn't quite know where he is. You could hear him trying to lift the sadness off his words as he said them, but the end of every sentence fell away under the weight of it.

I'm impressionable—lacking in good boundaries is how the psychologists put it—and that may be why I didn't think much about the feelings I sometimes had as I stood at the vanity or took a shower or started to walk down the stairs. A sense of great sorrow would wash over me, and I would think of her. I would think how weak and despairing she must have been as she stood in those spots, and it was as though those same emotions swept through me. As I tell it, this sounds spooky and strange, but it wasn't. I didn't stumble or gasp or do anything dramatic. I just felt a wordless kind of knowing.

It didn't scare me. I would pause and let the feeling linger for a moment. It seemed as though, in acknowledging it, I was there with her, extending a sort of tribute to her. What I felt seemed like solidarity and common humanity. I didn't wallow in it. I paused, felt it, thought of her, and went on. It was a feeling so deeply embedded in my interior self that I never considered mentioning it to anyone.

From the first moment we walked into the house I knew it should be ours because I felt such a sense of love and peace and gladness. When those other feelings came—this is strange but true—I felt as though the woman who had lived in the house before us was lingering there, being with me to bless and affirm our having bought it.

I'm tempted to say that I didn't take it seriously, even that I didn't quite register it consciously, but I must have. About six months after we moved into the house I was at my sister's, thumbing through a book on Feng Shui, when I came across this advice: always clear your house of lingering spirits by repainting. If you can't do that, spray orange water around the baseboards and in the corners.

I hope what I did next doesn't sound heartless. It wasn't that I wanted to chase her out of the house, but feelings of weakness and despair are not so very pleasant, and they weren't going away. Like the nurse listening to the Archangel Michael, I didn't want to trifle with a state of mind that might not be healthy. If the house's former inhabitant really was there, this would release her. If my feelings were created by some strange fixation of my overactive imagination, maybe a little ritual would steady me.

I didn't think about it that much. When I went home, I bought some orange extract, mixed it with water, and sprayed it around the baseboards.

The feelings left and never came back. I sometimes think of her when I catch a whiff of what seems to be perfume. I'm usually in the basement, my closet, or the pantry when I smell it. So the smell is probably wood, sachet, or something that I can only smell when my allergies are under control.

A few days after I remembered this story, I mentioned it to medium Greg Kehn.

"You're right. That is who it was, and it was also her when you heard the footsteps," he said.

"I didn't hear footsteps," I said. Then I searched my memory. Oh, yes. I had. I was in the bedroom one day when I heard footsteps so clearly that I thought my husband was walking across the wood floor downstairs. I called to him, but he wasn't home. Like a thousand women in spooky movies, I shrugged and thought, *That's funny.*

I hadn't told Greg anything about the good feelings I had toward the woman, so maybe what he said next was just another coincidence.

"She wasn't trying to scare you," he said. "She just wanted you to know that she was glad you were in the house, and, since her illness was the only thing you knew about her, she used that as the way to identify herself."

15

After dinner the night I attended Patricia Price's reunion, her students gathered in her living room, which was furnished like a turn-of-the-century parlor—lace curtains, overstuffed, wine-colored furniture, old photos on the wall. In the bookcase were carved busts of Native American men.

The time-honored way to develop gifts of spirit contact is through the kind of home circle that we were about to have. Mediums often liken their gift to singing or playing the piano. Everyone can learn to play the piano, they say, but not everyone can be a concert pianist.

For more than 150 years, people who want to develop their Spiritualist abilities have gathered in someone's home, sat in a circle, and practiced on one another. For most people, becoming a medium is a long road. It takes years. Some Spiritualists criticize public circles and classes, saying they encourage people who have no gift to imagine they do. But almost no one becomes a medium without some sort of support, and they don't get it from the outside world.

Medium Beverly Burdick-Carey is an example of the close-to-home criticism many face. Although "Rev. Bev" is highly regarded in Lily Dale for her skills, her family doesn't always like what she's doing. One of her children has converted to evangelical Christianity. "She thinks I eat babies for breakfast," Rev. Bev said. "Dead or alive, it doesn't matter." I noticed that a number of the Spiritualists' adult children were conservative, rather disapproving Christians. I wondered whether the loosey-goosey ways of their parents had sent these children scurrying toward faiths that give them certainties and firm doctrine.

Patricia dimmed the lights and put a trumpet on the table. We traced a circle around it so we would know whether it moved. It didn't. We started as usual by singing to get our vibrations up. Vibrations are a big thing. Exactly what a vibration is I still don't know. I never saw anyone shake or quiver. That too seems to have gone out of style. Lily Dale's favorite put-down of an uppity medium is to quote a long-dead resident who said, "A quiver and a shake do not a medium make."

The only songs most people seem to remember are beginning piano songs or scouting campfire ballads. By the time we belted out, "Daisy, Daisy, give me your answer do, I'm just craaaaazy, all for the love of you," segued into "Twinkle, Twinkle, Little Star," and finished with rounds of "Row, Row, Row Your Boat," we were ready for any action the cosmos could provide. Patricia's circles also include a meditation backed by rhapsodic music and guided by her melodious voice. Then members are invited to give messages from spirits. On this night we sat in silence for a while.

Patricia is a tall, ample woman whose age I would guess to be somewhere in the fifties. She wore her brown hair shoulder-length that summer. She has a broad, kindly face and a low musical voice that blends beautifully with New Age music.

Despite the amount of competition in town and the occasional backbiting, I never heard anybody say a bad word about Patricia. During my second summer in the Dale, she shaved her head. Somebody said it had to do with letting hair dye grow out.

Someone else said it was a spiritual symbol. Whatever it was, people accepted it, even admired it.

"Girlfriend rocks," Shelley said.

Sometimes Patricia would hum a little during circles or, if the energy felt low, start up a new song. Then silence would fall over the group again. Patricia told a married couple that their dog, Wolf, who had died recently, was pushing his head between them. I didn't see him.

Then there was a long silence.

"Welcome," Patricia said, addressing the air. "We're happy you've joined us again."

Her eyes appeared to be following something or somebody as it moved through the circle.

"A black leopard who has appeared in our circles before has entered the room," she told us. I squinted into the dim light. I didn't see him.

Apparently he and the dog didn't see each other either because Patricia didn't mention a ruckus. In an earlier circle, students had seen a layer of foggy vapor they called ectoplasm rise in the middle of the floor and spread to the edges of the circle. It grew until it was a foot high, they said. Everyone saw it.

On this night, I saw no rising mists. That's all right, they assured me. They didn't either.

One guy dressed like a biker was told he would be getting love in his life. The spirits had apparently promised this before. It had been slow in coming, Patricia said, with a deep-throated chuckle. He needed to be patient.

Some students gave each other messages. Then Patricia looked at me and said in her sweet, lilting voice, "May I come to you?"

I nodded. Then I remembered. They like to hear your voice. "Yes, please."

"Two spirits are standing behind your chair," she said. "They are former Lily Dale mediums. Billy Hammond is the man, and Lillian Braun is the woman. They were highly regarded mediums on the earth plane, and they're telling me that they've come back to help you. They're going everywhere with you as you walk about Lily Dale, and they're making sure that you meet the people you need to meet for your research."

"Thank you," I said.

"Oh," Patricia said, as if slightly startled, but looking pleased. "They're now telling me that you are a person of impeccable honesty, and I can believe anything you write in your book."

Such affirmation so disconcerted me that I forgot to say thank you. Impeccable honesty? Who has that? I'm not trying to sound dark or sinister, but, for pity's sake, I'm a reporter. Nobody says things like that about reporters, and they shouldn't. We're the enemy. People who let reporters into their lives are living dangerously, and some of them know it. It makes them edgy and suspicious.

I was surprised by how few people in Lily Dale tried to control what I would write. I often raised an eyebrow and grinned at what they said, clearly showing my disbelief. I expected them to whine or bluff or sic the spirit world on me. At least they might have indulged in a few dark predictions about what would happen if I crossed them, but they didn't.

Only one person flatly refused to talk with me. Gayle Porter was just graduating from a two-year Lily Dale school that taught mediumship and hands-on healing. When I asked for an interview, she said she would talk with me only if I took a two-part class called "Spiritual Insight Training." At the end of the class, I would be giving readings myself, she said.

I didn't think so.

"I can guarantee it," she said. "There's no way you will ever understand what's going on in Lily Dale until you take those classes."

I thanked her, took her telephone number, and said I'd call if I ever followed her advice, which I didn't intend to do.

Generally, the mediums seemed unafraid of my questions. Several even affirmed what I was doing, as Sherry Lee had when she said the spirits picked me for the work of writing about Lily Dale. Now Patricia's spirits were vouching for me. In Lily Dale, spirit words carry weight.

Maybe Patricia was buttering me up so I would write good things. Maybe Lily Dale mediums hide their competitive feelings under smiles and phrases such as "All is in divine order," but religion aside, they *are* in business, and businesses do well if they get publicity. Maybe that was what was going on.

Patricia didn't come to me afterward, however, and she never tried to draw me into conversation. She didn't seek me out or stop to talk when I saw her on the streets. I tried to set up interviews with her, and something always went awry. It was not as if she was avoiding me, but she made no effort. None. Not to be included. Not to explain herself. None at all.

When the circle ended, I walked to Shelley's house feeling aggrieved. Normally I would be embarrassed to repeat such a compliment, but normal doesn't apply in the Dale. I couldn't get it off my mind.

"Patricia says the spirits told her I'm impeccably honest," I said. I could hear petulance bordering on paranoia in my voice. What was Patricia trying to pull?

Shelley waved her hand dismissively and said, "Oh, anybody could see that."

"Impeccable?" My voice went high. "Even *I* wouldn't give me that."

Shelley grinned and said nothing.

"So is this what Lily Dale does?" I asked. "Butter people up, present them in some outrageously positive light? Affirm them in ways nobody based in reality ever would?"

"Maybe," Shelley said. "Is that what you think?"

"I don't know," I said, suspicious and scared of being too easily led.

I did not believe two dead people were following me about, helping me meet everyone I needed. And the dead-people part of it was the least of my problems.

Life is not like that. Finding truth is difficult. You work until your mouth is dry, your brain is fried, and your vision starts to blur. If you've interviewed one person after another for six hours and you're so tired you wobble when you walk and you're on the way home and someone wants to talk, you do the interview. I chide myself for carelessness, warn myself against laziness, lecture myself against letting up. The next person I talk to, the next book I read, the next document I find will be the one that makes the story sing.

I'd lived by this creed for twenty-five years. Maybe I was beginning to tire, maybe I'd stayed too long in Lily Dale and it was unhinging my mind, or maybe . . . I don't know why, but Patricia's nonsense wormed its way into my brain. Her story of mediums walking with me gave me a new superstition to fight the old ones. This one was crazier, sure. I never saw them or heard them, dreamed about them or sensed their presence in any way, but I played around with the idea. The next time I tried to interview someone and he shook me off, I didn't fret about it. I thought, "Guess Lillian and Billy didn't think I needed that one." With their imaginary help, I began to ease up.

16

No one but me seemed to notice the difference, which is often the way of spiritual transformations. They start small. Some weeks into my new life as a laid-back reporter, Shelley said, "Have you ever thought of relaxing and just letting things happen?"

"This *is* me relaxed," I snapped.

So I redoubled my efforts to let Billy and Lillian do my work. When someone gave me the dodge, I let them. When someone refused to answer a question, I said, "Do what you're comfortable with." When I failed to get what I wanted, I said, "Maybe the energy's not right. I'll get it later." And things worked out.

It was like a charm. I didn't believe in it; I just watched it. The person who dodged me would call, apologize, and set up another appointment. The question that hadn't been answered by one person would be answered by another. Those who refused to talk would seek me out later to pour their stories into my notebook.

What was this? All my life, I'd been thrashing around using every bit of energy I had to keep from sinking. Now it was as though I heeded some soothing cosmic advice: "Relax and you'll float."

Bill Fleeman was an example. If you see Bill Fleeman driving down the streets of Lily Dale, he will probably wave. Well turned out as usual in a black T-shirt so neat it looks pressed, his gray beard nicely trimmed, his eyes alert, his body relaxed, Bill might appear to be alone, but in the backseat are three spirit guides that only he and a few mediums can perceive. They are two men and a woman. He calls them the Teacher, the Protector, and the Comforter. They appear every morning and have for several years. They never speak, but Bill communes with them nonetheless, sometimes while he's shaving but more often in the bath. He questions and they answer with nods, head shakes, and eye rolling. More eye rolling than he likes.

Their presence makes him feel safe, Bill said, and that allows him to do his mission, which is to help other people free themselves from the kind of raging despair that once wrecked Bill's own life, cost him his family, landed him in jail, and drove him to drink and drugs. The self-help program he started for so-called rage-aholics, Pathways to Peace, has chapters in two states and in Ontario.

Bill and his wife, Jan, were often among those who sat in Patricia's Thursday night circle. He was invariably pleasant and rarely talked at length about his own perceptions. I heard him mention the guides who sat in the backseat of his car once, and I was eager to know more. But he wouldn't tell me. I sat next to him in circles, bumped into him on the streets, and sweated next to him in a sweat lodge, but he never told me a thing.

By the end of the summer, I would wave at Bill when I saw him and walk on. I heard that his college-age son was coming to visit. They hadn't seen each other since the boy was a year old. Bill prayed about the visit during the sweat lodge, and everybody prayed with him. All of Lily Dale was rooting for him.

One day, I was reading some old clippings in the Lily Dale museum when the two of them came in. Bill was beaming so hard it hurt my jaws to watch him. The boy was a journalism major, and

Papa was eager to talk of his son's accomplishments. I praised everything they told me and talked about the boy's bright future. I was about to leave Lily Dale for the summer, and I didn't think any more of it.

The next time I saw Bill, a year had passed. I nodded politely and looked away, but now Bill was eager to talk with me, to tell whatever I wanted to know. All I had to do was listen.

His father, a violent alcoholic, had left when Bill was an infant. The boy grew up blaming himself. At seven, Bill concluded that there was no Santa Claus and no God. One Sunday his grandmother sent him to the Methodist church with money for the collection plate. He walked past the church and spent the money on popcorn and peanuts at the Sault Sainte Marie locks. He grew up angry and without hope. He took any drug he could find and unleashed his fury on everyone around him.

At about thirty-five, he sobered up. Without drugs and drink to cushion reality, life was grim, and he started looking for a reason to live. He read Bertrand Russell and Albert Camus. He faced how powerless he felt in a world that lacked purpose or meaning, one in which his actions were dictated by cause and effect.

One night in 1977, after he had been sober for nine months—a period he finds most significant ("smacks of gestation, doesn't it?")—he came home after the second shift at the machine shop where he was a foreman. He began writing in his journal and suddenly, without warning or forethought, he popped out of his body and floated to the ceiling, where he hovered and watched himself writing. The room was filled with a bright white light, like the flash of a welder's arc lamp.

And the thought came to him as he looked down on his other self, *Man, he takes himself way too seriously.*

Then he had another thought, *You're half-right. You've been shaped by your circumstances, by cause and effect over which you have no control, because that's what you believed, but not anymore. From now on, you will shape your own life. You can never again point to the past as the reason for your behavior. You are in control.*

Then he popped back into his body. "It was the big 'Oh, shit' moment," he said.

As I listened, I wondered whether his unconscious mind had rescued him. He was in a period of great despair, having realized that rationality can make our lives quite nice in material ways but "cannot assuage our sorrow," as author Karen Armstrong puts it. Maybe his mind, with its infinite creativity, had begun to reach beyond the reasonable.

Bill went to the library looking for explanations. He found William James's *The Varieties of Religious Experience* and Jiddu Krishnamurti's *The Awakening of Intelligence.* Both authors assured him that others had also experienced such events. He was filled with excitement and energy.

But old habits hold on. Rage and despair still claimed him again and again. A year later, he awoke one morning to see a pair of huge, liquid eyes staring into his eyes. The eyes came out of a broad face with a gray beard. He could see only the naked torso of this figure, which was life-size and robust and appeared to be a human form of about the *Homo erectus* period.

"I am one of your guides. I have been every conceivable life form, done every conceivable act. I have been a priest, an amoeba, a virus. What you have done by comparison is child's play," the figure said.

To Bill, this message meant that all his guilt amounted to nothing. He should drop it and move on. The figure disappeared.

Bill went back to the library. There he found a book titled *Cosmic Consciousness* by Richard Maurice Bucke, who had had a similar experience after a poetry reading of Walt Whitman's work. That book presented stories of similar visions and asserted that they occur to many people between the ages of thirty-five and forty-five. He read *The Tibetan Book of the Dead* with the foreword by Carl Jung. He began studying the works of mystics. Eventually, he came to live in Lily Dale.

One day a couple of years ago, as he was driving toward Highway 60 on Dale Drive, he glanced toward the passenger seat. His friend had returned. Now the *Homo erectus* man was balled up and somersaulting at a furious speed. The apparition's whirling stopped abruptly. He turned toward Bill and made a comic face.

A few weeks later, the man moved to the backseat, where eventually two more guides joined him. Each has a distinct personality. The gray-haired man, whom Bill calls his Teacher and Healer, is fairly grim and rarely smiles. The second man, whom Bill considers his Protector, is brawnier and has some sense of humor. The third guide is a Native American woman who is his Comforter. "They are here to help me, to give me what I need so I won't screw up and pass to spirit too soon and hold them back again," he said. Whatever holds him back also holds them back, he said.

"I'm their project, and helping me is how they're going to get to the next level. They're in kindergarten just like I am."

He told me his story during a party at Shelley's house. We were sitting at the long table on her back porch.

"Are they here now?" I asked.

"Sure," he said. "They're always with me."

Where are they?

"The Comforter is standing behind you, right there beyond your left shoulder, so I can see her face. The Teacher-Healer is over there"—he gestured to his right—"and the Protector is there by the door, so he can see who comes in, and so I can see him and be reassured."

With the spirits around, Bill no longer needs rage. He has the comfort denied him as a child. He has the wisdom and healing that rationality failed to give him. And he has protection against his fears. These three figures give Bill more stability than he experienced in his rational past. Is he a little nutty? Or is he someone who has brilliantly saved himself by accessing the deepest regions of—of what? His own consciousness? The collective unconscious? Has he simply tapped into what's available in the universe if we have the will and the wit to call it forth?

And were Billy and Lillian the same kind of guides for me? When Patricia presented them as my helpers, she nudged me into accepting comfort and ease that my rational mind said didn't exist. Had she taught me to float by teasing me into the playful consideration that the impossible might be real, that heavy human bodies may actually bob along blithely on top of cosmic waves, and that everything a reporter needs might come to her if she simply proceeds with happy confidence?

Thinking such thoughts made me feel as though I was dropping from a tall building. The angels would not bear me up. I knew they wouldn't, and if I kept thinking such things I was in for a hard landing. I knew I was.

17

Here is the story Marian Boswell told about her return home to her perfect husband and their perfect life. She didn't think much about the surgeon's strange prediction. The idea that she might lose everything was too ridiculous, especially considering the great spiritual growth she was experiencing. She began meditating more than before. The colors that swirled before her when she shut her eyes became more vivid. They looped and circled like silk scarves being flipped about the room. She told me that Jack, who sometimes watched her while she sat, said he could see tendrils of her hair moving as if a breeze was lifting them.

One morning, she awoke to the sound of a woman's name. Jane. Marian knew a Jane, an acquaintance who was once an artist. Her body had been stiffened and stilled by a degenerative disease. She owned a studio in the small town where Marian and Jack lived.

The voice Marian heard as she came out of sleep said, "Go see Jane." Whether it was a voice in the air or a voice from her dreams, she never knew, but it woke her up, and Marian did as it directed.

Jane drew Marian into art classes and into a group of women meeting to talk of spiritual things. They discussed mystics and visions, their own and those they'd read of. Marian began to increase her sensitivity to what she believed were forces outside normal consciousness. The reading and meditating and praying began to take effect.

She and Jack had always relished power. He taught her how to negotiate, to bull her way through life, to get what she wanted, no matter what it cost others. To have money, to buy things, to impress people had been their life, and they loved it. Together they had created a world in which they were the most beautiful, glittering objects around, and then she changed. She put all that behind her. She didn't want to talk about winning anymore. She didn't want to go to corporate parties where she could be admired and envied. She wanted to talk about goodness and balance and love. She began to think those things ruled the universe and that nothing else was important.

The women in her group became more and more vital to her life. She began to see an expression on Jack's face that she'd never seen before. "I'd say, 'You're angry,' and he would say, 'Oh, no. I'm never angry.' "

At this point in Marian's story, I began to feel a little sorry for Jack. His money-loving, power-gathering wife had changed into a meditating, voices-hearing, God-is-Love kind of woman. That would be a nasty shock to any man who had married corporate Barbie.

He questioned her intently now about everything she did. He wanted to know everything people said to her. He was jealous and suspicious, but what of? When she tried to talk to him, he no longer listened as he once did. Now his face turned toward her, but his mind was elsewhere.

Her first clue that it might be someplace she couldn't go came on the day she was rummaging under the seat of his SUV. She found a Barry Manilow tape. They hated Barry Manilow. She would throw such a tape in the trash, and so would he. Wouldn't he?

Not long afterward, an even stranger clue came her way. They ordered a generator. On the day it was to come, Marian received a call from the distributor, who said he had sold the last generator and would have to order them another one.

A few minutes later Jack called. "The generator is in, and I'll pick it up."

"What?" she said. "Are you sure?"

"I talked to the man," he said. "It's in."

"It can't be . . ."

But Jack interrupted her. "I talked to him."

For some reason, Marian stopped protesting. Her husband was lying. He'd never lied to her. Why would he lie now about such a silly thing?

When Jack came home that evening, he didn't have the generator.

"It wasn't in, was it?" she said

"Sure it was. I just didn't have time to get it," he said.

Tired of the game, Marian told him what she knew. "You didn't talk to him at all, did you?" she said.

Jack admitted then that he'd lied. When she asked him why, he said he was a perfectionist, he wanted to please her, and so he'd fudged a little, hoping the generator would be there.

Knowing he would lie to her shook Marian, but how could she stay mad about something so silly? So she didn't.

Jack began to complain about her behavior, telling her that she didn't treat his children well. Once when she walked into the bedroom, he was on the phone, and something in his voice made her think he was talking to a woman and not about business. He broke off the conversation.

Jack was more and more removed from her and at the same time more demanding. Her perfect life was crumbling, but she didn't know why.

About this time, she heard about Greg Kehn, a Lily Dale medium who wintered not far from their house. She made an appointment.

Greg is one of the most highly renowned of the Dale's psychics. Plenty of people told me that police officers frequently call on him when they have trouble solving a case. In the summer, he has a waiting list of clients. A book about psychics describes him as being so good he can tell clients which spark plug is misfiring in their car engines. Car troubles are understandably a specialty. He trained as a mechanic. But Greg didn't talk to Marian about cars.

Before she had time to ask him questions or tell him what she came for, he said, "You feel like you're living with a stranger, don't you?"

She did.

One day, Marian went to the pharmacy to pick up some medicine. "Look under Boswell," she said. The clerk handed her a package of three pill bottles.

"This isn't mine," she said.

"Oh, that's right," said the clerk, handing her another package. "Those are for your husband."

The first bag contained psychotropic drugs. The dosages called for were high, staggering to Marian, who'd never heard of anyone taking so much of these medicines. She took them home and, when she showed them to Jack, he confessed again. He was obsessive-compulsive and hadn't wanted her to know. He said he was ashamed. She comforted him.

Marian was horrified, but she had a little of the disorder herself. At least this was something she could understand. Now she had a reason for their problems. They could work on this together.

Jack began to see a therapist. He joined a men's therapy group. The group was reading a book about controlling rage. Every night Jack sat in his favorite chair, turned on the lamp, read his book, and made notes in a little pad he kept beside it. He was outlining the book, he said. He often talked about the progress he was making in his therapy and the things he was learning from the other men.

Once, when he was away, she went to the table where Jack kept his book and the notepad. She flipped open the book. He had underlined three lines. She opened the pad. It was all doodles and lines from songs.

One evening, he arrived home from a trip in an especially good mood. He kissed Marian and told her about his day. It felt like old times. Marian should have been happy, but something kept telling her, "Look in the briefcase."

He went to bed early that night, leaving his briefcase on the floor beside his chair. Marian was thinking about bed herself, but the voice kept saying, "Look in the briefcase."

To anyone else, that might have sounded like the snake in the garden, but to Marian, who had begun to listen more and more to what her mind told her, it sounded like an old friend trying to help her past her illusions. She heard the voice again, "Look in his briefcase."

So she did. Inside was a financial statement that she had never seen. It showed that they were tens of thousands of dollars in debt.

Then the voice said, "Look in his computer."

It was sitting there, still in its carrying case. He took it with him every morning.

"Look in his computer," the voice said.

And so she did.

18

I hadn't known Shelley Takei a week before she invited me to stay in the lavender house on the hill where she lived. "I've got lots of room," she said, taking me up the green-carpeted stairs, past the little angels that sit on the steps. "Pick which bedroom you want."

Shelley and her sister Danielle each selected three bedrooms on the second floor to decorate according to her own taste. Danielle's bedrooms tend toward flowered wallpaper and color-coordinated bedding. Quite lovely and tasteful in an English sort of way. Shelley goes for a different ambience. Her rooms have themes: angel, goddess, and zodiac.

"I want this to be a sacred space," she said.

This is clearly a house where men have no say about decor. It contained 672 angels by the last count, and more have been added. Stained-glass windows made by Shelley's husband, Frank, cast a multicolored glow across the rooms. The living rooms feature gold lamps with cherubs cavorting around them, lampshades with long fringe, a crystal end table, and heavy-petaled artificial flowers languishing over drapery.

In the peach-colored angel bedroom, where I slept, there are more than one hundred images of angels. They're on a poster in the closet smoking cigarettes. They dance around the trash can, hold up the soap, tie back curtains, skip across the walls, and lounge on the dresser.

The downstairs bathroom, sponge-painted a rich purple, has stained-glass windows and a lamp that features a winged fairy. The house's upstairs bathroom is black and silver. Silver stars and moons dangle from the ceiling. Artificial magnolias grace the walls. A huge plastic shell filled with pink, orange, and purple bath fizzies sits ready for anyone who wants to relax. The shower curtain is white with the black silhouette of Norman Bates dressed as Mother, knife raised, ready to stab into the unsuspecting body of Janet Leigh—or if she's not available, whoever is.

Downstairs in the basement is the psychomanteum. A psychomanteum is a setup that's supposed to allow spirits to be seen in a mirror. Shelley's psychomanteum is screened off from the rest of the basement by panels of fabric that hang to the floor. A mirror is tipped up slightly so that people who sit in the chair before it can't see themselves but can see spirits if they materialize in the glass. The psychic explorer Raymond Moody, who said the psychomanteum had allowed a number of spirits to appear to him, suggested using a low-wattage light. Shelley has candles, which makes it even better. Shelley has never seen a spirit in the mirror, but at least one of her friends says she saw one. From the minute I saw the setup, I knew it represented opportunity.

What if we could make someone appear? I asked Shelley. What if we got some mediums together and tried to get someone to show up, someone like, say, Gretchen and Sherry Lee's brother, the late Chapman Clark? Shelley and Chapman had been great friends. On the wall leading to the basement, she had a picture of him mounted with the words, "See you, Chapman," next to it. Shelley believed that Chapman really might have had the power to communicate telepathically, to disappear, and to astral travel. She said he'd once described a room in her sister's hunting camp that he could not possibly have seen.

She was game to try. So we invited Gretchen and Sherry Lee to come over and see whether they could summon their brother. They brought a favorite book from his childhood and a bottle of liquor he'd made. We all took a drink of the stuff, which was pretty bad, and went to the basement. Sherry Lee took the chair, and the rest of us sat on the floor. Candle wax and brandy scented the air, which pressed closely around us.

A number of signs that Chapman might appear had occurred at other times. One of Shelley's guests, who'd never met him, dreamed that a balding, blond man tiptoed through the living room into the basement with his forefinger held to his lips, as though cautioning her to keep a secret. Another friend had seen wisps of smoky material coming up from around a little ceramic firedog that sits on the mantel. Chapman had been a fireman. Shelley's sister Danielle bought the dog to give to him, but he died first. So she put the dog on the mantel. She and Shelley had been watching it for two years, hoping that Chapman would come back and move it. So far he hadn't.

Gretchen had earlier given Shelley a message that seemed to bode well. We were in the auditorium at a Monday night circle during which anybody with five dollars can sit and get a quick message. When Gretchen came to Shelley, the medium's eyes filled with tears. "I have someone you know," she said.

"Is it Chapman?" Shelley asked.

Gretchen nodded. "He's saying something about the color blue. Does that mean anything to you?"

Shelley looked blank, and then she nodded. "Yes. I think so," she said, her voice practically a whisper. A few days before, Shelley had planted a garden at the side of her house in honor of Chapman. While she was digging, Sherry Lee came by, and they began to talk. Shelley looked up. When she looked down again, she saw a blue stone.

"It wasn't there before," she said. Chapman had blue eyes, and he often carried stones in his pocket to give away. Shelley immediately thought of him.

"I just knew he put that stone there to let me know he was around."

"It was him," Gretchen confirmed. "He wants you to know that he's with you often. He's been telling you things, but as usual you aren't listening."

Shelley laughed at that. Chapman always said she knew far more than she allowed herself to admit.

As we settled into our watch before the psychomanteum, my heart was thumping so hard I could hear the blood in my ears. If Chapman appeared and we all saw him, I'd have to be a believer. I wasn't sure I wanted that.

We stayed for about an hour, staring at the mirror in the dim light of a candle flame. The sisters said Chapman was there, and they gave several messages from him to Shelley. The messages were pretty cheeky. He talked about things like dancing with Shelley and sitting on her lap. Shadows roiled across the mirror, swirling into various colors. We all saw them, but it was hard to tell whether something was really happening or whether looking so long at the darkened mirror caused the brain to fabricate optical illusions. But Chapman didn't show up in visible form. We all agreed on that.

Some weeks later we tried again. Sherry Lee couldn't come. So we invited Anne Gehman. Years before, after the death of Anne's second husband, Chapman had courted her all one summer. He sat on the front porch of her big white and pink house, rubbing her feet and telling her stories about his psychic prowess. Anne didn't believe most of what he said but, when she told him so, Chapman merely laughed and told another tale. He talked to her of love and marriage, but the courtship stopped abruptly after two women came to Anne separately for readings, each crying over her love for Chapman and his unwillingness to commit.

Anne fasted all day to get ready for the psychomanteum. We prayed prior to the event and settled ourselves as before. Again, Gretchen relayed some slightly naughty messages for Shelley. None of the rest of us heard so much as a good moan, inside or outside our heads. As an apparition, Chapman was even less impressive than before. This time he didn't even make good shadows.

I was more disappointed than logic allowed me to admit. Anne still had hope for the psychomanteum and talked about trying again. We might need to sit several times to make sure conditions were right, she said. The messages Chapman's sisters delivered alarmed Shelley a little. She and Chapman had been friends, but nothing more. Over the years he had romanced a lot of Lily Dale women, but with her the flirtation had been innocent. "I'm a married woman," Shelley said. "I'd never do anything like that. I wonder if his sisters think I did."

She called Sherry Lee the next day to ask. When Sherry Lee said she wouldn't have cared if Shelley and Chapman were lovers, Shelley was really confused. Were the messages that the sisters gave in the psychomanteum actually from Chapman or were they the sisters' projections based on false assumptions?

"How can they not know that I would never do such a thing?" Shelley asked.

"Should they know better because they're your neighbors or because they're mediums?" I wondered.

"Both," Shelley said, exasperated.

As for our failure with the psychomanteum, Shelley shrugged it off. "I realized I'm more comfortable not having to commit either way," she said. "The tension of opposites is what interests me. That's where I like to play."

We spent hours debating different answers to the questions Lily Dale poses. Why weren't the mediums better, wiser people if they were in touch with all this infinite wisdom? Why did they do so many unwise things? Sherry Lee gave much the same answer that Dr. Neal, the physician-medium, did. The mediums are learning their own lessons.

"We're polishing our physical skills in this life. Every painful moment in your life is a spiritual birth pain," she said.

The mediums never claimed they were more holy or spiritual than anyone else. As Gretchen often said, "We're like a telephone just relaying what's given."

But Shelley and I still debated. If the spirits come to help heal people of their psychological wounds, why don't they heal the mediums? Why do the spirits say so many inane things? Why are the mediums so often wrong? Could the mediums be getting the same inklings that everyone gets but that most of us are too modest to make such great claims for? Could it be that the mediums' greatest distinction is merely an alarming inability to recognize that they are wrong more often than they are right? Are they merely sweet, deluded souls who puff up their own imaginings?

Shelley's willingness to debate questions no one else wanted to talk about allowed me to listen to some of her other ideas, ideas that were radical to me, and way scarier than dead people talking. She learned most of them from Lynn Mahaffey—the grandmother who spends so much of her time on five-mile bike rides while making intercessory prayers for the world.

19

Here is the short version of Lynn's creed. People's hearts are good. Love is in control of the world. People are on earth to connect with each other, with their own good hearts, and with the spirit of love around them. Connecting enables people to give their gifts, which is what humans are here for and what they want most. And, finally, people can trust the spirit of love to guide them. So people ought to follow their own inclinations, do what they like, and not do what they don't want to do. They ought to trust their own good hearts and their good sense, no matter what anybody says.

Most of that, especially the last part about doing what you please, I found scandalous. Dangerous even. I wasn't a Baptist anymore, but I still knew that people are bad and that you have to keep them tied down and trussed up. You have to curb their evil impulses. People can't go around doing what they want. The world depends on us to sacrifice ourselves for the good of others, and it doesn't make one bit of difference that doing so makes us miserable and ill-tempered and the kind of long-suffering cranks no one in his right mind wants to be around. We aren't here to be happy. We're here to be good. Most of us don't have what it takes to be good, of course, which means we have to be guilty.

Lynn wasn't the first person I'd heard espouse the idea that people such as Shelley, blithely confident souls who always listen to themselves, are on a higher track than the rest of us. Shakespeare said it: "This above all: to thine own self be true, / And it must follow, as the night the day, / Thou canst not then be false to any man." Joseph Campbell advised following your bliss and said it would align you with an inner knowing. Edith Wharton talked about the "inmost self where the unknown god abides." I'd heard it before, and yet to me Lynn's ideas smacked of soft morality and the license to act with utter abandon. They scared me.

Lily Dale's creed was informal, unwritten, and debated, but it matched Lynn's, as far as I could tell. I would have never taken this creed seriously or given it much thought except that Lynn said it was true.

And something about Lynn made me hold my doubts in abeyance. I didn't give them up so much as I set them aside while I listened to what she said. Why? I didn't exactly know. Maybe it was her humility. Some people are convinced by bluster and bravado, by big stories and great deeds. I'm not. I suspect such tales, and the people who tell them.

Lynn hardly ever spoke unless someone drew her out. She was too shy to attend Shelley's parties. If the crowd was over three or four, she would sit on the edge of the group, listening intently, fiddling with her hearing aid when she needed to.

I heard someone liken her to Clarence the angel in *It's a Wonderful Life.* She has a strong nose, a wide-open face, and a sometimes slightly befuddled air. One woman likened her to the absent-minded Fairy Godmother in Walt Disney's *Cinderella* with her spell-casting chant of "Now where were we, for goodness' sake? Bippety, boppety, bippety, boppety, bippety, boppety, boo."

Lynn doesn't cast spells, of course. She reads the runes, an occult system of divination that relies on stones imprinted with symbols. She isn't a medium and hasn't consulted a medium in years. She did once take away the pain of a woman named Joyce Parker. For years, Joyce suffered from back pain that nothing could allay. Lynn was reading Joyce's runes one day when Joyce mentioned the pain.

"Let's send it away," Lynn said.

"Can you do that?" Joyce asked.

"I don't see why not. You've carried it long enough. We'll pray and ask that it go somewhere else."

Then she put her hands on Joyce's back, and the pain left. That was several years ago, and it's never come back, Joyce told me. When I mentioned the story to Lynn, she didn't remember it.

Walking down the street, Lynn often becomes so engrossed in thought that she walks more and more slowly until she stops completely, often in the middle of a street. Lily Dale being the town it is, people rarely honk. They merely wait, engine idling, until Lynn finishes her thought and moves on. The cafeteria's three entrances invariably confuse her. She is always talking as she walks in, listening as she walks through the line to order her food, and completely disoriented by the time she has her loaded tray. "Which way is out of here?" she often asks Shelley.

When someone asks her opinion, Lynn sometimes says, "Oh, dear," and looks about the room in a vague way. It might take a while to give her thought words, but, when she answers, she never dithers and never equivocates. She always says something no one else has thought to say, and, to me, what she said always seemed wise, even when it seemed ridiculous. Ridiculously wise, maybe.

"She's the smartest person I've ever known. Not just the wisest, the smartest," Shelley said.

Maybe I listened so closely to Lynn because I agreed with Shelley, or maybe it was because her ego never enters the argument, and she isn't afraid of any question. Or maybe it was because of her laugh, which has a soft quality, like wrinkled chamois slipping across your skin. It often starts as everyone else is getting revved up about something they think is infuriating and stupid. Lynn's laughter sometimes takes over her body so that she draws her feet off the floor and throws out her arms. There is no meanness in her amusement, only purest delight and total faith that love is in control, no matter what life tosses her way. Shelley calls it "Lynnie's Buddha laugh." Her goodwill is like peace stealing into your soul. I had to struggle against believing every word she said.

Once she told me about a drive through the country with her husband. They passed a dead deer by the side of the road. Seeing such innocence and beauty turned into a carcass, Lynn was overcome with despair. Weighed down with a dark awareness that suffering is immense and everywhere, Lynn groaned inwardly and asked, "Why is there so much pain?"

As she did, she heard an answering voice in her head. It said, "I know, Lynn, but will you accept it?"

I could see that the story had great import for Lynn, and so its meaning was important to me too, but I didn't get it. Accept it? What did that mean?

"It meant, would I go on believing that love is in control?"

And do you? Can you?

"Of course," she said. "If it isn't, then forget it. Nothing makes sense. Nothing. That's the end of joy; that's the end of hope. But I do believe it. I believe that our greatest sorrows lead to our greatest joys. I believe they can."

If the horrors we see around us come into our lives, we will endure and find meaning in them, she said. "The bruised reed I will not break. The flickering flame I will not quench. That's the promise," she said. "This unconditional love is in you, and you can trust it."

Even if we die?

"What do you mean 'even'? Especially if we die. That's not the worst thing that can happen to us."

Lynn formed her beliefs through terrible times.

Her brother killed himself because he was unable to control his alcoholism, and her oldest son, Johnny, died in a car accident when he was twenty-two. Lynn was a Catholic and had been for years, but the faith didn't mean much to her then, and Johnny's death left her in a state of grief that threatened to kill all the light within her.

Her son had loved philosophy. After he died, she often sat leafing through his books, thinking about how his eyes had gone over the pages. She was taking a community education class from Frank Takei before her son's accident. A country girl and mother of five with only a high school degree, she didn't understand a lot of it, but she kept at those thick books of heavy thought, and eventually she unknotted their dense meanings.

After the accident, Lynn began studying in earnest, looking for some clue that would help begin her life again. As she studied, she felt close to Johnny. "I could feel him right there with me," she said. She marked up the books, underlining and highlighting the sentences she liked. Then she read them again and marked more passages, sometimes putting stars and exclamation points in the margins. She read the theologians and the mystics. She took everything they had to say, sifted it, weighed it, and made it her own.

As her personal theology began to take shape, Lynn looked around for verification. She found it in Shelley Takei. Shelley had been a quiet, almost shy, girl when Frank married her. Once after their marriage, during a rare visit to church, Shelley was asked what she thought God was like. She said she thought he was like Frank. But in truth, "I thought Frank *was* God," she said.

Lynn first came to their house for a class Frank was convening in their basement. One evening when Frank was teaching Carl Jung, Shelley put their two-year-old into her crib and settled the older children before an episode of *The Dukes of Hazzard* so that she could join the class. Shelley thought of herself as nothing special, somebody whom few people paid heed to, but Lynn seems to have loved her from the beginning. Perhaps it helped that Shelley was exactly Johnny's age and remembered him from grade school.

By the time Lynn knew her, Shelley had a huge collection of Christmas houses that she had hand-painted and displayed through the holidays. To her, they were wonderful and slightly embarrassing. "One of those things that you do when you're a housewife," she said.

But, to Lynn, the love and care Shelley put into the houses made them "an altar to the sacred." Shelley laughed at such a notion. "I don't even go to church," she said.

By now, however, Lynn saw things differently. When Shelley made a meal, when she planted a garden, when she talked with her children, she was giving her gifts to the world.

Everything Shelley did was magical, Lynn thought.

When Shelley disparaged some whimsy she was creating or denigrated some thought she had, Lynn said, "That's not true. You're right."

"She retranslated my life for me," said Shelley.

"No, darling, I held up a mirror so you could see who you were," said Lynn.

Lynn told Shelley that her ideas were right, that her actions were right, that everything she did was perfectly right. And, after years of hearing it, Shelley believed her. She started to follow her own thoughts and to see the value of them. At the same time, she questioned whether Lynn's ideas were giving her a false sense of herself, an illusion that shouldn't be trusted.

One day Shelley was sitting alone in her dining room when she experienced what she would now call kundalini rising or a spiritual awakening, but that wasn't what it seemed to be at the time. She began to feel bigger. She felt as though she were getting bigger and bigger and bigger. She was horrified. *This is ego,* thought Shelley, who was in graduate school at the time. *This is what they mean by overblown ego.* This terrible thing was happening because she was starting to believe what Lynn told her. Her ego was inflating monstrously.

She expanded to fill the room and the house and the block and Clarion, Pennsylvania, where she lived, until finally she was everywhere and everything. Then it was as though all the energy popped and rushed back into her. She began crying and hyperventilating, but in some quiet part of her mind she thought, *That was not ego. That was the force of love.*

"I finally understood the essence of what Lynn had been giving me," she said. "I trusted Lynn, and I trusted myself, and I knew I could give others what she had given me."

She began telling other women that they were right—in what they thought, how they acted, and who they wanted to be. She wrote a grant for federal money to start a displaced homemakers program. She got the grant, and, when women took her class, she told them, "Don't let that man knock you around. Don't let those people say you are stupid. Dream some dreams. You can make them happen."

When they believed her, it caused quite a stir in the little country towns around Clarion. In her class, which she called "New Choices," she told women with many kids and no education, women whose best job ever had been cleaning houses or taking money at the gas station, that they ought to go to college. She took them to college herself and signed them up, getting government money to pay for it. Weary-faced, quiet women who had once been perfectly reasonable and resigned started acting strangely—staying home from church to study, talking about things their husbands didn't understand, demanding that someone else cook dinner and do the wash.

Some husbands and boyfriends sent flowers and made lunch for the classes. Others protested. They hid the women's books. One rammed the family car into a tree. Several threatened to shoot themselves and their wives. One called out to his girlfriend, looped a rope from a beam, and was in the process of strangling himself when his girlfriend finally put down her books and came out to see what was wrong.

But the women didn't quit because of such resistance. Instead, they won scholarships, awards, and acclaim from their professors.

"People didn't like it when we started to think we could do more than rub our husbands' feet and take care of their kids," said Joyce Parker, one of Shelley's students, a single mother and former meatpacker who now has a degree in philosophy. "Well, that was too bad."

20

One weekend in July, a handful of New Choices women burst into Shelley's house bearing grocery bags filled with every salty, sweet, fried, or frozen junk food America allows. When they first came to Lily Dale ten years before, the women were on welfare. If food stamps wouldn't buy it, they didn't eat it. They had jobs now and could afford restaurants, but bringing groceries was a tradition of their annual Lily Dale weekend.

A little blonde with long wavy hair and deep cleavage came through the door first. "Mom," Dawn Ganss called out as she moved toward Shelley with her arms outstretched.

Next came Doris Goodman, with curly hair the color of butternut and a don't-mess-with-me set to her mouth that wasn't a lie. It was a look that warned those who wanted to abuse her—and there'd been more than a few—that they would have a fight on their hands. She had just left her job working at the Kmart snack bar when she heard about Shelley's class. Doris went on to be named most outstanding senior in her undergraduate class and most outstanding student in her graduate program.

Next, Darcy Kiehl bustled in with a grocery bag on her hip. Darcy could make your dinner and build your house. Darcy can do about anything, which is amazing considering how much bad luck had done to her.

She had been involved in forty-eight car accidents and two motorcycle accidents. A car hit her two weeks before she delivered her only daughter. Cars hit her from behind as she waited for lights to change. Cars coming against the light hit her as she went through intersections. Once a car ran up into her driveway to collide with her parked car.

Darcy had good reason to respect the kind of visions and dreams that rule Lily Dale. Her younger sister, Corinna, once dreamed that she would die in a red car and refused to buy red autos. When she couldn't avoid buying a red car, she had it painted white, but she was killed in a car accident nevertheless. A red car hit her. Darcy was not involved in that accident.

After Darcy's arm was caught in a machine in the glass factory where she worked, she was injured, sued the company, and lost her house to attorney's fees. Her husband left her. Her two granddaughters have cystic fibrosis. For years, she has been plagued with a long list of ailments. Sometimes it seems as if the only lucky thing about Darcy is that she doesn't know how to quit.

Joyce Parker came last, moving in a lanky, languid way, looking a little sleepy, missing absolutely nothing. In her pre-Shelley days, Joyce often stood at her kitchen window, smoking as she watched Monday's laundry flap from her neighbors' clotheslines. Monday was laundry day. Tuesday was trash-burning day. Wednesday was fill-the-car-up-with-gas day. On Saturday nights, she and her truck driver boyfriend drank beer with their friends. The women swapped recipes. The men told racist jokes and bragged about road warrior exploits. Everyone did everything the same way every week, and Joyce thought that she would go mad if she didn't break a rule real soon. Shelley helped her with that.

The New Choices women were first invited to Lily Dale because Shelley had a house there, and she thought they might like a weekend away from their children and husbands. Doris refused the invitation initially. She had never spent a night away from her husband and children. At first, the town scared the women. Joyce, who hid her tender heart under a gruff exterior, was afraid the mediums could read her mind. Dawn, the little blonde who wore her heart on her sleeve, was afraid she'd cry. And Doris? Doris was afraid she wouldn't fit in. You never looked at Doris that you didn't see those brown eyes looking back, figuring you out. They all did that. Especially on their first Lily Dale visit, under the laughter that came too quickly, behind the smiles, through the cigarette smoke that wreathed around them, they were watching.

Many of the women in Shelley's New Choices classes were well acquainted with families in which fathers had sex with their children, with marriages in which men beat their wives with fists and finished them off with words, with lives in which things were always happening and none of them were good. They'd been cheated on and lied to, humiliated, and told they were worthless from their earliest days. They'd had sex before they were ready and children before they were grown. Such experiences made them into excellent watchers. They watched for signs of what was expected and instantly molded themselves into whatever shape seemed least likely to draw attack. They couldn't remember a time or a place when survival hadn't required camouflage.

But Lily Dale was not like any place Doris, Darcy, Joyce, or Dawn had ever been. No one cared who they were or where they came from. No one objected to how they looked or talked or what they said. No one asked what they did for a living or how much education they had. No one was offended if they didn't believe Lily Dale's religion, if they didn't see ghosts or hear spirits. Without any effort from the New Choices women at all, people of the Dale liked them, told them how wonderful they were, and assured them they could do anything, be anybody they wanted.

At first, they felt it but didn't believe it. They watched faces, studied voices, contrasted what was said against what was done, and the answer kept coming up the same. Nobody wanted them to be anybody but who they were. That was a first. It made them feel dizzy, a little sick to their stomachs, like the floor had fallen out from underneath their feet.

"I was scared to death," said Doris. "I didn't know how to act. In Lily Dale I could be myself. But who was that? I didn't know."

None of them did. Lily Dale was going to teach them.

Dawn was pointed in the right direction her first trip to the Stump.

The medium was a little round guy with dishwater-blond hair. He picked Dawn out of the crowd and said he had a message from a male energy, someone whose name started with an *I*.

Dawn knew only one person whose name started with an *I*. Ian. The last time she saw him was at a ninth-grade dinner dance. Dawn was fifteen then, and pregnant. It was the last school dance she would ever attend, the last night of teenage romance and endless possibility she would ever know. The man she would soon marry was too old to attend a high school dance. Dawn danced with Ian all night. They were in band together and had long been pals. They flirted and told each other their dreams. Dawn loved Ian but never told him so. He was Jewish, she was not. He was free to go on living the happy life of an American teenager, she was not. And then the night was over. Dawn never saw Ian again.

She was a military wife and mother by the time Ian died in a car wreck. She cried and cried, and her husband, annoyed, said, "Why do you care so much?"

Dawn left her husband after twenty years of marriage. Nobody thought that was a good idea. Her mother called her foolish. Her sons shouted angry words into the phone. Dawn left them all, took a little apartment, and told no one where she was. She had a nervous breakdown, recovered on her own, and came to Lily Dale hoping only that she would not cry.

The medium said, "He wants you to know that he loved you." Dawn put her face in her hands and wept, deep heaving sobs from the center of her soul, tears for Ian and tears for herself, for the girl she had been and the woman she was, who could hardly remember the last time she had danced like that.

21

Lily Dale has always been a place where women find freedom, as psychic researcher Hereward Carrington himself found out in 1907. Being mindful that the best results are often obtained in the humblest of quarters—through the least-known mediums—Carrington wandered up one of the small side streets, off the general track of business, and saw on one of the houses, the sign MISS M.V. GRAY, AUTOMATIC MESSAGE BEARER.

He knocked, asked for a sitting, and thus began the part of his Lily Dale investigation that most excited and confounded him. Miss Gray had been the sport of spirits since her childhood. More or less an invalid, the child was controlled by spirits mentally and physically to such a degree that her parents had moved West to escape their influence. At the same time, they instituted a bedtime ritual of washing her thoroughly and putting her between clean sheets as a means of keeping the spirits away. If her parents failed in these precautions for two or three nights, the raps would begin again.

Such problems persisted into Miss Gray's adulthood but finally subsided, and she became a nurse. When her powers returned in adulthood, she dabbled in giving readings. Her method was to close her eyes and become passive.

In all this, Miss Gray was a perfect example of mediums during that era. She was female, her experiences began during a sickly childhood, and she was merely a channel for the spirit. None of the wisdom, strength, or knowledge were Miss Gray's. Spirits used her body and brain solely because she was weak and passive.

Although some men were mediums, many people thought strong-minded people couldn't be good spirit channels. Women and children, being weak-minded, easily led, and unlikely to have authority or much knowledge of their own, were much more amenable than men. It was even better if such women and children were further weakened by illness. In fact, almost all the well-known female mediums suffered with chronic illnesses before taking up their gifts. Even today, many mediums have suffered some sort of trauma in childhood that causes them to disassociate.

The idea that the words mediums spoke were not their own had some decided advantages for women, who had few rights, little education, and extremely limited options in the society of the time. Weakness and passivity anchored their femininity, while the spirit working through them pushed them into realms where they would have never dared venture under their own power.

In the mid-1800s, when women who tried to speak in public might well be booed off the stage and even attacked by rough crowds, female trance mediums were able to support careers with speaking engagements across the country. A key difference between them and other women was the idea that men were speaking through them. It was easy for everyone to agree that a woman couldn't know so much or speak so well, and therefore spirits must be involved.

The spirits were almost always males—as they often still are. Under spirit control, the mediums might swagger and make rough jokes, pontificate, and lecture. They were most free with their opinions and their advice. All of which was often unchallenged and thought to be highly amusing because hardly any woman would behave in such fashion on her own. Mediums protected the license allowed their spirits by carefully emphasizing their own lack of control and responsibility.

The unearthly power of female mediums and Lily Dale's ardent support of suffrage made the community a good place for an unmarried woman such as Miss Gray, her mother, and her younger sister to live and to make a small income off their gifts. Carrington was obviously quite taken with her. When their session started, Miss Gray sat across from Carrington and closed her eyes. She began to speak in a peculiar, high tone of voice characteristic of mediums. Her words were quaint and simple; she used *thee* and *thine* instead of *you* and *yours,* and, most oddly of all, the lines rhymed.

The cords in her forehead stood out, her neck enlarged, and her whole head appeared to be congested with blood, causing her skin to flush. Carrington seemed unalarmed, perhaps because such strange symptoms meshed with the odd behavior of other mediums during those times. Mediums sometimes went rigid and could be lifted and carried around the room like boards. Others became so insensible that their skin and tongue could be stuck with needles and they would not flinch. Emma Hardinge Britten, one of the most famous speechifying trance mediums, was cool and unruffled during her public appearances. In her autobiography she bragged that while under spirit power she could outthink hostile men and transform threatening crowds into awed believers, but during one less public session she was said to have rolled around on the ground and hissed like a snake.

Miss Gray correctly described Carrington's health, advised more exercise, and said he would be doing a lot of public speaking. She described his office and home in detail. After their session, she told him that she, her mother, and her sister produced many phenomena in private sittings. The spirit moved trumpets, produced lights, spoke from all parts of the room, rapped, played the piano, and even touched people in the room, she said. He immediately asked to be invited to such a sitting.

When Carrington arrived on the appointed evening, he was told that "Mike," the control spirit, didn't want him in the room; after some finagling, the investigator was allowed to take a seat with the three females in a darkened room, and, sure enough, the spirit of whom so much was promised did appear, and he did produce. He spoke from all about the room, lofted trumpets to the ceiling, gave messages, accepted fifty cents from Carrington, and even kissed the investigator's hand. The kiss was wet and warm, Carrington noted, quite human. The most stunning moment of the evening occurred when the spirit began playing the piano, singing, and making thumps on the floor at least six feet from the piano. Then the spirit blew into one trumpet and talked through another one at the same time. As the spirit talked, Carrington noted that the two older women were also talking and so could not have been part of the show.

The researcher left that night amazed, excited, and almost convinced. Miss Gray and her mother were entirely honest, he was sure.

"Of the little girl, I was not so sure . . . I will merely state here that the child is shy, quiet, reserved and rarely speaks to strangers; she is anemic, and might suffer from chlorosis; in fact, she is a typical poltergeist girl," he wrote in his report.

At the next session, Carrington calmed himself and watched even more closely. All his attention was on that pale, quiet child. He decided that she might easily have plinked random notes on the piano while reaching her foot across the room to make a thumping noise. He suspected and later confirmed in his own experiments that it is possible to hold two trumpets on either side of one's face and blow into one trumpet with one side of the mouth and begin easing air into a trumpet on the other side at the same time. These machinations were enough to produce the effect he heard when the voice seemed to be speaking and playing at the same time. He surmised that the little girl might stand on a chair, hit the ceiling with a trumpet, and then quickly lower it so that it would thump on the floor and thus make sounds that seemed to be coming from different directions. By creeping about in the dark and putting his ear near where the voice was coming from, he also convinced himself that the girl was speaking.

"I distinctly heard her speaking into the trumpet at the moment the voice came (apparently) from the air over my head, near the ceiling, in the center of the room."

Before both sessions he noted that sulfur matches were sitting on the piano near the little girl. When wetted and rubbed, such matches would glow and produce dots of lights like the ones the "spirit" was manifesting. This time he distinctly heard a hand groping for the matches. And, once the lights began, he peered through the darkness to see the girl's face shining faintly behind them.

Two days later, Carrington met the girl walking in Lily Dale and confronted her. Although she did not confess, Carrington said she laughed with him about the phenomena and did not contradict his idea that she had produced the strange happenings.

So much for his great finding. Once again, all he'd found was fraud.

My reaction to his report was slightly different. What a kid! A little girl, encouraged to be meek and self-effacing, probably poorly educated and definitely sickly, turned out to be resourceful almost beyond belief. Somebody sign that kid up. She's a wiz. It's almost easier to believe in spirits than to believe that a kid with such ingenuity and skill didn't grow up to be somebody.

Whenever the New Choices women come to Lily Dale, they go to the Stump at midnight. They never carry flashlights because they want to trust that they won't run into the trees. So far they haven't. Once Doris lay on the Stump and felt her body begin to vibrate. Another time, in a sweat lodge run by Dr. Neal, she saw the figure of a Native American woman in the smoke. It was her great-grandmother, she believes. Neal told her to breathe in the smoke and the spirit of her grandmother would reside within her.

In Doris's first reading from a medium, a woman with a big bun and round tummy appeared to lay pink roses on her lap and thank her for taking such good care of John, Doris's husband. The spirit was Doris's mother-in-law, she told me.

Later, Patricia Price told Doris that her late mother was present and enjoyed walking with her in the flowers of Lily Dale. Patricia didn't give any identifying details about her mother, but Doris knew she was present.

"I just knew it. I felt it, and that's all I needed," Doris said. "I'm learning that I don't have to understand what's happening at Lily Dale. I just have to experience it. That's enough."

The first message Darcy got at a Stump service was from her sister Corinna. The medium didn't give a name. She said she had a female spirit with bruises across her chest. Those were from the seat belt, Darcy thought. A male spirit was with her, and they had a motorcycle. That was their cousin who loved motorcycles. The two of them were having a great time, the medium said. Darcy took the message home to her mother, who was having a hard time adjusting to the death of her daughter.

The summer after I met Darcy, Shelley saw her in the Dale. She was taking "Spiritual Insight Training" classes and had gone "all sparkly," Shelley said. I asked what that meant, and Shelley said it was the look people get when they're first discovering all that Lily Dale is about. Some weeks later, I talked to Darcy, who told me that she planned to become a Spiritualist minister. One of the other New Choices women had laughed at her aspiration, but Darcy was firm. "I think I can do it," she said. "Why not?"

In all the years that Joyce visited the Dale she never heard anything as stunning as the other women heard. In a reading, Lauren did tell her that she had met her current boyfriend in a bar and that his drinking would cause her to leave him within a year. She was right on everything but the timing, Joyce said.

A medium at the Stump once told Dawn that a female spirit, an elderly woman with a bump on her head, was present and wanted to say that she hadn't drowned but had died of a heart attack. Dawn knew this was her grandmother, who had died one winter day when she went out to shovel snow and stepped on the septic tank cover, which was covered in snow. The cover collapsed, and Dawn's grandmother fell in. The bump on her head was from the shovel, which hit her as she went down. The shock of the fall jolted her heart, and she was gone before she hit the bottom of the septic tank, the spirit told Dawn.

These messages and others affirmed Dawn's ideas that the universe is a benign place of equality and love. She began noting that babies always smiled at her and decided that was because they could see her aura and liked the color. Ideas the Dale fostered began to affect her work as an aide in a home for mentally and physically disabled adults. Once when she was asked to feed a man strapped to his chair, wearing a helmet, another aide advised her to hit the back of his head to make him open his mouth.

But Dawn had read that medium Sylvia Browne says people with such disabilities are sent by God to teach us. She didn't want to hit him. Instead, she rubbed his cheek softly, the way she once rubbed her babies' cheeks when she wanted them to eat.

"He opened his mouth right up," she said.

Dawn, Doris, Joyce, and Darcy get together regularly throughout the year for what Shelley calls Lily Dale South. They sit in a circle sometimes, meditate, and share their stories. It's their way of capturing a little of Lily Dale's spirit when they can't be there. For one meeting, Dawn made little white boxes with gold trim that she called their "give it to God boxes." They were to put troubles and worries inside the box and seal them away. Doris's box had an especially tight lid because Dawn knew that she would want to take her troubles out and work on them.

She was right. Doris did want to, but she didn't. "I'm learning to trust," she said.

22

Every morning at ten to nine, I stumbled down Cleveland Avenue with my eyes still puffy from sleep. Nights went late at Shelley's house, and once in bed, I usually couldn't sleep. I'm a good sleeper outside the Dale, but insomnia plagued me on every visit to the Spiritualist camp. Once when I mentioned my troubles to Neal Rzepkowski, Lily Dale's physician-medium, he said I needed to get away from the Dale to break the intensity. I followed that advice twice, and, sure enough, when I came back I could sleep.

Hardly anybody in Shelley's house got up before ten, and I usually asked myself why I did as I walked in the door of the Assembly Hall and took my seat in the Reverend Anne Gehman's class for spiritual enfoldment. Mornings were cool, and I often shivered through my sweater as the cold metal of the folding chair hit my back. I crossed my arms to keep warm and then uncrossed them to avoid looking closed and disapproving. Old portraits of women in high-necked dresses and men with bushy beards glowered down on us. Newer portraits from the thirties through the fifties looked more welcoming. Plump women smiled benignly, and men in suits stared into the camera with great confidence.

I picked Anne's class because of Hilda's recommendation. Students who attended her class the year before said a heavy four-legged table floated around the room completely off the ground. I'd go for that. I'd go for a little ectoplasm, a few hazy spirit forms—even a bent spoon might convince me if I did it. So far all I'd heard were secondhand tales.

Anne was often already sitting in front, perfectly turned out in an elegant, ankle-length dress, her hands in her lap. She liked to have a few moments of quiet meditation to prepare herself, a student told me. Once the class started, she stood behind the lectern where Sunday speakers for the Church of the Living Spirit delivered their morning addresses. Spiritualists never call those talks "sermons." That sounds too churchy. They like to emphasize that they are skeptics and freethinkers, just as earlier Spiritualists were. Spiritualism scientifically proves the afterlife, according to one Spiritualist principle.

For 150 years, believers have completely ignored the fact that the great majority of scientists think Spiritualism is nonsense and hasn't proven anything except that vast numbers of people are foolish and credulous. Anne made much of Spiritualism's scientific credentials. A Canadian journalist in the class tried to reason with her on that point, but it was no use. Anne slid right past him, as I knew she would. Spiritualists are a lot more practiced at dealing with skeptics than most amateur skeptics are at dealing with them. I never saw a Spiritualist get angry or yield a bit of ground. They just fuzz the issue.

I'm not saying they mean to. Other religious people do the same when faced with disbelief. Even when believers earnestly explain how things are and disbelievers earnestly listen, disbelievers go away unchanged because facts are the least of their differences. It's perception that separates them.

That's how it is, and that's how it has always been. Those who must see to believe don't believe enough to see. And those who believe enough to see won't stop believing, no matter what they see. One of the most famous experiments in psychic phenomena tested that truism and has been repeated many times. It indicated that people who think psychic power is possible score higher than normal on tests of such power, while people who don't score lower than normal. A later experiment with Mensa subjects indicated that extrasensory perception and other psychic phenomena, often called PSI, may be less common among people with high IQs. One interpretation is that intelligence tests often rely on what's called left-brain thinking, while PSI relies on right-brain perception. People who excel at left-brain thinking may reject interference with their reasoning powers—or they may be too smart to fall for such hooey.

Anne told the Canadian that he needed to read the hundreds of experiments that started in the 1800s and continue to this day. Researchers have documented plenty of strange things. Some of the most extensive tests and documentation were conducted by the British Society for Psychical Research. The society's presidents included three Nobel laureates, ten fellows of the Royal Society, one prime minister, and numerous physicists and philosophers. One of them, Sir Oliver Lodge, was among the outstanding physicists of the nineteenth century. His experiments with the transmission of drawings from one person to another person are somewhat like those of Upton Sinclair and even more astonishing.

Investigators for the British and American Societies for Psychical Research recorded thousands of cases of psychic phenomena. Researchers often tracked down other observers and witnesses and looked for every possible way that the evidence could have been faked. They found a lot of cheating, imaginative projections, and willingness to be duped, but they also found evidence that's pretty interesting. Professor Gilbert Murray, twice president of the British society, experimented for at least twenty years with thought transference. He would go outside his parlor and shut the door, while inside his guests would think of a subject and write down a description. Then the professor would return and tell them what they had written down. Out of the first 505 experiments, 60 percent were hits, according to those who participated.

In the middle of the 1900s, J. B. Rhine at Duke University conducted what are probably the most famous experiments in mental telepathy. He devised a set of symbols printed on playing cards. In some tests, the experimenter would look at the card as the test subject tried to guess what was on it. In other tests, the experimenter, who was sometimes in another room, would lift each card without looking at it, and place it face down in another stack. Dr. Rhine's tests showed that some testers could identify far more cards than was likely to occur randomly. One particular subject, a ministerial student, was so good he became something of a star.

But Rhine had a problem he couldn't overcome. Accuracy declined if a test went on too long, and even the best testers lost overall accuracy as they continued testing over weeks and months. The ministerial student held his record longer than anyone else. Then his girlfriend dumped him. Plunged into depression, he lost his psychic concentration entirely and never regained it.

J. B. Rhine didn't give up. He continued to experiment with PSI, but the national excitement generated by his early findings dwindled when other investigators had trouble reproducing his findings.

One of my favorite experiments was conducted by an Austrian, Paul Kammerer, who thought that the universe operates on a principle of unity that draws like to like. From the age of twenty until the age of forty, he kept a log of coincidences. Carl Jung also kept such a record of his patients' responses to coincidences, which he said were amazingly strong. Kammerer believed that coincidences occur without physical cause and in groupings. To prove that, he would sit for hours in public parks, classifying people who passed using criteria such as sex, age, dress, or even such trivial matters as whether they carried umbrellas or parcels. Controlling for such factors as weather and time, he found, for example, that on a given day he would see a far higher number of groups of three, while on another day a higher number of foursomes made up of two men and two women would stroll past. He believed this data showed that like attracts like, demonstrating that a principle of unity exists in the universe. Later Jung and quantum theory giant Wolfgang Pauli worked together on a theory of synchronicity, which more or less fit with Kammerer's observations.

Modern researchers at Princeton University have documented times when thoughts were able to affect the operation of highly calibrated machines. They also found many examples of people being able to transmit mental pictures of scenes to others.

Critics say all the studies showing PSI are faulty. Even supporters admit that many of them have not been duplicated. And both sides must concede that the effects shown are relatively small. Many are so small that they show up only when thousands of tests are run.

In addition, some of the PSI claims are so weird that even the open mind wants to click shut. Anne Gehman, for instance, mentioned to the Canadian journalist that scientists in the 1800s weighed mediums before and after ectoplasm came from their bodies, and the mediums had actually lost weight after the manifestations. Anne was right. I read experiments where gooey streams of ectoplasm were coming out of people's noses and ears and who knows what other orifice. Sometimes, observers showed that the stuff was made of cheesecloth and glop. Other times, they weren't able to find out what it was, and they did weigh people, but those experiments were like all the others. Maybe they proved something, maybe they didn't.

Like journalist Arthur Koestler, I find all the evidence for paranormal phenomena to be "unfortunate," because some of it pushes me toward belief and I don't want to go there. I like the universe to be rational and predictable. I like reality to be something that we can all more or less agree upon. Unlike Koestler, who analyzed the evidence and came away convinced that something beyond consensus reality was going on, I was not convinced by the evidence pro or con. Probably that is because I will never be able to analyze all of the data myself and I don't trust either side. No matter what I read, one part of my mind is saying, "Yes, but . . ."

William James believed that it might take one hundred years to come to grips with the realities of psychic occurrences, but that we finally would. Science as it is usually conceived "will look small for its insistence that only what it can measure, only that which is material can exist," he believed. He was wrong about that, so far.

His own description of psychic phenomena might explain why scientists have had little luck tracking it. "These experiences have three characters in common: They are capricious, discontinuous, and not easily controlled; they require peculiar persons for their production; their significance seems to be wholly for personal life."

The day Harry Houdini came to Lily Dale, he paid his gate fee and headed straight for slate-writing medium Pierre Keeler's house at the edge of the lake on Cottage Row. Nobody remembers the exact date, because the Dale's official histories don't record that Houdini ever came to the community; but Ron DeChard's mother lived in Lily Dale during the mid-1920s, when Houdini was earning his self-applied title as the "scourge of spirit mediums," and she told her son the story.

Everyone in town feared the flamboyant little magician and was on the lookout for him, she told Ron. He made headlines by showing up in mediums' parlors in a fake beard and mustache and wearing thick glasses. Once he figured out a medium's tricks, the magician would rip the disguise from his face and shout, "I am Houdini! And you are a fraud."

The renowned magician and escape artist faked Spiritualist tricks himself early in his career and later befriended one of Lily Dale's most famous physical mediums, Ira Davenport. Mr. Davenport's specialty was a spirit cabinet. He or his brother would be bound in a chair inside the cabinet. Once the door was shut, raps, tambourine rattles, and bell ringings were heard. Ghostly hands came from openings in the cabinet. The act garnered international fame for the brothers, and no one could figure out how they did it.

Houdini said Davenport revealed the secret of his tricks and told him that the brothers never made contact with spirits. Later Houdini refined their methods in his famous escape stunts.

That might have been all the contact Houdini would ever have with Spiritualism, but, in 1913, his mother died. The magician's grief was enormous.

"What would be more wonderful to me than to be able to converse with my beloved mother?" he wrote. "Surely there is no love in this world like a mother's love, no closeness of spirit, no other heart throbs that beat alike; but I have not heard from my blessed Mother, except through the dictates of the inmost recesses of my heart, the thoughts which fill my brain and the memory of her teachings."

Some people think his fierce hatred of phony Spiritualists came from his rage and disillusionment because they couldn't bring his mother's spirit to him. When he became friends with one of Spiritualism's most famous and ardent converts, Sir Arthur Conan Doyle, Houdini tried contacting his mother through Conan Doyle's wife, who sometimes gave readings via automatic writing, a form of mediumship in which spirits supposedly guide what's written.

The Conan Doyles believed their spirit contact with Houdini's mother was real, but the message was a disappointment to Houdini. It began with Mrs. Conan Doyle drawing the figure of a cross, something Houdini's mother would never have instigated because she was Jewish, the wife of a rabbi. The writing continued with an insipid, unspecific message in English. Houdini's mother didn't speak a word of English.

When Houdini expressed his doubts to Conan Doyle, the author replied that his wife always drew the shape of a cross at the beginning of her messages. Conan Doyle's confidence in Spiritualism was so strong that he believed Houdini himself was more than a mere magician and said that his tricks could only be accomplished with spirit help, which the fame-seeking magician hid so that he could take all the credit.

At one point during a carriage ride, Houdini showed Conan Doyle a simple trick often done for children in which the magician's thumb seems to disappear. According to Houdini, the creator of the ultrarational detective Sherlock Holmes was as impressed as any child. The two finally fell out in bitter public arguments.

Poor Pierre Keeler. Or lucky Pierre, depending on your perspective. By the time Houdini got to him, Keeler had been exposed over and over again, but each time he outlasted his critics and kept working. After Houdini threw off his disguise in his usual flamboyant way, he left Keeler's house and began knocking on doors, according to Ron's story. But word spread faster than Houdini could walk. Lily Dale's mediums all locked their doors and hid. Finally, realizing that his prey had gone underground, Houdini left Lily Dale.

That was not, however, the last of Houdini's dealings with Lily Dale's finest. Houdini made compacts with about a dozen people to communicate with him after they died. He agreed on secret handshakes and code words that would prove who they were.

"They have never come back to me! Does that prove anything? I have attended a number of séances since their death, the mediums have called for them, and when their spirit forms were supposed to appear not one of them could give me the proper signal. Would I have received it? I'll wager I would have," he wrote.

Before he died, Houdini left instructions with his wife, Bess, to continue his mediumistic inquiries by trying to contact him. She would know it was him if he delivered a secret message they had agreed on.

Three years after Houdini's death, Lily Dale medium Arthur Ford appeared at Bess's house to deliver what he claimed was the correct message. Bess wrote a statement confirming that Ford's message, delivered in the couple's secret code, was from Houdini, and two newspaper reporters covered the event. But one of the reporters later accused Ford of fraud, saying he told her the code the night before, enabling her to write her story before the event. Many who were skeptical of the reporter's veracity questioned why she ran a story she knew to be false.

But that was not the end of the criticism. Others noted that the code had already been published in a book. Ford supporters replied that his message was much more than merely the code. Then Bess herself was accused of having conspired with Ford. One Lily Dale medium told me she knew for a fact that Ford and the widow were having an affair and that she had given him the secret message. Eventually, Bess retracted her statement and to the end of her life denied that her husband ever communicated from the grave.

Séances to contact him are still held on the anniversary of Houdini's death. Organizers say the magician has never shown up. Spiritualists say he has no need to since he already proved his point in 1929 when he communicated with Ford.

23

Anne Gehman was obviously a woman who wanted to lead us into the deeper meaning of her faith, and she spent hours trying. I was pretty much bored, as I had been by the Spiritualist church services. Lily Dale churches may have no appointed ministers, but they have lots of reverends because many mediums and healers are licensed as ministers. Healing is part of the service, and so is giving messages. Different church members speak from the platform each week. Some Spiritualists expect speakers to arrive without any preparation so the spirits can take over. Judging from the times I attended, the spirits don't have much umph.

Lectures tended toward "Let's love each other" and "We ought to try to be nice." That may be good enough, but guilt and shame and a God ready to throw sinners into everlasting, roasting hell do make for a livelier meeting. The Weak Willie way of Spiritualist lectures made it hard for me to take them seriously as religion. I approved of what was being said, but my mind kept wandering.

Before Lily Dale, I had a pretty good idea of what Spiritualists would be like—old, bloodless, soft-voiced, hopelessly hopeful little folk who had watched the world pass them by and didn't quite know it yet. I was right about the hopelessly hopeful part. Spiritualists don't believe in hell, and they don't talk about sin. They think humans are basically good. They think that everything we do comes back on us. "Kick a dog and you'll answer for it," said medium Betty Schultz.

No savior can rescue humans, according to Spiritualists, but there's also no cutoff for changing your ways. You can do it now, or you can do it after you die. Spirits and angels are always gathered around us, watching and guiding and trying to beam messages through.

I couldn't believe that. What kind of loafing-around spirits would be wasting celestial time on me? And what kind of dopey egotist would I be if I thought they were?

In class, Anne talked about the principles of Spiritualism while we waited for her to give us what we came for, which was the tricks. That eagerness to see her perform made me feel a little like those rude men who yell, "Show us your tits," at earnest young women trying to get a serious message across. Maybe other people felt the same way, because no one tried to steer Anne toward the good stuff during class. But none of us discussed her religious ideas afterward. We were all too entranced over her stories of spirit doings.

She said her mentor used to brag, "Anne isn't happy until the men cry and the women wet their pants." Both events were part of her history, she said. A client who gave her a false name had once wet her pants in fear and consternation when Anne revealed that she knew the name was phony. And a skeptic who once tried to humiliate her during a lecture was brought to tears by the message she gave.

She told us of the evening her long-dead sister appeared before her and several friends. She gave details of the afternoon she was sitting in her living room feeling terribly depressed when she looked up to see a perfect rose floating across the room toward her. She recognized it as having come from her garden. Later she went to the garden and saw the stem where the rose had been. It was carefully clipped.

Anne was never stagy or particularly dramatic as she told these stories. She seemed almost bemused by them herself. She never raised her voice or varied the tempo of her speech. Her voice was soft, and she had a disarming way of interrupting herself with a bubbling little laugh that made me think she might be fun if you ever got past that ladylike surface, but I didn't think I ever would. Her eyes were arresting, almond-shaped and not easy to read. "She's got witch's eyes," a classmate hissed one day. When I looked at her in surprise she said defensively, "Nice witch."

Our class of about thirty included a lawyer, a former policeman, an artist, a couple of students, therapists, health-care workers, hypnotherapists, and experts in massage. This was the second week of a two-part class. I hadn't been in the first class, and neither had the Canadian journalist and his wife, who were in town researching the possibility of a book on Spiritualism. According to one student, the energy had been better the week before. They saw all sorts of psychic phenomena and gave each other astonishing readings, she said, but having journalists around messed with the vibrations, and this week wasn't nearly as good.

I resented that, but I could see how it might be true. I often felt like a black hole as I sat there brooding about what I heard. A television crew also showed up that week, and Anne's decision to let them film the class upset some students who didn't want outsiders to know they were involved in such lessons. Anne often looked toward the Canadian and sometimes called on him for comments during her talk. I could see why. He was tall and dignified. He had best-selling books, and he looked alert. Unlike me, yawning and as red-eyed as a drunk just in from an all-night bender.

Anne so rarely looked at me during the class that I began to have an odd sensation of being invisible. Sometimes her eyes ran down the row of people, and when they got to me I could have sworn they blanked out. When I raised my hand, she didn't seem to see me. She agreed to an interview, but when I got to her house, no one answered the door. Later she said she hadn't heard me knocking. How could that be? Her house is not that big.

The idea that someone might feel invisible came up during my first conversation with Shelley, when she was talking about stages of what she called the heroine's journey. Shelley asked me whether I'd ever had the feeling. I had, so often that I never think people are going to remember me when I meet them a second time. I generally like feeling invisible. It leaves me free to watch. But in Anne's class I had too much of a good thing. According to heroine's journey theories, the feeling of being invisible comes most often when people are beginning a spiritual journey. They feel as though others don't see them because they are changing and are not the solid selves they usually feel themselves to be, Shelley said.

Then one day in class a strange thing happened. A woman named Anna sat toward the middle of the room, and I sat on the left side. She had attracted my attention early in the week when she mentioned that she felt so in touch with her dead son that he was as much support and help to her as her living children. This day Anna was sharing some point with the class when she leaned over, looked directly at me, and said, "There are great advantages to being invisible."

I should have caught her after class to ask what she meant, but I didn't. I had never mentioned my feelings of invisibility to the other students, and Anna's comment made me feel like a stranger had shoved me. She didn't have to tell me the advantages of being invisible. If I was being needy and childish about the lack of attention, I didn't want her giving me lessons.

Hilda was right about Anne being a born medium. She wowed our class with many fabulous stories from the days of her childhood as the youngest of eight children in an Amish-

Mennonite family. Cutlery and dishes would move at her end of the dinner table. Her father would lay his big hands on her head and pray that this strange affliction be taken from her. She remembers once being sent to bed as punishment. As she lay there, the table beside the bed began to rise. She heard her father's heavy footsteps coming toward the room, and the table crashed to the floor. Once she returned home to find her mother lying on the floor so sick she couldn't move. Anne placed her hands on her mother's body and began to draw the poisons out. As they left her mother's body, Anne's hands and arms turned dark, and she had to wash them repeatedly before they returned to their normal color.

In the community where she grew up, children weren't expected to go past eighth grade. So Anne left home at fourteen, determined to finish high school and go to college. By then the family was living in Florida, and she moved to a small town not too far from their farm. She worked in a nursing home and took care of an old lady in return for lodging. She was so lonely and lost that one day she bought as many over-the-counter sleeping pills as she could, took them all, and lay down on the bed. She awoke vomiting and too weak to rise from the bed. As she lay there, a female apparition appeared at the foot of her bed and said, "If you will follow me, I will lead you into a new way of life."

When she was strong enough to get up, Anne felt compelled to get in her car and drive to a nearby Spiritualist camp called Cassadaga, named after Lily Dale's lake. Her car kept stopping at a certain house. She got out and knocked on the door. It was opened by a man named Wilbur Hull. "You're a natural medium, and I want to help you develop your gifts," he said. That morning the same spirit that had appeared to Anne appeared to Wilbur and told him that she was sending him the greatest natural medium she had ever known. Over the next few years, Wilbur taught Anne what he knew about the spirit world and helped her develop her gifts.

She lived for many years in Florida. Several people told me she made a bundle when spirit told her to buy some land, which she eventually sold to Disney World. The story wasn't quite accurate. She didn't sell directly to Disney World, but she did make a lot of money, she said. "But it's gone now. I made other bad business deals," she said.

Other mediums encouraged her to become a physical medium because of her skill with objects, she told us, but that didn't interest her. She wanted to help people grow and heal.

People in the Dale were always talking about how the manifestations of spirit ought to help people on their path to spiritual growth, but I didn't get it. Mediums differentiate themselves from psychics in emphasizing that their primary goal is to prove the continuity of life by contacting the dead. But most people who come to the Dale are more interested in what is going to happen in their own lives than they are in talking with the dead. So the Dale's mediums give people what they want. I couldn't see how foretelling the future had anything in common with spiritual growth. People come because they want money or love or power. They aren't looking to become better people. And most of the time, they aren't looking for dead people.

Lily Dale's visitors today are mostly people of modest means, mainly working people. The women are secretaries, clerks, factory workers, beauticians, school cafeteria cooks, and women whose main task in life is cleaning houses and keeping children, sometimes their own and sometimes the children of others. The men are carpet layers, carpenters, mechanics, firefighters, and policemen. Those who aren't in unions probably vote Republican. In recent years, Lily Dale has drawn increasing numbers of schoolteachers, physicians, nurses, professors—people with education and a good bit of social status.

Those who come are often middle-aged or older and, like the rest of America, overweight. Sunshades are clamped to their heads and cameras swing from their necks. Those not wearing sandals are most often shod in the enormous, blazingly white athletic shoes that identify American tourists everywhere in the world. They wear shorts, although many are long past the age and weight when they ought to have given up such revealing wear, and they often sport tans with the peculiar beetle-shell look that comes from tanning beds.

They are cheerful, easygoing people and not at all fools. Unlike people whose intelligence or education has puffed them up, many Lily Dale visitors take in what the town has to offer with easy shrugs that accept and dismiss in equal measure.

Once I interviewed people in the Monday evening line outside the auditorium on five-dollar reading night. On these nights, six people sit in a circle with one medium, who will go from one to the other, giving short messages that last maybe five minutes. One medium complained that the people who attend Monday night messages are often greedy for more than their money buys them a right to. They press the mediums, argue with them, and sometimes treat them like sideshow performers, which the mediums don't appreciate. Incidentally, mediums make no money from this event; all proceeds go to the Lily Dale Assembly.

Hours before the event started, a French girl, dressed in black, smoking a cigarette, was in line. She was visiting the area, heard about Lily Dale, and came to see what she might find out about her future. Yes, she did believe in all this. She'd gotten a good reading from a medium in Belgium, who told her about what would happen with her job and her love life. Asked for specifics, she blew a column of smoke and said she didn't exactly remember. A group of sixty-ish friends was there from nearby Jamestown. They didn't want to give their names. They came every year. "For five dollars, it's worth it," said one.

Oh, yes, they'd gotten good advice and heard true things. One woman was told that she would have problems with her lungs. She wasn't smoking, but her face had the lined look and her voice the husky growl of a longtime heavy smoker.

Did you stop smoking?

"No," she said.

Did the prediction scare you?

"Sure."

I asked people in the line whether any of them had changed anything in their lives because of the mediums' predictions. That got a laugh.

"No."

"Of course not."

"I'd never do that."

They shook their heads and grimaced, amused at the idea.

But you say the mediums are often correct?

"Sure." "That's right." Lily Dale patrons don't have to be consistent. This isn't science. It's life.

Nobody mentioned contacting dead relatives or friends, which might be just as well.

"It's getting harder and harder for spirits to prove that they're who they say they are," medium Lauren Thibodeau told me.

"People don't remember anybody from past generations," she said. "When you add the number of adoptions and divorces that split families apart, you've got a real problem. I might very well be bringing in Grandpa, and no one knows enough about him to believe that he's really there."

Spirits don't often talk about life after death, and the Spiritualists themselves differ on what happens. They don't agree on how long the spirits stick around to converse. Some think spirits aren't available right after death because they're too mixed up about their status. Others think spirits linger for only a short while and then go off to do whatever spirits do. And then there are those who think that the spirits stay available as long as anyone on earth still remembers them.

Some Spiritualists believe in reincarnation; some don't. "There's going to be skid marks on the clouds if they try to make me come back," Lily Dale historian Joyce LaJudice said.

Spiritualist heaven, called Summerland, does not have streets of gold, but it does have flowers. Lily Dale resident Richard O'Brocta said his dead wife has visited him many times and taken him on a tour of her Summerland home.

"She lives in a little white house with a stream running by it," he told me. "It has flowers around it. She's taken me there to see it. I've been inside. She works in a hospital taking care of babies that died. She helps raise them. Everyone has a job. People are the age they were at their happiest time in life. I'll be thirty-two."

I never heard anybody talk about their dead relatives having met God. The most specific inquiry regarding divine whereabouts that I ran across came from a book by the late California Episcopal bishop James Pike, who believed he had contacted his son. This particularly surprised the bishop, because his liberal theology hadn't convinced him that life after death exists, but the messages that came from his son did. The bishop asked the boy whether he had seen Christ. His son answered through a medium that he had been told he wasn't ready to meet Jesus. He also said Jesus was talked about in the afterlife as a seer and mystic but not as a savior.

Perhaps not coincidentally, the message, which came through a medium, dovetails with Spiritualist thinking about Jesus. There are Christian Spiritualists and some Lily Dale devotees who claim membership in traditional faiths as well as adherence to Spiritualism. But the predominate philosophy in Lily Dale is not Christian. Many Spiritualists speak of Jesus as the greatest of all mediums, and they sometimes use his healing miracles as examples to bolster their contention. They don't believe he died for our sins or that he was the Son of God, except in the sense that everyone is a child of God.

As an aside, the Dale's Arthur Ford once gave Bishop Pike a reading on Toronto television. The information Ford relayed from Pike's son was so convincing that it made international news. Later, journalist Allen Spraggett, who set up the interview, wrote a biography of Ford. In looking over Ford's papers after his death Spraggett discovered that the medium had researched the boy and that many of his amazing revelations came from newspaper clippings.

Ford's fraud shook Spraggett's confidence in him but didn't destroy it. Like many before and after him, the journalist held to his contention that "something" real was happening amid and despite the fakery. This ability to hold to faith in the face of contradictions maddens Spiritualism's critics. Justly so, I think.

But blind tenacity isn't confined to Spiritualism. It's the heart's blood of religious experience. Religion says people will be transformed into new beings. They aren't. And faith sails right on. Religion says God will answer prayers. He doesn't. And faith sails right on.

I saw it happen with the Taiwanese who came to Garland, Texas, believing God was going to appear there before ending the world. Right before the Almighty's scheduled appearance, the prophet changed his story to say that God in His infinite wisdom would not appear in person but via television. A horde of reporters gathered to see the Almighty take over the airwaves. When he didn't, we expected great wailing and gnashing of teeth, at least a shamefaced apology.

But no . . . at almost the exact moment that God became a no-show, a sudden breeze caused the clouds to go skittering across the moon. That was all the Taiwanese needed. God *had* appeared, they told us. He had come as a great wind and had entered into our hearts. He now dwelt among us as He had promised. And He was going to delay ending the world because everything would be different now.

The sociologists and psychologists, the scientists and the journalists, all have explanations for such credulity—just as they do for Spiritualism. Good, solid, logical reasons. I believe them all and feel securely superior when reciting them.

Most of the time. But sometimes the bright face of a true believer shakes my certainty. Sometimes as I look into the clear, guileless eyes of faith, I wonder if the rest of us are missing something. Have they taken the dross of ordinary, drab, death-and-taxes life and turned it into some kind of gold? If there is no "more," why are so many people finding such richness in living as though there were?

Unlike the scientists' explanations, these questions don't cause me to feel secure and superior. They make me think I'm missing something. Worse than that, they make me think that I'll have to be a little gullible, maybe even a little crazy, in order to figure out what that something is. I hear a lot I would like to believe. White light, for instance.

One of the most widely discussed and debated gifts of spiritual thinking is the white light that people report seeing while in comatose, near-death states. White light also figures prominently in Spiritualist thinking. "Go to the light" is often what mediums tell poltergeists, whom they believe are merely confused spirits that don't know they're dead yet.

Anne, a firm believer in the white light, also gave us some hints about what would happen once we entered the glow. Jesus didn't figure in her stories, but a sense of purpose did. She told our class that we would all have tasks in the afterlife. We would use our skills to help others. At the break, as we stood outside the building, the former policeman asked me what I thought of Anne's ideas about heaven.

"I don't know," I said.

"I'm not interested," he said flatly. "Sounds boring. When I go to heaven, I want to be a Viking."

I laughed. "I don't think there's going to be a lot of rape and pillage, if that's what you want."

"I can do without that," he said. "But to do battle. To risk everything you have, even your life, in the cause of something you believe in, to help other people, to save them, that's the greatest thrill in life. That's what I'd like more of in the afterlife."

When I repeated that story to Jackie Lunger, a diminutive medium who once wore a T-shirt that read, "Small medium at large," she replied coolly that Anne's ideas were right and heaven was probably pretty boring. "That's why everyone wants to come back here," she said. "This is where the action is."

24

I believed I killed my son," Pat Naulty said. "I was convinced of it." She knew that John needed her in those weeks before he shot himself playing Russian roulette. She knew that she should have gone to Indiana immediately and taken him back to California with her, but she didn't. Her guilt was so intense that she would have killed herself to escape it, but her other son, Willie, held her to the earth. She'd killed his brother. She couldn't kill his mother.

For a year, Pat could not say the words "John is dead." Her tongue could not form the words. The breath to speak them stuck in her throat. On the first anniversary of his shooting, she went alone to a cabin in the woods. There she wrote a song for John and a eulogy.

The next day, she set out to walk up a nearby hill. She brought flowers saved from his funeral and photos his grandmother had taken of him in his casket. She hated those photos of his body and had never looked at them because she didn't want to remember him that way. She also carried her guitar, a pen, and a pad in case she needed to write something. She followed a clear path to the top of a hill. Looking over the land, she sang the song and read the words. She buried the photos.

John had once asked her what she thought about life after death. She replied that she believed in it, but she didn't know what she believed about it. He said that he believed the universe is filled with amazing energy and that after death souls float up to the energy and join it. Pat couldn't forget the sweet dreaminess of his voice when he said those words.

In the years since John's death, as she struggled to stay sane, a new fear came to her. It wasn't anything rational, nothing other people understood. She worried that her grief might be holding him back, keeping him from moving into the energy of the universe.

She finished her lonely ceremony and sat sobbing on the hill. When she could stand, she said, "Good-bye, John," and turned to walk down.

The path that had been so clear on her ascent had disappeared. She struggled through the brush, weeping as she went, her guitar clanking hollow against her legs, until she came to a fallen log. As she sat on it, she began to cry again. She curled into her body, keening. Her ragged cries, rough as a crow's dark caw, tore through the clear air of the silent, empty woods. When she could cry no more, she sat there a while, wet, limp, exhausted. Then she pulled out the pad and pen and began to write a letter of apology to her son, the letter she had not finished, the one that had sat on her desk because she was too busy, and then because John was dead and it was too late. She begged his forgiveness for not being present when he needed her.

She finished the letter and began to weep again. A breeze started from behind her, high in the top of the trees. She heard the shiver of their leaves, a trembling that started far away and moved toward her, over her head and past her.

"I knew that was John. I'd been able to release him." She stopped crying and raised her face. Slowly the trees came into focus. She saw the path that led down, right before her.

She had released her son, given his soul permission to leave her, but did he go? Or did her grief snap him back? She didn't know.

Pat's reading with medium Lauren Thibodeau didn't start well, at least not on the surface. The medium said she had a name, but it wasn't John. It was a name Pat didn't know and forgot almost immediately. Lauren asked whether Pat's son had died. She said that he had. She told Lauren his name and how he died. Giving that kind of information may not be a good idea when consulting mediums. It might help them too much.

But Pat wasn't skeptical. She wanted to help Lauren because even before the medium spoke Pat was certain that her son was present. As she entered the reading room, she began to hear a refrain.

Diddle diddle dumpling, my son John.
Went to bed with his stockings on.
One shoe off, one shoe on.
Diddle, diddle dumpling, my son John.

It was the nursery rhyme Pat had sung to John when he was a little boy. Each son had his own. Willie's rhyme had been "Wee Willie Winkie." She couldn't remember the last time she had thought of those verses, and now John's rhyme was tripping through her head like a children's chorus chanting. John was in the room.

"I knew it. I felt it," said Pat.

"He says to tell you drugs were involved," Lauren said.

"I didn't know that," Pat said. "I suspected it."

"He's in a wonderful place," the medium said. "It's just beautiful. I see him lying on a table of some kind, and people are standing all around him. They're laying their hands on him, and he's being healed. Everything is wonderful."

But was he free to move on? Now while she had the medium's attention, Pat asked her question. "Ask if I'm keeping him back, if I'm keeping him from going on," she said.

Lauren smiled, shook her head. "No. No, he's telling me that the ceremony you had released him. The song and eulogy. They released him."

No one knew about that ceremony. No one could have known.

Did he forgive her? Pat wanted to ask, but she couldn't. What right did she have to ask for that? And what if Lauren said something that made it seem that he didn't forgive her? She couldn't bear it. As it turned out, Pat didn't need to ask.

"He's telling me to say that the love you two have for each other is always with you," Lauren said.

Pat thought, *She used the present tense. The love we have. Not the love we had.*

"Anytime you want to feel it you can just call it up," Lauren said. "Think of him, and he'll be right there with you. Always."

25

Our class's star pupil was Sean, one of those thin, serious kids who looks so intense he'd quiver if you touched him. He held objects and got visions. He tuned into spirits and brought messages that amazed everyone. He came with a buddy who giggled a lot, but Sean was solemn. On the third day of class, he was not looking so good. His eyes were round and scared.

"I couldn't stop thinking about them all day," he told the class. "I couldn't make the images go away."

The day before, when we practiced giving messages, Sean had seen a dark-haired, slightly built young man hanging dead from a backyard swing set. The boy's mother was standing inside the house, looking through the window at her son's body.

"She couldn't make herself go out," Sean said, his voice a miserable croak.

Sean didn't know this family, but Anne did. "That happened to one of my clients," she said. "You're right about it all. He killed himself. The mother saw him, but she couldn't go out."

Her voice was soothing but matter-of-fact.

"Just let the images go. As soon as you have them, release them," she said.

But they didn't go away. The next day, it seemed as if Sean had been taken over by this evil scene. When it came time to raise our vibrations by singing, Sean was silent. Afterward, he announced that he couldn't sing. He was still captured by the vision of death. It wouldn't go away. We all looked at him warily. Was he being haunted? Anne didn't give the idea a second to grow.

"You can control it," she told him firmly. "Just let the thoughts go as soon as they come to you." Then she went on with the class as though there was no reason to discuss it further. Later, the Canadian journalist and I quizzed her. Again she minimized the incident.

"Sometimes . . . ," she said, and then paused, searching for words, ". . . sometimes artistic people dramatize too much. A good teacher downplays any attention they might get so that they won't hang on to things they ought to let go. That's part of learning to be a medium."

Oddly, Lily Dale mediums often seemed determined to downplay every sexy aspect of their profession. They refused to say that their gift was anything that everybody doesn't have. Messages they brought from the spirits were so bland as to be boring unless you were the person they were for—and sometimes even then. William James complained, "What real spirit, at last able to revisit his wife on this earth, [wouldn't] find something better to say than that she had changed the place of his photograph?" One researcher during James's day likened their fuzzy, strange performances to that of a drunken messenger. Others noted that the spirits seemed not in full possession of their faculties.

When it came to evil spirits, possession, and hauntings, the community really fell down. People rarely mentioned evil spirits without prompting, and if they did, they passed over them without much fanfare. Betty Schultz did say her father wouldn't allow her to dabble in otherworldly communication when she was a child.

SPIRITUALISM'S MOST REVERED SHRINE The Fox cottage, where children Margaret and Kate Fox first heard knocking sounds that their family believed to be made by a dead peddler, was the 1848 birthplace of modern Spiritualism. The cottage, originally located in Hydesville, New York, was moved in 1916 to Lily Dale, where a medium produced similar "spirit raps" and sold pieces of wood said to be from the cottage's original foundation. The cottage burned in 1955. *(Courtesy of the Lily Dale Museum)*

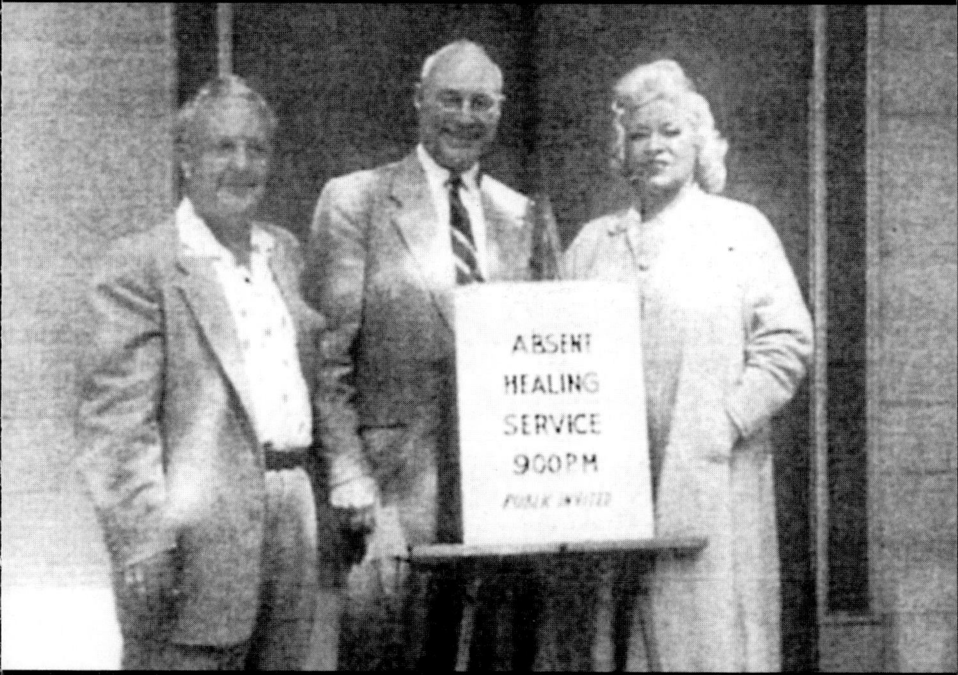

MAE WEST AND HER MEDIUM Mae West was a fan of Lily Dale medium Jack Kelly (left) and once came to visit him during his summer residency there. After Kelly's death, she claimed that he appeared to her dressed in a tuxedo. *(Courtesy of Hilda Wilkinson)*

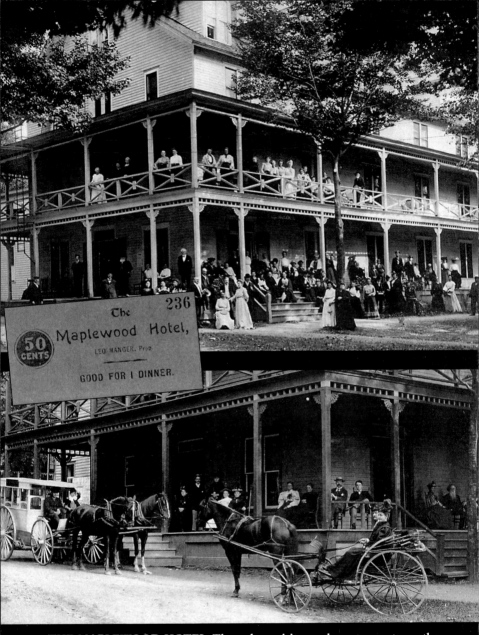

THE MAPLEWOOD HOTEL These days, visitors who congregate on the veranda of the Maplewood Hotel are more informally dressed but often are just as avid about their belief in spirit communication. A sign in the lobby warns against conducting séances and circles in the public rooms, but the side parlor is sometimes used for such. Tales of roaming spirits, bumps in the night, and furniture inexplicably moved are common as tourists testify each morning about their night's adventure. *(Photo at top courtesy of the Lily Dale Museum; photo at bottom courtesy of Hilda Wilkinson)*

THE CAMPBELL BROTHERS' SÉANCE ROOM The Campbell brothers' 1905 séance room gives a view of Lily Dale's lavish style during an era when the crème de la crème of Spiritualist society gathered there for the summer camp season. The Campbells made their fortune in the import-export business, but their fame came from the spirit paintings they produced. *(Courtesy of the Lily Dale Museum)*

VICTORIAN LILY DALE Lily Dale's fondness for gingerbread ornamentation, seen here on Melrose Drive, roused Sinclair Lewis's esthetic scorn when he visited in 1917. Complaining that architects on the astral plane had failed to aid the community much, he wrote, "It is a shabby collection of much-porched, drab-painted, scrollwork-decked houses of the school of 1890." Today, that same look gives Lily Dale a charm that few communities can match. *(Courtesy of the Lily Dale Museum)*

A SUMMER'S IDYLL Lily Dale's early popularity was furthered by a nearby train stop that allowed visitors easy access. They often came and stayed for weeks, renting low-priced rooms from year-round residents. Such long-term visits gave the mediums plenty of opportunity to learn stories about the tourists and their dead relatives. Visits are usually shorter now, but tourists still rent rooms with shared baths and pay prices as low as $35 a night. *(Courtesy of Hilda Wilkinson)*

LILY DALE IN ITS HEYDAY Lily Dale entertained Victorian visitors with a Ferris wheel and a formal ballroom. The community also once boasted a bowling alley and a newspaper of its own called *The Sunflower.* Today those attractions are gone. *(Courtesy of Hilda Wilkinson)*

THE MEDIUM AND THE SCOURGE OF SPIRITUALISM Harry Houdini (right) claimed to have learned some of his most famous tricks from Ira Davenport, an internationally famous Lily Dale medium. Later, the magician became one of Spiritualism's greatest enemies. So feared was he that, when he came to Lily Dale, the mediums are said to have locked their doors and hid.

(Courtesy of the Sidney H. Radner Collection, Houdini Historical Center, Appleton, Wisconsin)

THE CITY OF LIGHT In 1903, Lily Dale was called the City of Light because it was one of the first communities in upstate New York to have electricity, but many people claimed the name for its more spiritual significance. City of Light remains one of its more laudatory nicknames. Today, the less reverent call the settlement Spooksville and Silly Dale.

(Courtesy of the Lily Dale Museum)

SUSAN B. ANTHONY Suffragette Susan B. Anthony (seated at far right) was a frequent visitor to Lily Dale, where she was invited to speak at annual Women's Day celebrations. Her signature is in a hotel register preserved in the Lily Dale Museum. Although not a Spiritualist herself, Anthony did visit a medium and got a message said to be from her aunt. Anthony's response was, "I didn't like her when she was alive, and I don't want to hear from her now. Why don't you bring someone interesting like Elizabeth Cady?" *(Courtesy of Hilda Wilkinson)*

PEACE RALLY
Early Spiritualists rallied for peace and other progressive political causes. Present-day Lily Dale stays far away from such advocacy, preferring New Age–type workshops that deal with topics such as psychic pet communication, vibrational healing, and understanding out-of-body experiences.
(Courtesy of the Lily Dale Museum)

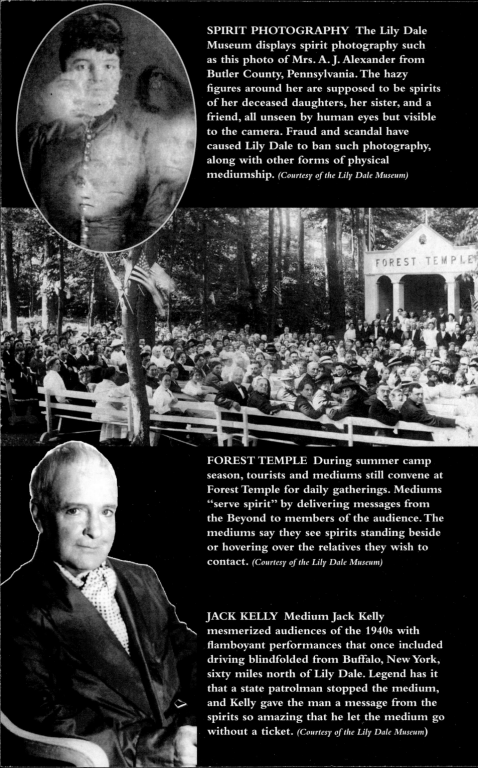

SPIRIT PHOTOGRAPHY The Lily Dale Museum displays spirit photography such as this photo of Mrs. A. J. Alexander from Butler County, Pennsylvania. The hazy figures around her are supposed to be spirits of her deceased daughters, her sister, and a friend, all unseen by human eyes but visible to the camera. Fraud and scandal have caused Lily Dale to ban such photography, along with other forms of physical mediumship. *(Courtesy of the Lily Dale Museum)*

FOREST TEMPLE During summer camp season, tourists and mediums still convene at Forest Temple for daily gatherings. Mediums "serve spirit" by delivering messages from the Beyond to members of the audience. The mediums say they see spirits standing beside or hovering over the relatives they wish to contact. *(Courtesy of the Lily Dale Museum)*

JACK KELLY Medium Jack Kelly mesmerized audiences of the 1940s with flamboyant performances that once included driving blindfolded from Buffalo, New York, sixty miles north of Lily Dale. Legend has it that a state patrolman stopped the medium, and Kelly gave the man a message from the spirits so amazing that he let the medium go without a ticket. *(Courtesy of the Lily Dale Museum)*

"I would never allow a child to do it either. They're too open," she said. "Murderers and rapists are looking for a way in. They're on that level.

"As my teacher Gertie Rowe always said, 'Just like you wouldn't let a stranger into your house, don't let a stranger into your mind.' "

Once when Joyce LaJudice was opening up the Maplewood Hotel for the summer, she called Betty and said, "Get over here and get the damned ghosts out." A woman in a long gown had been seen walking the stairs. Joyce and Betty blamed a few guests who had brought Ouija boards to their rooms the summer before.

"Anything like that attracts the lower vibrations," said Betty.

I asked a bit breathlessly, "What did you do?"

"Just what anybody would do," she said. "If an ordinary person was bothering you, you'd say go away. It's the same with spirits." Even the worst are easily banished. "A 'God bless you' will stop them cold," Betty said.

"They're not evil, just confused," was a description I heard many times. Mediums often talked about misdirected, unprogressed, or lower spirits.

Even the late Arthur Ford, grand old mediumistic showman that he was, dismissed the idea that bad vapors might take over the unwary. He told audiences, "When evil, obscene spirits come to you, look in your own heart—that's why they come. You reap what you sow. A good, normal type of person does not become obsessed."

Again and again, mediums tossed away stories that might have been fiendishly well told. Lily Dale healer Tom Cratsley once counseled a man who felt his dead lover was inhabiting his body. "I don't know if he was really inside his body," Tom said. "But inter-dimensional codependency is as real as codependency between people on earth. People don't change their tendencies because they go to another dimension." The dead lover had dominated Tom's client before his death and was continuing the pattern.

"I supported him as he claimed his own power," Tom said of the living client. When the spirit moved on, everyone in the room knew that a moment of grace had occurred. A great burst of energy come up from the floor and tears came to their eyes, he said.

Spirits don't victimize people, but people do project their own problems and hang-ups onto spirits, Tom said.

"The whole fear thing is overblown, enormously and immensely. The danger, if there is one, is mainly in self-delusion," he said.

Tom has been called upon to exorcise ghosts from houses, a process Spiritualists call spirit rescues. They never use the word "ghost." "Earthbound spirits" or "lost souls" or "spirits who haven't gone toward the light" are preferable descriptions, according to Lily Dale thought. Tom calls them stuck souls.

"I usually take a group with me and build up the love energy and then invite the poor stuck soul into it. Most of the time they just want to be understood. If someone living comes in and says, 'I understand that you're pissed,' that begins the [telepathic] conversation. Once you do that, you can discuss with them their problem."

He was once called to a house where one resident believed an ancient Mesopotamian demon lived in the basement. Tom found nothing so alarming. The spirit of a woman who had lived in the house earlier was still waiting for her ship captain husband to return from the sea. Tom told her the quickest way to find her husband was to go to the light.

One resident wouldn't accept that. Perhaps he believed Tom was covering for the Mesopotamian demon. Tom laughed. "His imagination got the best of him."

I did find a few stories of spirits that didn't have goodwill toward humans. On his Lily Dale visit during the 1920s, the psychology student George Lawton wrote of a service held in an eastern camp during which a popular medium began making filthy and obscene remarks. He had been possessed by an impersonating spirit, Lawton was told, "one of the vilest specimens of depravity that ever could be imagined." Several men overpowered him and carried him off the platform.

It's standard practice for Lily Dale mediums to begin their sessions with a prayer requesting only the highest and the best. "You have to set your intentions," the mediums tell students. "It's your intentions that control what happens. If your intentions are good, nothing bad will be attracted to you."

The idea that spirits might roam looking for unwary bodies to inhabit has been around for a long time. Some mediums flatly reject the notion. Others say mental illness might sometimes be caused by such spirits, but nobody seems to feel menaced.

One of the scariest stories I heard came from Marian Boswell, who told me that several nights when she was sleeping alone she awoke feeling certain that someone was in the bed with her, that the someone was male, and that his intentions were sexual. Once she felt a hand stroking her hair. Another time she saw the blanket move. She asked Greg Kehn what he thought was happening.

With the kind of insouciance that's typical of Lily Dale mediums when discussing such matters, he said, "Oh, yeah." Those were spirits roaming around looking for someone alive to be with. They were attracted by her warmth, he said.

"Just tell them that you aren't going with them, and they'll go away," he said.

Lily Dale's spirits don't give bad news, and if they do, the mediums don't deliver it. If there's something in the future that people need to be warned about, they soft-pedal it. If it looks like lung cancer, they say, "I'm seeing something in the chest area. Maybe you ought to have it checked out."

That seems irresponsible to me, but as several pointed out, "What if we're wrong?" The future, especially knowing when something might happen, is particularly tricky, they said.

"You always have free will. If you change what you're doing, the future will change," is the standard explanation.

The spirits Lily Dale brings back are almost saccharine in their goodwill. They praise people and tell them that things are going to be great. Parents who disapproved of their children while alive are especially likely to come back saying that they didn't understand and now they do. They ask for forgiveness, show remorse. I couldn't find one story of anyone who came back saying that upon reflection and with the benefit of their new expanded view, they had been right in treating their kids badly and they wished they'd been meaner.

Inexperienced receivers such as Sean pick up images of death and destruction because those images have the heaviest energy, and people who haven't learned to increase their own vibrations come into contact with heavy energy first, said medium Lauren Thibodeau. She saw all kinds of scary things when she was young.

In grade school, Lauren would sometimes become angry at another child and say something like, "You're going to fall and break your teeth." And then the kid would, she told me, which didn't help Lauren's popularity. When classmates began calling her "witch girl," she stopped telling her visions, and the premonitions went away for years. In the tenth grade, she moved to a new school. One day, as she stood at her locker, a blond senior wearing an angora sweater walked toward her. Lauren saw a gray coffin with pink roses on it floating before the girl. She fainted.

The doctor blamed hormones. Her mother called the episode a

brownout. Whatever it was, the girl's mother had breast cancer and died two weeks later, Lauren said.

"Every paranormal thing you can have happen happened to me. I couldn't escape it," she said. "All I saw was death and destruction." She was beginning to feel like some real-life Carrie.

"Most people who have these experiences sit on them and hope they go away," she said. Lauren didn't do that. Instead, as she refined her gift, she began to draw happier visions.

26

Before he died, Noel Lucas used to say, "If I'm the first one to go, and you feel someone pinch your fanny, it's me on the other side."

"There are a hundred and one better ways than that for you to let me know," Carol would reply.

It had all been a joke, of course, back in the days when their respective golf scores were of more pressing concern than illness or death or grief. Noel hadn't come back to pinch her, and if he had, Carol probably would have thought she imagined it. The messages Martie and Sherry Lee gave her—about golf lessons and dangerous tires—were convincing partly because they were so unexpected. They were nothing she could have ever imagined.

But, in truth, it wasn't only the mediums' words that swayed Carol toward believing a reality beyond reason might exist. She believed Noel's efforts to communicate with her through extraordinary means began when he was in the hospital for the last time. The first instance was one midafternoon when Carol, exhausted after a night at his bedside, left his room to take a nap. She fell asleep quickly and began to dream that Noel was coming toward her out of a blank background. Nothing was around him, and he said nothing, but the feeling was ominous.

She jolted awake thinking, "Noel's dead."

Carol rushed back to the hospital. He was still in a coma. While she was there, a doctor told her that he didn't think Noel was going to survive. She and their daughter Stephanie put on a tape of a thunderstorm because Noel so loved listening to thunder and rain, and they began to talk to him. His heartbeat steadied for the first time. He was taken off all machines except the ventilator.

As the night wore on, Carol began to fear the moment of his death. She told her daughter that she wasn't sure she could bear it, but she also couldn't bear to leave. One of the unhooked machines began to beep. Carol left to call a nurse.

"Mrs. Lucas, there's no reason for that machine to be beeping," the nurse said as they met in the hall.

They walked back into the room, and Stephanie said, "He's gone, Mom."

"That was Noel's last gift to me," Carol said when I talked to her after her visit to Lily Dale. He had somehow caused the beeping so she would not have to endure watching his last breath. "I believe that."

A month after his death, Carol took her coffee and newspaper to the back deck. She sat in Noel's rocking chair so she wouldn't have to look at it squatting there as empty as a human lap. Everywhere she turned there was some gap left by Noel's disappearance, a thousand little jolts a day. She could see the water garden he made for her birthday and the wind chimes he hung in a too-sheltered spot. They never rang. He often mentioned moving them, but he never did.

She sipped her coffee as she gazed toward the golf course where they had played together so many times. South Carolina can be muggy even in May. This morning was cool and fresh but already airless.

Setting the coffee down, she pulled the newspaper off the table and snapped it open. She was trying to focus on the news when she heard a silvery sound. More than a sound, a commotion. It was the chimes. She could see them, shivering across the yard's dappled shade as though someone had reached out and given them a hard shake. She looked at the tops of the trees. They were motionless.

She got up. What was this? She walked toward the pond. Not a leaf moved, but the chimes were agitated, excited now into a cascade of sound. They were fairly jumping on their strings. She looked around for a squirrel or a bird. Had something fallen on the chimes? Nothing was near. Nothing was on the ground around them. She saw no animals.

Just as the wind chimes were about to fall silent, they leapt again as though someone had swiped a hand through them.

Was it Noel?

She stood close to the chimes. There was no breeze, but they were still swirling as though caught in a whirlwind.

It was Noel. She could almost feel his presence.

Carol said, "Okay, dear. I get the point."

She turned, went back to the porch, and sat down. The chimes stopped. As is often the case with such occurrences, Carol didn't feel excited or strange. She was calm and almost matter-of-fact. Without Lily Dale, she might have passed the moment off as her imagination, but after spending time with Martie and Sherry Lee, Carol reassessed the moment and counted it as a blessing.

On another morning Carol awoke to the sound of a door opening, and then she heard Noel's voice.

"Carol, are you up yet?" he said, as he had on a hundred other mornings.

For a moment Carol believed that his death had been the dream and that his voice was the reality. Then she came fully awake, and life fell about her like a sodden blanket. She might have sunk under the weight of it and been filled with renewed despair, except for Lily Dale.

The mediums said that Noel wasn't dead. He was alive. Out of his body, but still alive and still in touch. Carol believed it. They had convinced her of it.

"Nobody is going to take this away from me," she said of her new belief. "I won't let them."

Every day we learned a little more about Anne.

She now lives in Virginia, where she has earned her reputation as one of the most popular mediums in Washington, D.C. She confirmed that highly placed people consult her regularly but would not give any names. It wouldn't be ethical, she said. Police and family often consult her to find missing persons, she said. She told the class about how she helped catch serial killer Ted Bundy when she was living in Florida. She saw part of his license plate and described his van. She got the names Brady or Bradley and Ed or Ted. She said they could catch him through fraudulent use of credit cards and described the hotel where he was staying. I checked with an FBI friend about confirming that story. He laughed. Nobody in the FBI would admit it even if it was true, he said.

Anne also said she helped W. W. Keeler, the chairman of Phillips Petroleum, find oil. She studied geological maps and then directed pilots to fly her to certain areas. After walking over the ground, she selected a spot and knew that oil was underneath. She stood over the spot and lifted her arm into the air. Then she brought it down like a lever, up and down, up and down. Each pumping of her arm represented so many feet of depth.

Keeler wrote the preface to a book about Anne. He definitely believed in her powers, but his testimonial to her powers didn't mention that she had found oil.

I wanted to believe Anne. I was pretty sure she was of sound mind, and I didn't think she was a liar. Her Georgetown University professor was once a Jesuit, and she told me that Georgetown had asked her to teach a class about Spiritualism. And she could do amazing things. When she and four other mediums were tested by University of Arizona psychic researcher Gary Schwartz, they were 83 percent correct for one sitter and 77 percent correct for a second sitter. The sixty-eight control subjects who tried to give messages were 36 percent accurate.

I was practiced by then at accepting stories that would have been too bizarre for comment in the outside world, but the oil story strained me. I might not understand the mysteries of the universe. I might not understand the force of love. But I knew a lot about the power of greed. Those oilmen wouldn't care if she had three heads, clucked like a chicken, and spoke pig Latin. If Anne could make them money, they'd all be asking her to dance. I asked her why the Phillips deal fell through.

"Well, Mr. Keeler died," she said, "and my contract was with him. So that ended it."

When I repeated that story to Shelley, she said, "Anne wouldn't lie about it." Maybe Keeler didn't tell anyone else. If Anne was his golden goose, maybe he didn't want anyone to know. Or maybe finding oil with a psychic embarrassed him and would have run off his investors.

So what was going on? One of the first lessons I learned in Lily Dale was that truth is slippery there. It's always good to ask, Whose truth are we going by?

Was everyone lying? Were they rearranging the facts to make them fit a good story? Or were they imagining things? Was anything real at the core of these stories? And if there wasn't anything, why were so many people telling so many stories? A mass case of wishful thinking?

I was increasingly aware that my quest for "just the facts, please" might be missing the reality of what Lily Dale is about. If Jung were around, he might say that the people of the Dale are tapping into consciousness beyond their individual minds to find archetypes that reflect their soul's hopes, allay their fears, and assure their inner selves. He might say they are reacting to a world that has gone too far into rationality, cutting its inhabitants off from deep wells of meaning.

Maybe Lily Dale's stories are like ancient myths that don't have to be literally true because facts aren't the point. The point is that such stories resonate with us spiritually. They answer our deep need to believe the universe contains order and purpose. In a post-modern culture, perhaps perfectly sane but spiritually adrift people retreat into their own visions because there are so few alternatives. Maybe Lily Dale fosters that, and maybe it serves a good purpose.

But I was a journalist, and facts were all I knew. My soul's desire was to see something that I couldn't reason away.

At the end of class on Wednesday, Anne announced that we would tip tables the next day. At last. Here was my chance to see something with my own eyes.

27

When table-tipping day arrived, we were as wiggly as schoolchildren. Finally, Anne told us we could move our chairs to the side of the room. For almost a week, we had mucked around in theories and murky stories and prophecies that might be only good guesses. Now we were going to *see* something.

I was not entirely a novice at table tipping. My family once sat around a card table with our hands placed flat, the tips of our thumbs and little fingers touching as we chanted in rumbling unison, "Up table, up table, up table, up." My uncles cheated somehow, probably by pushing one edge of the table until the other side rose. They were good enough frauds to thrill my grandmother. My eyes were pretty wide too, but when Grandma began plying the table with questions about whether any money was coming to her, my uncles fell away from the table, clutching their bellies, guffawing like donkeys, and the game was over.

A hundred years ago, communicating tables were a commonplace example of physical mediumship. Families all over America and Europe gathered, dimmed the lights, and turned ordinary kitchen tables into oracles of cosmic wisdom. One group sat every night for seven weeks before their furniture so much as wobbled, but such was the faith of the times that they didn't give up. In

France, the pastime was so popular that actors would tip tables in the wings of the theater while waiting to go on.

As usual with Spiritualist practices, chicanery was a problem. Mediums devised many ways to make tables do their bidding without otherworldly aid. They fastened poles under their wrists inside their sleeves so that when they bent their arms to place their hands on the table, the rods extended under the rim and could be used to leverage the table upward. In the dark of the séance room, they might slip the toe of a shoe under one table leg and use the force of their hand to balance the table as it rose.

In our class, the lights were on. Three tables were to be used. We didn't want them to rap answers to our questions. We just wanted them to move. One table was the big, solid, four-legged table from the Maplewood Hotel that students told me had floated last year. I was stationed at a small, but stable and sturdy, pedestal table. Two of us could fit on each side. We put our hands on the tabletop and began singing.

"Do rounds," somebody yelled.

The table to our left started "Row, Row, Row Your Boat." Our table joined after the first line, and then the third table came in. A dizzy clamor of melodies filled the old assembly hall. Some students leaned close, crooning over the flat dark surfaces, "Come on, table, come on, get up." Others pleaded, "Please, please, table, rise. We know you can." Others prayed, "Spirit, help us. We need your help." One woman seemed almost in a trance as she bent over the table with her hair hanging around her face, swaying back and forth, moaning.

I watched my fellow students' hands. No one seemed to be pushing. I didn't think they would, not consciously. We wanted the spirits to do their stuff, and at least three-quarters of the group had no doubt that they would. The tables had no cloths, and we stood with our hands, legs, and feet in plain sight. Others stood watching.

Our table rocked the tiniest bit. Then it stopped. Encouraged, we launched into a heartier round of "Row, Row, Row Your Boat." The table rocked to the right and then the left. I looked to see whether anyone's fingers seemed pressed too tightly. Mine rested so lightly that they slid when the table moved. Others seemed to do the same.

Then the table rocked again, left to right, left to right, left to right. Now it was tipping like a ship in a storm, up and down. Then it rocked forward and back, left and right, forward and back. We started to laugh with excitement. The table began to move in circles, hopping around like some crazed Cossack dancer. Our hands slid about on the surface. And then we ran, trying to keep our hands on the table as it twirled round and round, across the room.

"Keep singing," someone yelled. "Keep singing." I was out of breath, woozy with too much circling and laughing. The table bobbed about, tilting wildly in one direction and then skipping to the next leg. It was like something alive. And we shouted out to it, as though it could hear us, "Keep going, table. You're doing it."

Then, with one lunge to the left, it fell completely over.

"Don't stop," Anne called to us from another table. "Keep the energy going. You can get it up."

I didn't see how. We sang and we pleaded and we prayed. And nothing happened. The table was completely on its side. It couldn't possibly rise. And it didn't.

"Don't give up," Anne shouted above the voices all around, and we didn't. We knelt and canted our bodies to the side so that we could keep our hands in place. We called for reinforcements, and other students gathered around to add their hands and their all-important energy.

"MERRILY, MERRILY, MERRILY, MERRILY, LIFE IS BUT A DREAM." We were roaring by now. All of Lily Dale must have heard us. But the table was dead, keeled over, exhausted probably, as dead as it had been before we transformed it. We were gasping ourselves, but we kept trying. We had the faith now.

Nothing happened. Then Anne, singing along with us, moved to our part of the room. She put one hand on the table's perpendicular surface, and damned if the thing didn't start to come up. I looked at her hand, studied the nails to see whether they showed any white from being flattened. She put her other hand on the table. The fingers were touching, and then the palm. Could I see daylight between the table and the heel of her hand? Sometimes I could. I looked at the muscles and the bones in the back of her hand. No hard ridges of strain showed. If she was pressing any more than I was, I couldn't tell it. But the table was coming up. I looked at everyone else's hands and then their faces. Were they cheating?

They were looking at my hands and my face with the same suspicion. So maybe none of us were.

Steadily it rose. The heavy top was rising against gravity, tilting itself upright again. Nobody pushed from the top edge. Nobody braced the legs. I couldn't believe it, but there it was, sitting upright and then dancing again.

Anne left for the four-legged table. Students were working themselves into a frenzy around it, but nothing moved. Then our table stopped suddenly, as though someone had gripped the legs and pulled them down. For a few minutes it did nothing. Our song became shouted choruses as we beamed energy into our hands. The table rocked, and then toppled, and once again we couldn't get it up until Anne's hands touched the surface. Even if she was pushing the tabletop, I didn't see how she could move the heavy wooden top from a complete sideways standstill to an upright position. It didn't seem possible, but I saw it happen.

We left that day chattering and laughing. What happened? Something real. We'd seen it. We'd felt it. We knew it. The world was not as static as we thought. It was full of marvels. Anything could happen next.

That night I told everyone at Shelley's about my table exploit. "I don't know what it was," I kept saying, "but I saw it happen. I did." Only one thing bothered me. The four-legged table didn't move. Why not?

I went back to the Assembly Hall. As I stood over the pedestal table, I pushed on its edges. It was solid, heavy, and sturdy, not rickety. I placed my fingers on it and ran them across the surface as I had before, lightly and gently. Nothing happened, but as I kept at it, not cheating, just letting my energy rise, I applied pressure to one edge and felt a shift. I continued moving my fingers back and forth. The table began to rock. Now I was using no force whatsoever, just letting my hands slide and slip, and the table was bucking all over the floor on its own momentum, just as it had in class. Drat.

The magic was gone. The mundane rules of the physical universe were once again in place. A top-heavy table. A pedestal base. Excited people. No spirits needed. We didn't cheat. Not consciously. Nobody had to.

I told Anne what I'd discovered. She didn't contradict me, just looked at me with that calm, unreadable face. *She knew it all the time,* I thought bitterly. *She knew about that table.*

"What about the times it came up from the ground?" she asked quietly. "How did it do that?" The look she gave me then was a mixture of sadness and something else. Resignation? Was that because she believed and was weary of having her proofs rejected? Or was it because I'd exposed the trick?

"I don't know how it came up from the floor," I said. My voice was flat with disappointment. Once fooled, twice wary. I would never believe it was spirits.

28

Much of Lily Dale makes me roll my eyes, but I am not alone. Oddly enough, Lily Dale prides itself on skepticism. Everyone in town has what sociology professor Charles Emmons calls an eye-rolling threshold. Charlie's wife, Penelope, for instance, is a medium, but she draws the line at believing the teeth they found in their kitchen sink were from her dead grandfather.

Charles, who teaches at Gettysburg College, laughed at himself as he told the story, but he swore it was true. They were having plumbing problems. The plumber would arrive, tinker around, give them a bill, and go away. Then the leaks would start again, and the plumber would come back. This went on long enough that Charles, a patient man, was pushed beyond his good nature. One day, after the plumber came again, Charles discovered a set of false teeth in the kitchen sink.

The message in that? "Getting things fixed was like pulling teeth," Charles said. "That was the message he was sending us." It was a little spirit humor from Penelope's late grandfather, a dentist.

They took the teeth to a living dentist, who told them they were probably from a fourteen-year-old girl and looked to be a set used for demonstration in a dental school.

Penelope shook her head at the whole idea. She didn't know how the teeth got in the sink, but it wasn't a ghost joke, she said.

"Well, what was it?" Charles asked.

"Somebody must have left them there."

Anne Gehman's eye-rolling threshold is reincarnation. The National Spiritualist Association of Churches, of which Anne is a minister, does not endorse reincarnation. She once researched the subject by having more than one hundred past-life readings done all over North and South America. There was so little overlap among them that she couldn't believe any of it could be true.

Past lives are popular among Lily Dale mediums, but, in a very Lily Dale kind of way, some of the mediums who do past-life readings don't believe in them themselves. More than one told me that past-life readings might not be literally true, but they contain psychological insights people can use.

I sat in several circles where students practiced giving past-life messages. I recall being told that I was a midwife who delivered hundreds of babies and twelve of her own. Maybe that's why I have so little interest in motherhood. I got over it in a past life.

In one scary session, Tom, a kind-faced man sitting across the circle from me, said he saw me as an old Cherokee woman clinging to a horse. I was fearful and sorrowful, weakened by age and the loss of everything I loved. It was freezing. I was sharing the horse with children. Only old people and children were allowed to ride. Everyone else was walking.

My grip on the horse's mane slipped, and, as I slid down the horse's side, the children pleaded with me to hold on. Anyone who fell on the Trail of Tears was killed by the soldiers, but I was too weak, and so I fell and lay in the dirt. A soldier stood over me, his gun pointing down.

The circle leader warned everyone against giving bad messages. So what was this? Tom apologized.

"I hate to tell you this, but I'm supposed to say that it's why you feel such sadness and grief in this life."

Afterward he approached me looking worried. "I hope you don't feel sadness and grief," he said. "I felt I had to give you the message, but I hope I was wrong about it."

He couldn't be more wrong. I am an upbeat, cheerful person. I experience some foreboding when the phone rings, when my husband goes to work, when I drive to get a pizza or must make an unexpected trip to get milk, when my dog's nose is hot, when anyone suggests a vacation that requires leaving my yard, or when everything in life is too perfect. I have a perfectly reasonable sense that happiness is fleeting, that death, pain, and destruction could befall me and the people I love any minute. That's normal, I think.

Margaret Mary Hefner, who channels the Virgin Mary, triggers a lot of eye rolling. In channeling, the spirit speaks using the medium's body. Once Margaret Mary was channeling Mother Mary while a guy on the other side of town was channeling Jesus. When Hilda heard what was going on she said, "Shouldn't someone go over and tell Mary that her son's in town?"

One afternoon each month Margaret Mary and her husband, Bob, stand outside, pray, and scan the skies for a vision of the Holy Mother. At first, they held their vigil outside the Lily Dale Spiritualist Church, but that caused some people to behave quite rudely. One woman told Margaret Mary to take it elsewhere or else. So now Margaret Mary and Bob hold their vigil, which they call Mother Mary Energy Day, in the field near the playground equipment.

Energy days help them get ready for the Virgin's imminent arrival on earth by changing their DNA so they can transmit greater amounts of energy, said Margaret Mary, who is widely known in Lily Dale as Marge. She now prefers Margaret Mary because the

Virgin asked her to use her full name, which has better energy. Mother Mary Energy Days leave the Hefners weak in the knees sometimes, and the couple always requires a nap afterward.

One day I joined them in the field. First we chatted a little. Margaret Mary told me that she and Bob dowse when they make a decision. When I asked how, she took off a pendant and held it by the chain so that it dangled.

"What does 'yes' mean?" she asked. The pendant swung left to right.

"What does 'no' mean?" she asked. The pendent swung back and forth. "You see?" she asked.

I did.

"We do that with everything. We dowse all the food we eat."

"Not all of it," Bob said.

"Yes, we do. Once we were in the grocery store, and I dowsed some cake to see if it had ingredients in it that would hurt us. A woman saw me doing it and asked me to show her how. Pretty soon other women gathered around, and the ladies behind the counter were watching. Everyone wanted to try it on their own food," Margaret Mary said, laughing. "We did bread and cookies and all sorts of things."

Margaret Mary had an extra rosary so I could join them in reciting Hail Marys. As we chanted, we squinted into the sun and scanned the clouds. The Virgin had appeared once when Margaret Mary, Bob, and a friend were looking for her. She was mostly a cloud shape. Their friend thought it was an angel. Margaret Mary was pretty sure it was the Holy Mother.

We were almost finished with the Hail Marys when I spotted a configuration of clouds that looked exactly like the outline of Mary's figure. She was wearing a long gown, and her head was covered. She was facing straight on, her hands folded as they often are at about waist level. There was no halo.

I blinked. She was still there.

I looked at the Hefners. They didn't say anything. I looked again. Still there.

If I spoke up, Margaret Mary and Bob would get one of the great thrills of their lives. I would go down in Lily Dale history as the reporter who saw Mother Mary in the field near the playground. I would go on record as having experienced something so farfetched that even Lily Dale rejected it.

Why didn't they say something? I looked at their upturned faces. I had to speak. It was too cowardly.

I glanced back at the sky. She was gone. The clouds had moved.

Imagination. The mind is strange. It plays tricks. You have to watch it, corral your thoughts, be careful what you see.

Joyce LaJudice, Lily Dale's historian, loves history, and she loves Lily Dale. It might seem that drawing the line would be especially tricky for her. Not so.

Joyce, who had heart trouble, diabetes, high blood pressure, and a bit of a wheeze the summer I spent in Lily Dale, has devoted more hours than anyone can count to gathering scrapbooks and setting up displays in the little museum that was once a one-room schoolhouse. During the summer season, she stands behind the glass display cases that hold Spiritualism's treasures for far longer than she ought to, thrilling tourists with tales of the old days and setting the record straight. It wasn't Eleanor Roosevelt who came to Lily Dale. It was Elliott Roosevelt, Eleanor's son. Mahatma Gandhi didn't visit the town, despite what many people say. It was another Gandhi. William Jennings Bryan did speak on the Lily Dale platform, and so did Robert Ingersoll, who was known as the great agnostic. A hotel register with Susan B. Anthony's signature shows that the great suffragette really did visit Lily Dale.

Joyce's house and the back room of the museum are stuffed with files of clippings and playbills, old photos and pamphlets. She's slowly working her way through them, compiling records of how the community developed and who has lived in it. Like most residents, she was happy to admit that mountains of fraud have been committed by mediums, but none of it shakes her faith.

Floating trumpets? Sure, that happens. Joyce and Betty Schultz sat for years trying to move one, and it never left the ground, but she has newspaper photos of mediums doing it. Joyce also has photos of ghostly figures floating around and about the figures of live humans. Spirit painting? That's real too, Joyce said. Just go over to the Maplewood Hotel and look in the lobby.

A painting of Napoleon and a painting of a spirit guide named Azur are displayed there. So is the portrait of a young girl painted after her death. The child's mother was thrilled with the likeness, but she died not long after taking it home. Her relatives believed it was the work of the devil and returned it to Lily Dale.

The spirit paintings are a long way from masterpieces, even to my untrained eye. If God sends spirits back to the earth to paint, why doesn't he send the best? Michelangelo or Rembrandt would be happy for the work, and just one of their paintings would end Lily Dale's money troubles forever.

What mystified me most was how the Spiritualists seem to view the pictures. "Did you see the paintings?" they asked, as though the mere existence of the canvases would convince me they were painted by spirits. It didn't.

Joe Nickell, a researcher for the Committee for the Scientific Investigation of Claims of the Paranormal, has come to Lily Dale repeatedly. When he wanted to look at spirit paintings, Joyce was more than glad to help him. She tells everyone about his story on the painters who worked in Lily Dale: two sisters known as the Bangs Sisters and a gay couple in the import-export business who called themselves the Campbell Brothers. Joyce is cited at the end of the critique Nickell wrote for the *Skeptical Inquirer* magazine, which is published by the Committee.

"Joe's my buddy. He's just like me," Joyce said. "He's skeptical of anything that can't be proved."

29

You only have to see one white crow to know that not all crows are black, wrote William James. All it takes is one. For him, the white crow of Spiritualism was an uneducated Boston housewife named Leonore Piper.

James was convinced that her knowledge about the small domestic matters of his family came from a source beyond normal consciousness. She told about their son's tantrums and his nickname, "little Billy-boy"; the contents of a letter from his wife's aunt warning against all mediums; his loss of a waistcoat and his wife's loss of a rug; how he had killed a gray and white cat with ether and how it had spun around and around before it died; how a rocking chair creaked; how his wife heard footsteps on the stairs; and how their child's crib creaked at night.

"A normal person, unacquainted with the family, could not possibly have said as much; one acquainted with it could hardly have avoided saying more," he wrote.

Mrs. Piper and her family were followed by private investigators and tested in a number of ways. Unannounced clients were brought into the séance room only after she had gone into trance. Other clients came as proxy sitters, meaning that they asked questions for third parties, strangers they didn't know.

Richard Hodgson, one of the world's fiercest psychic debunkers, investigated her over a period of years and became so convinced that Mrs. Piper was genuine that he promised to speak through her after he died. Hodgson's new belief in the afterlife turned him from a cynical, rather obnoxious man into a person whose love of life, serenity, and general glow of well-being were amazing to see, said James.

When Hodgson died, James and others tested Mrs. Piper to see whether their friend was able to return through her. The medium spoke in a manner that resembled the investigator's and gave messages that amazed his friends. But James was never convinced. The spirit's mannerisms were sometimes forced and seemed overdone, not quite genuine, he wrote. Perhaps another spirit was impersonating Hodgson, or perhaps Mrs. Piper's subconscious mind was supplying information that allowed her to mimic Hodgson. The accurate information she received might come from telepathy or other sources not yet understood.

One intriguing speculation was that perhaps the spirit of Hodgson or fragments of his personality had come through in early sittings and given bits of information. Once some hazy image of that personality was impressed on Mrs. Piper, perhaps her own mind embellished and amplified it. She might be entirely unaware of such a creation, James hypothesized.

As I watched Lily Dale mediums, I often thought of James's analysis. How can any of us know what our minds are actually doing? Nobody knows what consciousness is, how far it extends, whether it continues after death, or where it resides before birth. James, who called the gap between one mind and another the greatest in nature, also wrote that "our normal waking consciousness . . . is but one special type of consciousness whilst all about it, parted from it by the filmiest of screens, there be potential forms of consciousness entirely different."

James thought the brain might be a "temporary and partial transmitter of cosmic consciousness into individual consciousness. The power of those transmissions might rise and fall so that we are sometimes aware of things not normally conscious and other times are insensible and dull, unable to form an eternal, cosmic consciousness."

James used German philosopher and psychologist Gustave T. Fechner's analogy of the brain as a kind of dam or threshold for consciousness that already exists outside the individual and can exist after death. "We need only suppose the continuity of our consciousness with a mother sea, to allow for exceptional waves occasionally pouring over the dam. Of course the causes of these odd lowerings of the brain's threshold still remain a mystery on any terms."

Whether our thoughts are manufactured solely by our brain or imposed upon it is impossible for us to know. So how can a medium know where imposed thoughts leave off and her own thoughts start? She can't. Not entirely. Even if the mediums are getting spirit messages, they're bound to insert errors from their own ideas, their own interpretations, and their own projections.

30

My own white crow was Sherry Lee Calkins. I didn't feel a particular need for a reading. I didn't want a message or need guidance, but I heard so many stories about Sherry Lee's prescience that I had to try her out.

Her reading room is austere. A little couch for the client sits low enough that I found myself perching on the edge. Sherry Lee sat on a straight-backed chair behind a small table with a blank sheet of paper and artist's crayons. She talked fast and started as soon as I was seated.

"I have a young man here. Tall. Dark hair. Nice-looking young man. He has, what's that? Oh. He has a straw in his mouth. A piece of hay, and he's chewing on it. He's leaning against a tree, very relaxed. Do you know who that might be?"

No.

As she spoke, she was furiously drawing lines and dates on the paper. She said that in July 1997 I started something new. In February 1998 I finished a phase of my life.

I didn't know what she meant.

August was a big change, monumental, she said. That was right. I'd moved to Wisconsin. In January, another big change, she said, and this one freed me up. Vague, but right again. That was the month I stopped working for the *Dallas Morning News.*

In March, my new life really began, she said. That was the month I returned to Lily Dale. Pretty good so far. Then she hit a snag.

By June of next year, I would have completed the book on Lily Dale.

Not possible, I thought. *She doesn't know enough about books, and she thinks that giving me a year to finish will be enough*. She said a few more things about how I write and my grandfather's character. Nothing that meant much to me.

Then she picked up the blue pencil and began drawing up the side of the paper.

"Your husband became very sick before you started dating, almost died. He also almost died in the country when he was in his twenties. His guardian angel saved him."

She was right on the first point, but slightly off. "We had already started dating," I said.

"But you weren't serious about him yet," she said.

True. As for almost dying in his twenties, I would check.

She grabbed the brown pencil and began sketching ground from which she drew stalks of wheat. "The young man might be your grandfather. Yes, that's it. He's your father's father."

Now she drew back and scrutinized the paper. Her eyes narrowed.

"I'm seeing an initial. I can't tell what it is," she said. "What was his name?"

"Dyson."

"No. It's not a 'D.' What was his first name?"

"I don't know," I said. "I don't remember knowing him. I barely knew his son."

She squinted at the paper. "It's an 'L.' Did his name start with an 'L'?"

"I don't know," I said.

"Check it out," she snapped.

Now she was tapping the stalks of wheat. "There are three for his children. How many children did he have?"

"I don't know," I said. "I think two."

"Three," she said. "And this one," she tapped the shortest stalk of wheat, "had something wrong physically. He may have died early."

I shook my head. "I don't know."

"I see you teaching," she said as she filled in the right side of the paper with yellow.

"Not likely," I said.

"You will," she said. "Come back in a few years. You'll be saying I was right." Sherry Lee never backs down.

After the reading, I called my husband. "Did you almost die in the country?"

"Of course," he said. "I told you about that car wreck. The car was totaled."

"How old were you?"

"In my thirties."

I called my mother. "What was Tommy's father's name?" As I waited for her to answer, I tried not to hold my breath, but I couldn't help it. By the time she spoke the blood pounded in my ears.

"Leon."

I gasped. "How many children did he have?"

"Let me think. Three maybe, but there was something wrong with one of them," she said. "A miscarriage, or he died young. I can't remember."

"Oh, my Lord," I said. "She was right."

When I saw Sherry Lee later, I said, "You were correct about my husband almost dying in the country, but he was in his thirties, not his twenties."

"He looked younger," she said.

I told her about Leon and the three children. Sherry Lee didn't look impressed.

"Of course," she said.

"But I didn't know that myself," I said.

"You didn't have to, dear," she said briskly. "I'm not a mind reader."

Sherry Lee got eight things right. She mentioned perhaps half a dozen things that I didn't know or didn't relate to. She gave dates I couldn't connect with. She predicted three things in the future that might or might not happen.

Three things she told me were completely wrong: my husband's age when his car was hit, that we hadn't started dating when he almost died, and that my book would be finished in June. I'll accept her excuse on his age and on our dating situation, but it would be a stretch to give her points on the book. The research was finished by June, and I did finally know what I was going to write, but the writing itself was far from done.

Of the eight things she got right, the three dates that supposedly mark changes in my life were the iffiest, because she was general in what she said and because there was a slight chance she might have known them from other sources. So that leaves five facts: my grandfather's initial, the number of his children, that one child died early, and my husband's two brushes with death.

Could she have researched those things? Perhaps. But the name of my grandfather and details about his family weren't facts she could have found out without a lot of work. My birth certificate was changed when my stepfather adopted me. It didn't contain my original last name. Even a crack detective would have found only a handful of people who remembered me from Oklahoma City, where I was born. They would have been hard to find and certain to report that they'd been questioned. If she did get my grandfather's name in a normal way, why not give it? Why just the initial? My husband's two brushes with death never made the papers and weren't experiences I'd discussed with people in Lily Dale.

The wrong, general, or suspect messages far outnumbered the five correct messages, but I expected her to be wrong. That's the norm. Even William James was occasionally too disgusted with Mrs. Piper's "tiresome twaddle" to note it down. But the five times Sherry Lee was right were not coincidence, not good guesswork, not things she knew beforehand. And they were not facts she elicited from me. Those five messages defied any explanation I had. She said the information came from spirits. I didn't think so, but nobody was coming up with a better story.

31

When Marian Boswell fired up Jack's computer, she checked e-mail first. Among the messages in the delete file were notes from women in Colorado, Australia, New York, Ohio, Pittsburgh, and Florida. They wrote that they'd had a good time, they loved the gifts, and they looked forward to his next visit.

Then she checked the notes he'd sent. He gushed and flattered, recounted romantic evenings, promised love and more fabulous good times. Marian recognized this blather. It was the kind he sent her. As she read, Marian's shock gave way to numb horror. For the first time, the words she heard on that afternoon in Lily Dale seemed as though they might be true. Maybe she was going to lose everything. Marian didn't sleep much that night. When she did drop off, her dreams were all about Jack, a menacing, angry Jack who wanted to hurt her.

The next day she heard the voice in her head again, "There's more."

He's lied to me. He's cheated. He's in debt, she thought. *How could there be more?*

In the following weeks, Marian's dreams contained messages that led her to other evidence against Jack. She found a box of papers hidden in the garage. She tapped into computer files he thought were safe. She found that he was looking for another job and had résumés in at companies in New York and Chicago. He had debts and bank accounts she hadn't known of.

She went to a lawyer, who instructed her to gather more information. Every time she suspected something new, she took it to medium Greg Kehn, who confirmed her suspicions. "He never told me anything that I didn't at some level already know," she said, "but sometimes it seemed as if he was just waiting for me to find out what he knew."

Marian and Jack began to argue. They started sleeping in separate beds. One morning she awoke hearing her name called. She went into the kitchen. No one was there. As she was making coffee, Jack walked into the kitchen, sleep still blurring his face. "Did you call my name?" he asked. "I thought I heard my name."

She hadn't. When she took the story to Greg, he said, "You both got wake-up calls. You both can respond if you want to."

One evening, Jack and Marian argued. As the disagreement grew more and more heated, Marian became afraid. She retreated to the bathroom. Jack was behind her, still yelling. He seemed out of control, furious beyond recall. She slammed the door and crouched in the corner, thinking, *He's going to kill me.*

He kicked the door open. Her back was to him, her head in her hands. She felt the air stir. A cool breeze seemed to be circulating about the room. She looked over her shoulder. A purplish haze was filling the air, rising between her and her husband, she said. As she watched, it seemed to her that it formed itself into a big wing. Jack looked surprised, Marian said. He hit out at the form, and his hands stopped as though they'd encountered a wall. He hit it again. It didn't give way. Marian said she saw fear in his face. Then he turned and ran from the bedroom.

Not long afterward Marian packed and fled to her father's house. She filed for divorce and returned to their home only after Jack had been ordered to leave.

The marriage was over. The divorce would drag on for more than a year. Marian's weight shrunk to seventy-eight pounds. She chattered compulsively about the strange turns her life had taken. She was terrified that Jack would hurt her. In February, she had a nervous breakdown and committed herself to a local mental hospital.

While there, she woke up one morning to find a young woman sitting at the foot of her bed sobbing. Her husband had committed her because she was seeing colors swirl about the room, the woman said. Marian believes the meeting was ordained. She convinced the woman that such colors weren't a sign of mental illness. She told her about the purple wing that she believes saved her. They talked for days, and when Marian left, she felt ready to take up her divorce battle again. Soon thereafter the young woman also divorced her husband, Marian said.

Marian got a job and sold her house to help pay taxes, unpaid debts, and attorney's fees.

"It was just like the woman said, I lost everything," she told me, "and yet I've never been better. I had to know the truth. I prayed that I would know the truth. Now I do."

Once Sherry Lee Calkins gave me those five things she couldn't have known, I waved bye-bye to rationality and walked into the great, glorious unknown. Why not? Despite all its silliness, exaggeration, and downright falsehood, Lily Dale was full of stories I couldn't refute. Why not join 'em?

My season of belief was a heady time. Life would go on forever. Life had a plan, and I had a starring role. Everything would turn out all right. There was no way it couldn't.

Before Lily Dale, I'd possessed a limited array of powers—quite limited, in fact. Now I could call upon the universe, cosmic consciousness, Mother/Father God, all the angels, including the Archangel Michael and my own personal guardian angel, all the ghosts including the Holy One, Jesus, Mother Mary, fairies, alien beings from other planets, the discarnate entities who've never lived, and the elementals who reside after dark in Leolyn Woods. Many of these personages, if I may refer to them as that, were gathered around me on a fairly constant basis. Judging from the stories I'd heard, they would perch on the headlights of my car if I needed to drive through a blizzard, get me parking places, appear in dreams, materialize in meditations, and pop up in the real world to save me from my folly—maybe not all the time, but sometimes, which was more than I had expected. I didn't have to constantly whine and wheedle to get their protection. They were so eager to offer it that all I needed to do was to be aware of them and use them.

If I was doing what my cosmic contract called for—or giving my gift, as Lynn would say—the powers would conspire to help me. "We live in a responsive universe," said Mary Ann, the therapist who sees dead people.

I'd never be lonely no matter how old I lived to be. "The people who've passed over are all around us," Greg Kehn told Marian. "I wish people could see what I do. They would realize that they never need to be lonely."

And death? I could laugh at it. It was nothing more than walking through a door. Easier even, since so many relatives came forward to help.

I'm overstating. I didn't believe all those things. I remembered Anne Gehman's warning, "There's a fine line between believing what's true and turning into a person who's talking to the toaster." I didn't want to cross that line.

But hope, a big grand hope like this one, with endless surprises, all of them good, is a wonderful thing. I basked in it.

I didn't believe it all. No, I didn't. But I could. I had permission now, enough proof that I could believe anything that seemed real to me. Just to me. I didn't have to prove it to the rest of the world.

I merely had to listen to what I perceived, to know what I knew, to believe what I believed and move forward on it.

The test of that? It was the same one I'd started with from my first days in Lily Dale, the one that old Willie James gave me: How did it work, how did it play out in my life? How did it change me?

It worked pretty good.

I found myself breathlessly telling my friends and relatives what I'd found, which was that the world is full of wonder. I was less afraid. Work was easier. All failure was temporary. Everything counted to the good. Lessons that I learned late were as valuable as lessons I learned early because I had all eternity to use them.

And, as I began paying attention to the true things I heard instead of snagging on the untrue things, Lily Dale began redefining me to myself. It happened with Lauren Thibodeau.

Lauren volunteered to give me a reading. That was typical of her generosity. When I wanted to visit Niagara Falls, Lauren worried that I wouldn't have enough change for the tolls and offered to give me quarters. When I admired a sweet wine called an ice wine that's made in Canada, she tried to give me a bottle to take home. We put the reading off and then weren't able to meet and then almost gave up, but she persisted. And so one day we sat down with a tape recorder, and she started telling me what the spirits said.

I didn't connect with much. She thought she had my father's father again. I was not thrilled to hear from him. To paraphrase Susan B., why didn't he move aside so somebody interesting could come through? He couldn't tell me much that would be evidential because I didn't remember him. He didn't give his name or even his initial this time. The reading was something of a bust, I thought.

Then Lauren smiled and gave me a tender look. "I'm hearing that a lot of men from your past remember you with great affection."

The look and the message embarrassed me. So I said, "I was kind of rowdy," which embarrassed me more. I was putting myself down, and the men too. Why did I do that? The spooks must have been mum about the less praiseworthy parts of my past because Lauren shook her head.

"No. It's not that," she said.

"These men wanted to marry you. I'm getting the number seven." Now she smiled another in her repertoire of sweet smiles. This was the one I'd seen her turn toward Shelley every time Shelley challenged some mediumistic belief. My face must have been showing doubt.

"You've really been loved. They're telling me that those men still think of you as someone who was very special in their lives. Do some of them keep in touch with you even now? I'm getting that."

"Some," I said grudgingly.

Even so, this was another miss. My love life had been one disaster after another. In my twenties, I married and divorced. In my thirties, I had one dark affair after another. When I married happily for the second time, it was God's own miracle. Nothing else could have done it.

A week later I was on the road, driving the interstate for six hundred miles toward home. As the semis blasted by my little white car and the radio blared, I remembered Lauren's words. Seven? That was the stupidest thing I'd ever heard. There had been one or two, but not seven. Anyone who had seven men wanting to marry her would be well loved, I'd give Lauren that.

How many men *had* wanted to marry me?

I started to count. The two I'd married wouldn't be in the list. So let's see, there'd been . . . seven. Exactly seven.

How could that be? I counted again. Six. Six and two halves? I wasn't sure about all of them. But maybe. Maybe seven.

And I'd failed to notice? I'd dated a long time, two decades. That could explain it.

I went back over those men. One treated me fairly rotten before we split. Only one? I winced as I remembered how often I'd been the partner who pulled away. They'd all risen above it and continued to wish me nothing but good fortune.

This was not good news. For more than twenty years, I'd considered myself a victim of love, a helpless, often scorned woman, a total loser miraculously rescued. If that wasn't true, who was I? A woman blessed?

Couldn't be. I would have noticed.

My new belief also empowered me to push Shelley and her mentor, the bicycle-riding, praying-for-the-world Lynn, on their beliefs.

First, how could anybody be right all the time, as Lynn said Shelley was? And if it was true of Shelley, was it true of everybody?

It was true of Shelley, Lynn said, because Shelley listened to her true self and did what she wanted to do. It would also be true of others who listened to themselves and followed what their own spirit was telling them.

How could people do what they wanted to do and be right?

"Because what they truly want to do is what spirit is guiding them to do," Lynn said. "Whatever we don't want to do is not for us to do. Spirit takes care of those things." Lynn meant God when she said spirit, but she tried not to use a theistic term in deference to Shelley, who didn't believe in God. Or said she didn't, although I thought she did for all practical purposes.

I don't believe Lynn's ideas. Hitler was doing what he wanted. Was that right?

"People can get away from their true selves, which is that bit of God within us that speaks to us all the time," Lynn said. "If we block that voice, then we get off the path, but that's not what we really want to do," she said. "It is not what we're born to do."

"But sometimes we have to think more of others than of ourselves," I objected.

"Well, of course," Lynn said. "But when you feel you don't want to and you're a loving person and you've been doing it so far with love, that's the signal that you're to move over and another spirit will take over. And it will. It will."

What about old people living in nursing homes? If nobody wants to go see them, that's all right?

"Sure," said Lynn. She laughed at how easy it was. "If you don't want to go, you shouldn't. It's not for you to do. That's a do-gooder doing something for somebody because they think they should. That's sinful.

"Somebody else will do it. Somebody who wants to. And if they don't, spirit will take care of it. You have to trust that that's so. We're trusting universal divine love."

This was dangerous, and I did not believe it. We could learn to listen to ourselves, yes. That was good. But we could not be trusted to do only what we wanted to do. We could not trust those spirits. Ask anybody who lived through the Holocaust. Or the Rwanda massacres. The world is too evil a place for me to trust Lynn's universal divine love as she does.

One day, during one of our many debates, somebody mentioned the Dalai Lama, and I said, "I met him. Did I tell you that story?"

32

It was one of my last jobs as a reporter for the *Dallas Morning News*. The Tibetan Buddhist leader was coming to Bloomington, Indiana, to conduct an important ceremony that had never been conducted in the United States. People from all over the world would be there.

I arrived at the end of the first day just as all the pilgrims were being let out. My car was mired in crowds coming out of the meeting. The people carried fronds of some kind that they'd been bidden to sleep with under their left side, while they held some other plant in their right hand, or some such thing. Although I have great respect for Buddhism, I was out of sync with this event from the beginning.

We reporters were kept at the back of the crowd so that we could barely see the Dalai Lama, which made me even more churlish. I did my job with fairly poor grace until the last day, when it was announced that the Dalai Lama would conduct a press conference. We were all excited—buzzing about, jostling, ready to be awed in a very unreporter-like way. He might shake our hands, we were told. This really psyched us. Some people think the Dalai Lama is a god on earth, and we were going to shake his hand.

As we milled around outside waiting, I noticed a young woman in a miniskirt. Everyone noticed her. She had long legs and long hair. She was beautiful, and a crowd of men stood around her, smoking, watching, making her laugh. I was watching her too. Ruefully. I had once been the center of such crowds, perhaps not quite so large or so entranced, but I'd had my day. It was over. I would never be the center of such attention again. Usually I was reconciled to that, but sometimes it pained me. This was one of those times.

The organizers called for us to come into the tent. The *Dallas Morning News* is a big name in religion journalism, as the publicist must have known. She put me on the front row. The crowd was large, and everyone wanted to ask a question. She made sure I was recognized.

As the Dalai Lama began shaking hands, coming toward me down the line, I heard a wail behind me.

"I want to shake the Dalai Lama's hand."

I turned around, and there she was, the beautiful girl. Big, pleading eyes. Sad face. Begging for her chance.

Good grief. How could I reach for the hand of a god with that wailing in my ears?

I couldn't. Her pleading voice ruined it. Where were her male admirers now? I sighed, turned, stepped back.

"Quick," I said. "Take my place." Maybe we could both shake his hand.

She reached out, took his hand, let go, and moved back so I could touch him too. But it was too late. He had moved on.

The Dalai Lama finished the line of greeters and turned to walk away. No more questions. No more handshakes. It was over. *How stupid I am,* I thought bitterly. Always hanging back, missing out, trying to be some kind of goody-good, never taking care of myself.

Then he turned back.

He looked directly into my face and said, "I want to shake the hand of this woman."

And he did. He reached across the barrier, and he grasped my hand. His was bigger than I expected, and warmer. I could feel the heat of it long after he was gone.

I ended my story to Lynn by asking, "Did he know, or was it a coincidence?"

"He knew," Lynn said. "Of course he did. And you know what he was telling you, don't you?"

I shrugged. "I guess. He wanted me to know I wasn't such a fool. He wanted to let me know that I was right to sacrifice my own chance for another person."

But Lynn had her own take. "You did what you wanted to do. You followed your heart, not because someone told you to but because you wanted to. He was saluting you. As one Buddha to another."

There it was again, that Lily Dale lavishness. Buddha? No.

"Yes," Lynn said. "You were a Buddha. We all are."

There was nothing else to do with that except make a joke of it. So we started bowing to one another, saying, "Buddha. Buddha. Buddha." I was laughing and shaking my head at the same time. No. No. Maybe we are the Buddha sometimes, but it can't be that our deepest, truest selves are the Buddha. That would be too good. Too easy.

Maybe death is just walking through a door. Maybe the dead are always with us. Maybe life has purpose, and nothing is ever lost. Maybe we live in a responsive universe that conspires to help us. Lily Dale was full of such lovely maybes.

"Merrily, merrily, merrily, merrily. Life is but a dream."

That night as I lay awake, my mind too restless for sleep, I thought over the grand universe that Lily Dale lived in, and I remembered the God-voice that Lynn heard after she saw the dead deer on the road.

"Yes, Lynn, but can you accept it?"

As Lily Dale's glowing vision intruded itself into the dour landscape of my mind, I could hear the question being put to me: "Christine, can you accept it?" Could I accept this dazzling new hope?

I ran over the evidence for Lily Dale. Dozens of people had told me their stories, and I had my own story of a spirit in my house, which Greg confirmed. Gretchen pinpointed a disruption at my uncle's funeral, told me how he died, and gave a version of his name. I'd seen the Virgin Mary shape in the clouds and refused to believe my eyes. Lauren Thibodeau redefined my love life. The two dead mediums Patricia Price said were helping me caused me to ease up in my work. But all those things had been so embedded in wrong calls and cryptic sayings that they had not changed my mind.

Then Sherry Lee told me eight pretty convincing things. I was certain that five were facts she could not have known by normal means. I'd seen my white crow. So, yes, I would accept that there might be knowledge and pattern and purpose and force in the universe that worked toward the good. Now the question was, Would I follow my white crow into the thicket of beliefs that Lily Dale embodied?

33

I entered the evening development circle in high spirits, ready to chat. The young woman on my left said she became interested in mediumship after attending a class on communicating with animals.

Sure. I was in the groove now. I knew people could do that.

Alive or dead?

"Oh, alive," she said. She didn't have an animal of her own, and so the teacher gave her some pictures of animals. As she flipped through, the photo of an Andalusian stallion appealed to her right away. He was the one. So she began communicating with him.

He talks?

"Telepathically."

What's he say?

"He invited some people to a party once. His owner didn't know it until they started showing up."

I didn't grin as I once would have. I didn't shake my head. I didn't nod either. If I'd been a true confirmed believer in Lily Dale, I might have rolled my eyes and let it go, but my faith was too new. I didn't believe a word of that stallion story. Couldn't. And I didn't want to count myself among people who did.

The bulletin board outside the auditorium noted that Patricia Price was going to teach a class in materialization. I took that to mean that spirits would appear before our eyes. Chapman Clark's failure to show up at the psychomanteum had been a disappointment, but, as Anne said, we might have needed to sit longer. If Patricia Price was confident enough to advertise a circle dedicated to materialization, she must be pretty certain she could conjure up a few spirit forms. I wanted to be there when she did.

When the circle was full and the meditation was over, Patricia brought out a flashlight covered with a red filter. Once the overhead lights were doused, we were to hold the flashlight under our chins as it traveled around the circle, and we would look at each face as spirits materialized before them.

Patricia seemed dead serious about it. The red light was supposed to help us see spirit forms. It worked, after a fashion. Held under people's chins, the light threw their features into ghastly contortions. It hollowed their eye sockets and made their noses translucent in a most unattractive way. Hair fanned out around their faces like spider webs. Bushy eyebrows grew into caterpillars of monstrous size.

A man with craggy features had Abraham Lincoln's spirit before him, my fellow circle sitters exclaimed. When a woman with a big shock of red hair held the flashlight, people all around the circle saw the spirit of a fox before her. George Washington came from the face of an older woman with a straight nose. A beautiful dark-skinned woman wearing a shawl held the light slightly before her face so the shadows fell in lovely patterns. A Middle Eastern princess, they saw, a belly dancer, an Egyptian queen. I was an old lady again. Not American Indian this time, just old.

Good grief. This was a kid's game. Were these people serious? Yes, they were.

By the time we came to the end of the circle they were seeing the full bodies of manifesting spirits.

I was disgusted into complete silence. Afterward my fellow sitters excitedly compared spiritual revelations. I didn't speak to anyone. How could I have ever been taken in by such foolishness? Self-delusion, wishful thinking, fantastical imaginings. These were at the heart of Lily Dale. Was that all there was?

The next day I saw one of my classmates, a young man who was spending the summer in the Dale, helping out with classes and attending as many as he could. He was a nice guy and seemed perfectly sane.

"Tell the truth," I said. "Did you really see spirits last night?"

He did. Lots of them.

"I didn't see a thing except a bunch of people letting their imaginations run away with them." I didn't usually speak so bluntly, but I'd stayed too long in the Dale, and it had bruised me.

He said I failed to see anything because I was using my rational mind. I needed to let go of it, put away my notebook, and enter into the next group without skepticism. "You know what the definition of insanity is, don't you?" he asked.

"I do," I snapped, hoping he wouldn't oppress me with that old chestnut. He didn't even pause.

"It's thinking that you can do the same thing in the same way again and again and get different results."

"Thank you," I said sarcastically.

Only in Lily Dale could somebody be called crazy for holding to her rational mind. All the fury of a betrayed believer engulfed me. Let go of my rational mind? The thought gave me vertigo. If the secrets of the universe revealed themselves only to people who blathered about, letting themselves be led by anyone with any kind of crackpot idea, I'd have to live without the secrets.

The summer season was almost over on the day I left. The truths of Lily Dale had only partially convinced me, I guess, because it didn't take much to send me scurrying back to consensus reality. I liked it there, nice and cozy with all the respectable, reliable, living people gathered around talking about verifiable facts that everyone can see and agree upon. Maybe I was too cowardly for big revelations, or maybe I was too sensible. Whatever it was, I once again contrasted the marvels of Lily Dale with the disappointments, and now the disappointments swamped me.

What had I really witnessed? I had heard about spoons bending, but I never saw one. I hadn't seen anything really, except the Virgin Mary in the clouds, and that *was* imagination. The table in Anne's class had only seemed to dance by spirit power.

My faith in Anne had taken another hit when I finished reading Harold Sherman's book about her, the one with the preface by the oilman. It was written in the early 1970s and included Anne's predictions for the future. By the year 2000, people's houses would be held together by magnetic forces, she said. No nails or wood would be used. Curtains would hang without rods, and pictures would attach to walls by themselves. Furniture would be suspended in the air. Clothing would be radically changed. Smoking tobacco would be outlawed. Her predictions were so off that reading them embarrassed me.

During my time in Lily Dale I had seen no dead people, felt no energy, and received no visitations. Chapman hadn't shown up. All I had was talk: other people's accounts and my own experience with mediums who made some good guesses amid a mountain of bad ones.

Lily Dale almost drew me in, almost counted me among the people who look to Andalusian stallions for party invitations. I'd made a narrow escape, perhaps; but I was out. Disgusted with the whole place, I left early one August morning, happy to be going home. I wasn't going to blast Lily Dale as a community of lying frauds and crazy people. I was just going to walk away. Shrug and walk away as millions of other people have walked away from Spiritualism since it began.

And that might have been the end of this book.

34

I might never have come back to the Dale if it hadn't been for Gayle Porter. Gayle was the student medium who refused to talk with me until I took a two-weekend workshop called "Spiritual Insight Training." She said I'd never understand Lily Dale without that training. If I took the workshop, I would be giving messages myself, she said, and then she would talk to me.

Her contention that she knew what I did or didn't understand was presumptuous, I thought. I also didn't believe her. I would not be giving messages at the end of such classes. But she had reached a long finger into my psyche, pulled up one of my many fears, and dared me to ignore it.

If I walked away, I'd never know for sure. Someone could always say I'd failed to do all the research that presented itself. They could say I'd been a lazy reporter. I couldn't stand that.

I signed up for a September class certain that it would demonstrate how misguided Gayle was. As soon as I mailed the check, I began to dread it. I knew the drill. Insufferably perky leaders isolate a group for a weekend, create false intimacy, and cause people to cry, hug, and give maudlin testimonies. I hate that stuff, especially the hugging. I hate doing it, and I hate being the only little tight end in the class who won't. If people are hugging, you have to hug. What else can you do when they come for you? Dodge under their arms?

Giving spirit messages was part of the weekend. So was healing, which particularly spooked me. In one healing class that summer, people sat knee-to-knee for ten minutes looking into each other's eyes as they took turns repeating, "I love you. I love you. I love you." The woman who told me about the class said she did this with a middle-aged male, who was a stranger to her. She said the experience healed her of deep trauma and a longtime hatred for men.

I was happy for her, and equally happy to keep my trauma and hatred if that was the only way to give it up.

I arrived a day early and spent the afternoon cruising the back roads of the rolling upstate New York farm country. I stopped at a park on the edge of Lake Erie and began to walk. I wanted to quit this project. The summer was over. I'd given it my best, and I still didn't know what was going on inside the mediums' heads. I'd asked, they'd answered, but nothing was clearer. My skepticism may have blocked understanding, but without skepticism, I'd be defenseless, open to any oddball fantasy.

I was also tired of journalism itself. All summer, when my research stalled, I'd stomp about Shelley's house muttering about adopting a Chinese baby. Rearing a child would be useful, a contribution to the world. It would not be a waste of time, as journalism, particularly this journalism, was. Writing a book is like crawling into a dark tunnel. It takes everything I have, saps the rest of my life, puts me into a daze, exposes me to ridicule. All those feelings had peaked by September, and, as I walked the edge of the lake, I whispered to myself like a sulky child, "I hate it. I hate it. I hate it."

In that mood, I returned to Lily Dale. On the porch of the Maplewood Hotel, several women introduced themselves. We all needed to eat before classes that night. I knew the way to Grandma's Kitchen in the nearby town of Cassadaga. Over plates of spaghetti, chicken fingers, and iceberg lettuce salads, we told each other why we had come. A vegan massage therapist wanted to communicate with the universe. A hypnotherapist wanted to see dead people. Another woman had lost her job as a waitress at Red Lobster and was looking for new direction. A fourth woman was there because her relatives wanted her to work in their new wellness clinic and thought this class would start her education in what she needed to know.

Later, I met a woman who hoped to contact her late mother. It took her two days to do it, and when she finally did, her mother said, "What took you so long? It's easy to do." Many students were there because they experienced premonitions or visions and wanted to know how to control and use them.

Our class of about thirty people, mostly women, met in the main room of the fire hall. Two teen girls were in the group because one of their mothers had paid the fee. She believed the training would help them keep a grip on what was important as high school life tried to push them around. We sat on folding chairs that were so hard some people brought pillows. A fire helmet hung on the wall. We could sometimes hear the squawk of a shortwave radio broadcasting various local emergencies. People's sneakers squeaked as they walked across the linoleum floor.

Elaine Thomas, founder of the School of Spiritual Healing and Prophecy, which sponsored the workshops, is a licensed Lily Dale medium who began her exploration into Spiritualism more than thirty years ago after consulting an eighty-three-year-old medium in Buffalo. Encouraged, perhaps unwittingly, by her rabbi, who taught her that anything of a religious nature ought to be questioned, Elaine began to examine and modify the beliefs she grew up with. When she became an elementary school reading teacher,

her students reaffirmed her belief that children can contact the spirit world but are taught to ignore what they know. Eventually she and her family settled in Lily Dale.

In 1987, Elaine and her husband, Mark, who is now serving as the county executive, began teaching classes that put principles of neuro-linguistic programming, also called NLP, together with Spiritualist ideas. Teaching people to make spirit contact often took several years by the old method of having people sit in development circles. The Thomases found that their new techniques, which focus on physical movements, belief systems, and guided meditations, could cut the process down to a weekend. For those who want more training, Elaine offers a two-year program that results in certification as a Spiritualist minister or healer.

Part of her method involves giving messages to members of the class while students concentrate on watching her body, especially her eye movements. If she looks upward, she is getting visual information. If she looks to the side, she is using auditory channels. If she looks down, she is going into the realm of feeling. Breathing is also important. Breathing high in the chest encourages clairvoyance, or clear sight. Breath from the diaphragm brings clairaudience, or clear hearing, and breath that moves the belly is for clairsentience, or clear feeling. By changing our posture, our eye position, and our breathing, we can change the spirit channels we are using, she said. If one channel is not delivering, we should switch.

Among the messages Elaine gave that day were some for me. Her guides told her I was extremely focused. She said I seemed easygoing, but underneath I was full of strong opinions. Elaine said I could stop worrying about how my work was going to turn out. It would develop as I did it, and I could afford to relax.

A jury of my peers might agree with the first two points. I didn't. I thought Elaine was projecting her own fears about having a journalist observe her class. As for the third point, I had heard it before.

Gretchen told me much the same thing in a more lyrical manner. "You're on the train. You'll get there," she said during one of the Monday night five-dollar readings. "You can relax."

Sherry Lee said the spirits had already written my book. "You can relax."

Patricia Price promised spirit guides were following me to make sure I got what I needed. "You can relax."

I had relaxed. It didn't suit me.

Then Elaine scored.

She said I was intent on a question, but it was the wrong question. Instead of asking whether I should be doing this, I ought to be thinking about how to make it fit with other things that I valued, such as family and friends. She never said what "this" was.

If I'd been listening as Elaine said that to someone else, I would have dismissed her statement as vague and all-purpose. But her message wasn't for someone else. It was for me, and I had spent the day before wrestling with whether to quit because writing required too much. Even if Elaine has twenty stock messages that fit everyone, she gave this one to me, and it reached into my deepest conflicts.

Elaine's message was so completely on target that I could feel it spreading through me like a wave. She skewered a central fallacy in how I think. I dramatize conflicts into either-or propositions. I know better, but in crisis I forget my own best advice. The answer is in the middle. It's not either-or. It's in the middle.

Elaine's words spoke so concisely to my thoughts and needs that I was shaken. I looked at my watch. It was 3:25 on Saturday afternoon. That was the moment when I crossed over from being someone who was amused and sometimes amazed by the mediums' occasional scores and became someone who considered that they might have something useful to say.

Had someone told her of my struggles? When I returned home, I called Shelley to ask whether she talked to Elaine about me.

"I'd never do that," she said. "You know I wouldn't."

Later Elaine warned me against telling too much about her workshop because she was writing her own book. Everybody in Lily Dale was writing a book it seemed. I reassured her. I wasn't doing ten easy lessons in how to talk to dead people. How could I? I still didn't believe it could be done.

If she was such a great medium, why didn't she know that? And why didn't she know that I wouldn't steal her stuff? There it was again. The Lily Dale bounce. Elaine gave me one message that convinced me, and, before it could settle, she said something else that took my confidence away.

I felt like Faye Dunaway being slapped by Jack Nicholson in *Chinatown:* "She's my daughter." *Wap.* "She's my sister." *Wap.* "She's my daughter." *Wap.* There was no right answer.

During a guided meditation we were to envision the sun coming toward us. We were also to think of a pyramid of light coming down and infusing our bodies with brilliance.

"Breathe in the Christ light," Elaine said.

How did Christ get in this? I wondered but didn't break the mood by asking. No one objected to Christ's appearance at our séance. The light and our breathing were vehicles we would use to move into temples of light and healing where we would contact those who could help us, Elaine said.

During one meditation, she took us down a path that led to three temples. We were to choose one and go in. In my mind's eye, I saw my grandmother and my uncle. He was standing behind her, holding her elbow in a protective, guiding way. It was a gesture I'd seen him make a thousand times as she prepared to cross a street or navigate a curb. I could see them clearly. They didn't say anything, but they looked wonderful.

After meditations, Elaine invited students to tell what came to them. A lot of people had seen relatives. Some saw ancestors they had never met. One woman saw her dog. She had recently put the dog to sleep. In her vision he was a puppy again, and he thanked her.

A student named Ann began crying.

"I saw my daughter, running toward me, holding out her arms. She was so happy," Ann said.

"I want you to know your daughter is at peace," Elaine soothed her. "As much as you want her with you, she's still just as solid and real as she ever was."

"She's not dead," Ann said.

Ordinarily I would have laughed, but Ann was in such pain that Elaine's mistake seemed terrible. Elaine didn't miss a beat. Mediums confuse the dead with the living all the time. Anyone who can't recover quickly won't last long.

"Is there some kind of estrangement?" Elaine asked. "It's as though she is dead to you."

Ann nodded. She was sobbing harder now and apologizing every time she caught her breath. "I don't usually do this."

"What you saw are her true feelings," Elaine said. "I'm going to tell you that within three years she will be holding you in her arms. Everything is going to seem like an obstacle to that, but it's going to happen. They're telling me there are walls inside of walls, but they will fall down.

"I'm getting chills over it," the medium said. That's her sign that she's right. It's the sign for a lot of people.

As part of our lessons, we were to allow ourselves to experience whatever we saw, heard, or felt, and then we were to say whatever came to us. We might think, *This is just imagination.* But that was not to stop us.

"We're imagining reality," Elaine said.

She gave us a prayer to say before beginning our message sessions.

"Oh, God, as we open the door to communication in the unity of the Holy Spirit, the great I Am presence of the Universe, we give thanks, for we know that the words spoken are filled with your love, truth, wisdom, and understanding of the highest. Amen."

Setting our intentions is essential, she said.

"When giving a message, we hold that person in the palm of our hand because we open up soul to soul. So if you don't have something healing to say, please keep it to yourself," she said.

Elaine never tells people they are going to die, even though she sometimes sees visions that make her think they might. The future is nothing more than probability unfolding and could be changed, she said.

"I've seen too many people who were supposed to die and didn't," she said.

At the same time, if our intentions are to help, we are not to worry that our messages might hurt anyone.

"If it's about healing and it's spoken in truth and a feeling of love, we can do no harm," she said. We could count on our perceptions just as she counted on her spirit guides.

"They've never let me down," she said.

She and her co-leader, a phone company employee named Charles, told stories about miraculous healings. A child healed of sickle cell anemia and a woman cured of multiple sclerosis were among the most dramatic, but backaches and headaches were also mentioned, as was one event during which Elaine said her children healed their father after transporting themselves astrally into his body and cruising around a bit. Charles told us he had participated in helping people recover from terminal illnesses.

"I know you might have the idea that this can't be done. Please set that aside. This energy can go through lead, through walls. Superman, Superwoman, they all do this. The energy is going where it needs to go for the highest and the best," he said.

Elaine assured us that we already knew how to do what she was teaching us. We'd done it as children but forgotten how. She urged us to give up our ideas about whether what we said was right or wrong. Focus on healing, she said.

I worried about the idea that so many people needed healing. Was she saying everybody was sick?

Not exactly.

"People have gotten so out of touch with their feelings and their gut that they need a mirror that's going to be kind and loving," she said. Our messages would be that.

I'd heard Lauren say much the same thing. "If people could get their heads and their hearts together, I'd be out of business," she said.

As green as we were at giving messages, Elaine said we ought to proceed with full confidence in our abilities. "It's not 'Oh, God, give me this.' It's 'Thank you for what you're going to give us.'"

Don't try, our teachers told us. And don't analyze. Experience. We could analyze later.

Late Saturday afternoon we sat in two rows facing one another. We were about to play spirit chairs. My row stayed put while the people in the facing seats moved to their left after having exchanged messages. As each person sat before us, we were to say our prayer and then look into his or her eyes.

My first partner was Jim. On the first day, Jim volunteered to say the prayer before breakfast. He stepped up to the task with such energy and gave such a resounding blessing that I decided to stay away from him. So much positive energy jangled my nerves. But there he was.

As I looked into his eyes, my mind went blank. Nothing. Not a word. Not an image. I could meditate a thousand hours trying for such a total void and never reach it.

I had to say something.

"You're someone who really throws yourself into what you do." This was weak, and I was cheating. Everyone in the room knew that about him.

I looked more deeply into his eyes. They were a soft brown.

"Oh," I gasped, and, then, as though we were at a masquerade ball and he'd taken off a mask, I said, full of surprise, "that's who you are."

In an instant I felt as though I'd moved from seeing what he looked like to seeing who he was.

"Being so out there costs you something, doesn't it?" I went on. "You're really quite shy and sensitive. You'd like to withdraw, but you don't. You're quite brave. You stay connected with people and keep trying because you know that's the way to live the best life. You seek the truth even when it's hard to do. You ought to be very proud of your courage."

The connection was so intimate that it rattled me. I began to talk faster and faster. Words flew out of my mouth before I thought them, and I knew I was right. I could read it in his eyes. I felt powerful and full of knowledge that I hadn't imagined five minutes before.

Then Jim gave me a message. He said I came to the workshop as a skeptic, but I was being changed. He said I was there for a spiritual experience. I'd heard that perhaps a dozen times in Lily Dale, and I was tired of hearing it. My spirituality was fine, if you please. I was there to write a book.

I thanked him, trying not to sound churlish.

Next came Sally. I said the prayer, and I looked into her eyes. They had a glint that Jim's didn't. They were less wide but full of life. In an earlier exercise, when Charles asked us to demonstrate joy, Sally had thrown her clenched fists over her head and let out a piercing whoop. The explosion startled us all. One woman clutched her chest and said, "Don't do that."

"You have a great fountain of joy in you," I said, talking slow, feeling cheesy because I was cheating again. Then I morphed into my new self—fast-talking Chris.

"You have to protect that joy. It's your great gift. It's a gift for everyone around you. You don't understand how important it is. Don't let anything cause that fountain to lessen. If you do, you'll be robbed, but so will all the people who need to feel that joy. You've allowed what other people think and want to come ahead of that joy, and you must stop doing that."

What the hell was I doing? I was gushing like a broken hydrant. I never tell people who they are. I never give advice to strangers. I don't tell. I ask. That's my business. To watch, to listen, to stay under cover.

Finally, I finished my spiel, came back to my true self, and asked weakly, "Does any of this make any sense to you?"

"Yes," she said. "Thank you. I've had some bad experiences in the past couple of years, and I think they really caused me to withdraw from other people. I was not as outgoing as I used be. I guess I had dampened down my joy."

"Oh," I said.

She hugged me and then gave me a message. She said I was smart and tended to underestimate that. She said I had knowledge other people needed. She said I shouldn't waste that intelligence.

I didn't want to hear this. For all my life as a reporter, I believed that if I used my talent and intelligence well, people would benefit. I believed that every story had the potential to change how people saw the world. But I'd stretched myself as far as I could. The world hadn't changed. I hadn't enlightened anyone. I no longer wanted to trot out my intelligence, my theories, myself, in pursuit of some big vision. I felt like a trained monkey always dancing around hoping someone would throw out a penny. Instead, they threw tomatoes—you're not dancing fast enough;

you're not dancing well enough; the monkey down the street is dancing better.

I thanked her. I didn't like her message, but, as Elaine did before her, Sally seemed to have picked up my current state of mind. Or was I reading into it? Was I taking general statements and using them in my own ways? I didn't know. Maybe we were all doing that. Maybe the whole class was using our mysteriously sharpened intuition to connect with another kind of consciousness and at the same time using the same intuition and consciousness to eke meaning out of whatever was said to us.

Another Jim was my next partner. He looked dazed.

"I can't believe what's happening here," he said. "I'm really getting things. This message giving was the part of the workshop I was most skeptical about. I never thought this would happen."

I knew he wanted to write a book because he had already told me so, but this time I didn't use what I knew. I looked into his eyes and started talking. Again my boldness startled me. He didn't seem interested in what I was saying, but I couldn't stop.

I urged that he be more open about his own sensitivity. I told him that like a snail he needed to come out of his shell in order to move forward. I was talking as fast as I could, and all of it was drivel. I sounded like one of the mediums at the Stump who tells all the men that they're misunderstood and all the women that they give too much to others.

I hate people who foist ill-founded opinions on others. Why was I doing this? I finally wound down enough to shut up. I think we were both immensely relieved.

Jim's messages to me were of a different nature. He was seeing pictures. He saw children's building blocks with letters on them. He saw the words "super heroes." Then he got a vision of a forest and fields and horses running. None of this meant anything to me. I told him so.

"Are you sure?" he asked.

Now that he had his legs under him, he was ready to run with those visions. Messages he was getting meant far less to Jim than the ones he was giving. I understood completely. Our own powers were so strange and so powerful that we no longer cared what people could tell us. We wanted to know what we could tell them.

My next partner listened to my impassioned, hackneyed message with smiling impatience. Then she interrupted.

"What I really want to know is where I should go to school."

Psychics had told her she should become a nurse, but she didn't want to. I asked a few questions about her career plans. I shut my eyes. Nothing. As we began to discuss her plans again, a trainer tapped me on the shoulder.

"Try not to talk to each other. You're often blocking what you can get from spirit."

I closed my eyes. In the upper right edge of the blackness I saw a little figure with a nurse's cap on.

"I'm sorry," I said. "All I see is a nurse. I know that's no good."

After the exercise ended, Elaine asked for comments. People flung their hands in the air and waved them like school kids.

"Now we know enough to be dangerous," said a tall young woman with a thick braid hanging down her back.

"I'm good at this," shouted Beth the hypnotherapist as she pumped her fist into the air.

"You're good now, but wait until tomorrow when you'll be really good," Elaine said.

I left the fire hall thinking I'd experienced a connection so intimate and so powerful that it was scary. Did mediums feel this? If so, maybe what I took to be a lack of communication skills was a shield that they put up to protect themselves. If they felt such intimacy with every person who sat in their parlor, no wonder they wanted to hide during ordinary conversations. Maybe that's why they seemed not to listen to others and why I always had the feeling that they might break off the conversation any minute. I'd do the same thing if I were hooked up to such intensity day after day. I'd get some reserve and keep as much of it as I could.

I was disturbed but not convinced. I had a ready explanation: I had been reading people's faces and body language. I had looked into their eyes, which is not something people often do. I had said things I observed and intuited but hadn't brought into consciousness. The workshop focused that consciousness, but not perfectly. I'd also made a kind of fool of myself.

The next day, we sat in circles of six, and a trainer sat with us. First we did physical healing. Our trainer for that was a cherubic-looking woman with long, wavy, blond hair. She often said, with great relish and anticipation, "Love me up." Lots of hugging was required. As usual, I felt no energy when healing or being healed. The only surprise was that when the healers worked on me they concentrated on my shoulders and neck, areas I needed help with and hadn't mentioned. But, then, who doesn't need help with their shoulders and neck?

Later, we practiced giving messages. Elaine called this verbal healing. We didn't try for spirits, just messages. We were to say whatever images, words, or feelings came to us. The lights were always left on.

The first task was to figure out whom to give a message to. Our teachers said we might see a spirit form around a certain person, as mediums often did, but more likely we would merely feel drawn to that person. We might sense energy around someone, or a color, or simply the inclination to pick a certain person.

When one student had trouble getting a message, our trainer suggested that she give a message about childhood. When my turn came, I tried the same technique. I picked a blonde to my left and asked whether I could come to her. She said yes. Then I sat there mouth-breathing, like an adenoidal dunce. I had nothing to say.

I closed my eyes. At first I saw only blackness. Then the skirt of a dress and the legs of a little girl appeared. One moment nothing, and the next moment they were there. I couldn't see the child's shoulders or head.

"I see a dress that has a full skirt and a petticoat under it." I was laughing skeptically even as I said it. "It's the old-fashioned kind of slip, a can-can that makes the dress bell out.

"The dress has a sash, a wide sash," I said. "It ties in the back in a big bow. It's rose-colored."

I felt foolish, and a refrain was singing at the back of my brain, *You're making this up. You're making this up. You're making this up.* It was unnerving me.

"I know that's ridiculous," I said. "Who wears a sash?"

The other members of the circle laughed, but I didn't open my eyes.

Like a diver about to plunge, I pulled a long breath of air into my lungs.

"That's what I see. The sash is rose-colored. The dress is off-white with flowers on it. Not flowers massed together but spread out on the background of white. And they're big, but not huge. Red and pink, I think."

I didn't think. I knew. I could see it. But what was it?

It's a desperate attempt to fit in, the voice said at the back of my head. *You've conjured up something because you don't want to be embarrassed. Cowardly to the core.*

Now my words started to speed up.

"You were a girly sort of little girl."

I stopped. Part of my mind was groping for how to put this so I wouldn't insult her. Another part was still trying to shut me up.

You're extrapolating, the voice of reason said. *You're building on what you've seen, you phony. The woman is wearing makeup. Nice clothes, well pressed. Her posture is good. So you've turned her into a priss. Admit it.*

"Not prissy, exactly, but girly," I said, "very feminine. You liked to dress up and wear fancy dresses. You thought that was just a wonderful thing to do."

You're being ridiculous, the voice said. *Imagining things and passing them off as truth, embroidering on what anyone could see and making it into some great revelation. Disgusting. Stop it.*

I opened my eyes.

"What kind of sleeves did it have?" she asked.

"What? I don't know. I didn't look."

"Well, look," she said.

I closed my eyes. The vision was gone.

"Were they short?" she asked.

"I'm sorry. I don't know," I said. "They might have been."

"Little girls did wear sashes fifty-one years ago," she said. "My mother made that dress."

The voice said, *She's being nice, you dimwit. Don't buy it.*

"Oh, come on," I said, sounding a little mad. "You're kidding me."

"No," she said. "I'm not. That was my favorite dress."

What could I say to that? I laughed.

Next, I picked a woman to my right. Again I closed my eyes and saw nothing. Then, in the lower right corner of the darkness, the figure of a little girl emerged. She had blond hair, cut short like the woman before me. She was a bit chubby. The woman had a stocky build.

That's so lame, said the voice.

I kept looking at the little girl in my mind. She was leaning against a silver-colored pole.

"It's a swing set," I said.

Great, jeered the voice. *You see a kid. You see a playground. Such a put-on.*

I sighed. Why was I doing this? I didn't believe in spirit messages or telepathy or whatever this was. Eyelids still shut, I lowered my eyes toward the middle of my body.

Navel gazing? the voice said.

I ignored it. A sense of sadness fell over me. Lonely. She felt so lonely. I didn't want to say that. So I fumbled.

"I don't know why. I don't see anyone else on the playground, but there are children there. Is anyone on the swing set? Why are you alone?" My words were slow this time. My voice sounded so small and mournful. This was bad.

What are you doing? the voice needled me again. *You've run away with yourself, haven't you?*

I couldn't stop now. I had to say something upbeat.

"You loved to swing," I said, trying to put some life in my tone. "You loved the freedom of it."

It was no good. I felt too sad. "But you're not swinging now. You're just standing there. I don't know why."

I opened my eyes.

"That was me," the woman said. In her face was all the sadness I'd been feeling. "I never played with anyone on the playground. I wanted to, but I was afraid. I stood at the edge of the swing set watching the other children to make sure no one fell off."

Once again I didn't know what to say. But this time, I didn't laugh.

My next try was a woman with short curly hair who looked to be in her thirties. Elaine suggested I tell her about her own children. I shut my eyes. Nothing. Then the images came.

"I see three children. Two boys and a girl. The girl is taller, and the boys are about the same age."

"Tell her something about one of the children," said our trainer.

"The girl has brown hair that has a little wave in it. She wears it about shoulder-length. She's a tall, thin child. She's about eleven, I think."

You're describing a young version of the mother, the voice said. *Flimsy whimsy.*

Was I cheating again? It was impossible not to. The things I observed with my physical eyes melded into the visions supplied by my inner eye. Of course they would.

Suddenly my mouth seemed to take off as it had the day before.

"This little girl is quite willful. She is intent on getting her way. In fact, her brothers sometimes resent her for being bossy."

Now I was insulting this woman's child. Where were these cheeky opinions coming from?

I opened my eyes. The curly-haired woman was laughing in a rueful way.

"That's my daughter. That's exactly how she is. When her big sister doesn't do what she wants she chases her around the house."

"Do you have two younger sons?" I asked.

"No. I have two girls, but the boys might have been other children in my life," she said. "There are two boy cousins."

"I was wrong about the boys," I said to the trainer.

"No. You're never wrong. There are two boys. You just don't know who they are," she said.

I'd like to accept that, but I don't. I was speaking to people about things I had no knowledge of. I was giving character assessments that my normal mind would have never ventured. If I was speaking from some kind of divine guidance, then all was well and good and true. But I wasn't. I was wrong. So now what?

The messages I got from Elaine and fellow class members were surprisingly congruent. They focused on things I'd been pondering, such as what to do next, how to manage so I would have some life while writing a book. Were they guessing? Putting together what I'd told them with impressions and calling it otherworldly?

Probably. I was doing that too. I knew I was, but something more was happening. If my brain was conjuring these images, it was doing so without my complicity. Despite what the voice said, I wasn't trying to fool people. I was telling them what I saw, felt, and thought. More important, people were claiming the truth I told them.

My classmates went home blissful and full of new power. I fell into a funk so deep that I didn't get out of bed the first day of my return home. What was this all about? Where did I get that information? If I accepted what my experience was telling me, who would I be? A dippy prophet person wandering around talking about signs and spirit voices.

A few days later my neighbor asked about the weekend. I told her. After hearing my visions of dresses and swing sets, she said, "It sounds like something you'd do at a slumber party."

Next she said, "I wonder what the probability is of someone being able to describe a dress from someone's childhood. All little girls have a special dress. And every child spends time on a playground."

I knew exactly where she was going. I'd been there a dozen times myself. But those images were so clear, and the people's reactions were so powerful. Like a good seeker of truth, I considered endless paranoid possibilities. Were those women plants? Were they acting? Maybe the whole class was a setup. Maybe everyone there was a plant.

My mother suggested I might have been hypnotized. Maybe so. Maybe we were all hypnotized. When I told Shelley what happened in the class, she began calling me Madame Christine, Sees All, Knows All. When I told my sister, she reassured me.

"Don't worry. In a couple of days you'll come up with a way not to believe it." She was right. I could do that. I would do that.

35

A month later I returned to Lily Dale for the second class. It was October. The leaves had turned to such a brilliant gold that the air seemed to glow.

It was Saturday, and we were doing past-life readings. It was my turn. I don't believe in past lives, but that was a minor matter to the teachers. Just do it, they said. It doesn't matter if reincarnation is literally true. Many people in Lily Dale think we have chosen the lives we are now living, but even if reincarnation isn't a literal fact, the stories and messages we give function as metaphors for psychological truth, Elaine said. Our intent is to give healing messages, and so we do. Our listeners take the meaning they need.

Don't analyze. Just do. Give what you receive.

We sat in the usual circle of six. The room was brightly lighted.

I gazed into the eyes of a woman named Liz, our trainer. My mind was blank. I tried to slow my breathing. I always panic if I'm not performing well. They were all waiting. Then I had it. Not an image, but a word. I pushed it from my mind. Then it came again. So clear, so strong, that it was as if someone was hissing in my ears.

Witch!

"What do you get?" Liz said. "Just tell me whatever you get."

The word came whispering again, full of menace. *Witch.*

I was going to tell this woman, our trainer, that she was a witch? It was insulting. It was ridiculous. It was a cliché.

"Huh. Well . . . ," I stalled. Everyone was waiting. I shut my eyes.

In the darkness I saw a woman dressed like a peasant. It was two hundred, three hundred, maybe four hundred years ago. How could I know how long ago? I'm not an expert in peasant fashions.

The image appeared in the lower left quadrant of my visual field. She was hustling across a village square.

Good grief, I thought. *This is so obvious. You see her in a long dress because Liz is wearing a long dress. How unoriginal.* But it was all I had. So I gave it.

"You're very busy and full of energy and bustling about. People are drawn to you, and you're a kind of center to the community."

"What do I do?"

"You mean for a living? I don't get that," I said. "You must be some kind of housewife or mother. All I see is that you're important to the community, and people come to you for help, and you're able to give it to them."

"What do I do?" she asked again.

"Do?" I asked. I was not going to say it. "I don't know. Maybe you're married. Maybe you're a housewife. I don't know."

"Are you sure?" she said. "Aren't you getting anything?"

"I don't get that," I said. "Sorry."

She looked amused.

"Okay," she said lightly. "What does this mean for now?" A rule of the past-life readings in Elaine's classes was that they must always have a present-day meaning. Otherwise, they wouldn't be healing.

I paused, opened my mouth, and the fast-talker was back.

"It means that you have that same kind of role in this life. It will be harder to understand how important you are because in this time we value established careers more than we value what is done for the community," I said. "Your true calling is to work outside formal professions in helping people, in binding them together and helping them."

Late that night, we were all grouped together for a walk through the Dale, toward the woods and Inspiration Stump. We were going to "play" medium, and we hoped the spirits would oblige by gathering around. At least my classmates were. I didn't intend to participate. Liz was ahead of me. I caught up with her.

"You know that message today? There was one thing I didn't say. This is embarrassing, but I kept getting the word *witch.*"

She didn't break stride. "I know that. I knew what you were going for. I was a witch. Lots of people have told me that. They burned me at the stake. I've gone back and felt the flames and the smoke. It was agonizing," she said, quite calm and matter-of-fact.

I dropped back. She went on. Just another Lily Dale evening. You'd think I'd be used to it by now.

I didn't expect that I would ever see spirit loved ones, but when it came time for us to give those kinds of readings, I did see what might have been one. I picked a woman who looked to be in her mid-thirties and said that I saw a figure of an older woman. She was portly, had blue eyes, I thought. I could hardly see her face, but I saw that she had fluffy white hair.

"That would be my mother-in-law," the woman said.

My eyes were still shut. I saw a table in front of the old woman. I said so.

"That fits," the woman said.

The table was laid out as if for dinner. The words "you are at the table" came into my mind. Too banal. I was tired of being a channel for cliché.

I opened my eyes, looked at the woman, and shrugged. She seemed about to cry.

"I'm so happy that my mother-in-law showed up. I came here hoping to see her. Thank you."

Afterward the woman came to me with more explanation.

"My mother-in-law and I were once very close. When her son and I were getting a divorce, I wanted to see her, but her son discouraged me, saying that I wasn't part of the family anymore and there was no reason for me to see her. Then she died. I never got to tell her how much she meant to me. I was afraid that she didn't know how much I loved her."

Now the words I hadn't said had some meaning.

"Well, she's here," I said, my voice taking on that mediumistic authority that I'd heard in others so many times. I might as well do it up right. "She's here. And she says, 'You still have a place at the table.'"

I felt a chill go through me as I said the words, and I saw the former daughter-in-law's eyes fill with tears.

At the break, instead of running for the snack table as I usually did, I confronted Liz.

"What is this?" I asked. "What's going on here? What are we doing?"

"What do you think we're doing?" she replied.

"I don't know. I'm asking."

"What I think doesn't matter. What do you think? You have to answer that question for yourself."

"All right. I'll guess. I think we're all connected in some way. People are. I don't know how, but we are. This class helped us to tap into that connection. That's what's going on here."

"Sounds good to me," she said, and then she walked away.

So, okay. There is a channel to increased consciousness and knowledge. We can access it. Sometimes. But I was still stuck, as no one else in the class seemed to be, over the fact that what came through the channel was often wrong. My first experience in the October class had reaffirmed both those realities. People know things. Is what they know right? Yes. Is what they know wrong? Yes. Was nobody else bothered by this?

At one point, we were instructed to line up in two circles, one inside the other. When the music began, one circle would move clockwise and the other would move counterclockwise. When the music stopped, so would we. We would look deeply into the eyes of the person before us and give a message.

I didn't get a thing. Time after time I'd look into someone's eyes and see nothing. Just two peepers staring back at me. I'd look up, look down, look sideways, shut my eyes, open my eyes, look into their eyes, say my prayer, and nothing. Nobody else seemed to be having the same trouble.

"You think you're here to do a book, but you're wrong," said the first woman. "This is about your heart." She motioned toward her own chest. "You're here to have your heart opened."

Right. My heart. I didn't care about my heart. I cared about my book.

She didn't get points for knowing about the book. During the introduction session I told the group that I was writing a book on Lily Dale. I always announce myself when I'm working because I don't want people to feel deceived. If they want to avoid me, they ought to. By now I'd recommitted to writing. The mystery of what was going on in Lily Dale had hooked me entirely. Her contention that I was fooling myself about writing a book caused my face to fill with such alarm that she began to stammer.

"You'll do the book," she said. "I'm not saying you won't, but that's not the purpose of your visit here. You're here for a spiritual experience."

I thanked her. Were these people ever going to stop with the spiritual talk? Did they say that to everyone? Sure they did. Did people collapse in a grateful puddle when they heard it? Maybe they did. I didn't.

The next time the music stopped I faced another woman. This one hadn't been near when I received the first message, but she too wanted to talk about my heart.

"Your heart is closed, but it's going to open," she said.

My smile was getting tight. I'll put my open heart up against anybody's. Not the Dalai Lama's or Jesus', but most anybody's. There's nothing closed about my heart.

She could see I wasn't receptive, but this newby medium wasn't budging. The third time she told me that my heart was going to open I muttered, "I think my heart's okay. Really. It's pretty open if you ask me."

"Well," she said, in that smug voice that I'd heard come from my own mouth at the last workshop. "It's going to open more."

Great. I'm going to go around loving everybody up and gushing about how much they all mean to me? I don't think so.

The music started, and I walked around the circle again, peering into my classmates' faces. The music stopped. Another woman was in front of me.

"I'm feeling a lot of energy around your heart," she said.

"Right," I said, putting up my hand to halt her. "Everyone wants to talk about my heart." I wasn't bothering with gracious. I was tired of defending my heart against these ninnies. It was too absurd.

"I know. I know," I said in a singsong voice. "My heart is closed, and my heart is going to open, and that's what I'm here for. Thank you very much."

"Oh, no," she said. "Your heart is wonderfully open. It's a strong part of who you are."

"I've just been told by two people that my heart is closed and I need to open it," I said.

"I guess you could open it more," she said, "but it's definitely open. I'm very good with chakras, and I know what's coming from your heart chakra. It's strong and open."

Thank God for that. I hate to be told who I am. I hate to be told what to do.

Saturday night we went to the Stump. We started out at about nine o'clock. It was a cool night. The moon was out, but the trees in Leolyn Woods are thick, and the path was unlighted. Several people had flashlights. Charles, our leader, asked us to leave our drinks behind and realize that we were entering a sacred space. Before we entered the woods, he directed us to stop while he said a prayer and asked permission to enter. If he sensed that other entities were using the woods, we couldn't go in, he said, because the woods were their territory and we were only visitors.

After a few moments of silence he said it was okay to go in.

We hunched in little groups, running into each other, giggling, apologizing as we stumbled after the dim flashlight beams, feeble against the black night. Dark swallowed us if we moved even a foot away. Leaves crackled and swished under our feet.

In the clearing where the Stump is located, we could see the moon and stars above. There was only enough light to see the shapes of each other's bodies. Leaves were falling in showers of gold all through the forest. We couldn't see them now, but the woods were full of faint shifting sounds as they fluttered loose, colliding in their flight, settling with a million sighs. We took seats on the hard benches before the Stump. I sat on a row by myself.

Charles said anyone who received a message should feel free to come forward and give it. An ebullient African American woman, who was the only person of color in the class, went first. She said that the falling leaves were a sign of how happy the spirits were with us. The leaves were like applause from them to let us know how glad they were that we were learning to be more aware of them. They want to help us, she said, and are so excited now that we will be better able to let them.

I sighed. How nice it must be to believe that you're the little darling of the universe.

A few more messages were given, and then a solidly built young guy got up. All I knew about him was that he and his wife had just had a baby.

"I don't know your name," he said, "but is the woman who looks like Annette Bening here?"

I slid down in my seat. He meant me. I had a new short haircut, something like the one Annette wore in that movie where the president of the United States falls for her, and ever since I'd gotten to Lily Dale people had been telling me that I look like Annette Bening. I don't. Except for the hair.

Everyone laughed when he said it. I didn't answer. How could I claim that?

A couple of women replied in mock fluttery voices, "Oh, dear. You must be talking about me."

"Are you here?" he asked again.

I cleared my throat. "Uh, yes," I said. "Uh, I'm here."

The dark shape of his body turned toward me. I couldn't see his face.

"The angels are all around," he said, "and they're smiling." His head tilted up and moved as though he was looking around at the sky. His voice was filled with awe.

"There are spirits joining them, and they're smiling too."

I looked around. Didn't see anything.

"They are so happy and pleased with you. They say that you're a kind, loving, generous woman, and they're so proud of you. You make them so happy."

The angels and the spirits were all gathered and now beaming over how perfectly perfect I am? There it was again. That Lily Dale extravagance.

I put my head in my hands. I'd already copped to looking like Annette Bening, as mortifying as that bit of overblown ego was. Now I was being lured into greater grandiosity. *If* I am a kind, loving, and generous person, and I'm not claiming that I am, but if I am, those are qualities I ought to lose. They don't do a thing for me in the market economy. For a journalist, they're a handicap. You fight such impulses. If you're a woman who wants to compete, they are a weakness.

The student medium wasn't finished.

"They say that you need to let your voice be heard," he said. "They say you don't speak up enough and you should."

Well, yeah. If people are kind, generous, and loving, they ought to speak up. The world needs them. I'll give the spirits that much.

The next day, as we were gathering our things to leave, I stopped at the table where Gayle Porter was selling books and tapes. We had talked a little during the classes, but not much. I reminded her that she had promised me an interview. She gave me her phone number.

"So what do I do with all this?" I asked as I was about to turn toward the door.

"You live with it," she said. "You use it in your life."

"What does that mean?" I asked.

"You'll find out."

36

It's as though we live inside a big egg, whose shell is made up of a million perceptions, comments, and occurrences that have hardened around us and blocked our view of anything else. All we see are the calcified remains of our experience, and every day the shell gets thicker. Lily Dale's spirits tap, tap, tap away until they break a tiny pinhole in the shell. A strange light comes through. And some of us start to kick our way out.

That might be true.

When I returned from Lily Dale I tried to use my new powers. I prophesized that Gore would win the election. He didn't. On Thanksgiving I was invited to my neighbor's house. Her parents and sister were to be there. I'd never met them. Before we left our house I carefully conjured an image of each of them in my mind. Nobody looked anything like I imagined. My sister and brother-in-law were trying to have their first baby. I told my sister that she would be with child by Christmas. On December 13 she called to say, "I'm pregnant." One out of three. Not too reliable, and I'd cheated on the last one. During a five-dollar reading, Gretchen had told me I would be holding a "chunk of a baby" next year. My sister came to Lily Dale while I was there, and Sherry Lee told her she would be pregnant or have a child by August. My nephew was born August 7.

I was a psychic flop. Whatever happened to me during Spiritual Insight Training seemed specific to that place. I called Gayle Porter. She asked what I wanted to do with the book.

"Set your intentions," she said, echoing Elaine. "That will determine everything."

I told her I wanted to write a true account of the mediums and the town and my experiences in it. She said that mediums and messages didn't interest her much.

"Do you think they can bring through spirits and tell the future?" I asked.

Yes, but she didn't want to be part of a book about that, she said. She came to Elaine's classes because she wanted to hook up with a force of love and energy that she believes is available to humans. She thinks she did that.

She wished me luck.

After Pat Naulty received messages she believed were from her son John, she left the Dale in such a state of bliss that the outside world seemed coarse and jostling. At the truck stops where she stopped for coffee on her way home everything seemed too loud. She and Shelley continued to meet for long lunches in which they talked about how women ought to trust their innate knowledge. Pat joined a Spiritualist church but left after a while because people seemed too content to settle into whatever knowledge they had. She wanted to explore change and potential and new ways of being.

Once she had a vision of John. He appeared to be about thirty and was dressed in a white linen caftan. He was just as handsome and happy and wise-looking as she hoped he would be. When she reached her hand toward him he reached back, and, just as their fingers would have touched, he disappeared. Before Lily Dale, Pat might have doubted that vision and convinced herself that it didn't mean anything. Now she treasured it.

She had ignored her intuition when she knew that she ought to leave California to be with her son. That failure to heed herself may have contributed to his death. Lily Dale comforted her and fortified her determination. She would never again ignore what her own mind told her was real.

She remarried. Her new husband was a physics professor whose wife had died a decade earlier, leaving him with a young son. Pat loved the boy. His mother had favored violets, and after Pat moved in violets began to come up all over the yard in places they had never been. She took that as a sign that the boy's mother approved of her. Once, when her new son dreamed about his mother, Pat told him that she believed he truly had been visited by his mother and that she was still with him.

Shortly after her marriage, Pat became so ill that she could no longer get out of bed. Poor health had always plagued her, but this was worse than anything she had ever experienced before. She had inflammatory bowel disease, arthritis, and fibromyalgia, which caused every fiber of her body to throb with pain. Lying in a darkened room all day gave her plenty of time to think about her old boast: "Just pop my brain out and put it in a computer. I'm all intellect." She sometimes laughed about that odd delusion as her body taught her a new lesson every day in how connected to it she actually was.

I spent a weekend with Carol Lucas seven months after Noel's death. She was fairly dazed by how well she was doing. "I'm not half a person," she said. "What happened to me in Lily Dale made all the difference. Just knowing that Noel is all right meant so much to me. I can go on. I never would have believed I'd be doing this well. I keep waiting for the other shoe to drop, but it hasn't yet."

"You don't have to wait for the shoe to drop," medium Mary Ann Spears told her. "It's not going to come crashing in on you. You have this knowledge that you didn't have. He is alive."

Carol is haunted now, not by any kind of ghost but by the recurring image of a butterfly breaking free from its cocoon. "It's leaving behind a dried-up, useless husk," she said. Like Noel.

She hasn't seen any visible manifestation of her late husband, and she realizes that she may never. But her four-year-old granddaughter says she has seen Grandpop, and Carol believes her.

As for Sherry Lee's other predictions, Carol doesn't have a male business partner/future husband yet, but she did find herself counseling a young girl who was part of a grief recovery group. The future marriage partner was the one item of Sherry Lee's reading that Carol never believed and never wanted to.

The first Christmas without Noel was difficult, as she knew it would be. She was feeling blue on her way home from her daughter's house and decided to stop by a small-town crafts market. After browsing a while, she got in her car and began working her way back to the freeway. Lost and searching for the way home, she glanced up at a street sign. It said: N. LUCAS.

She knew that "N" in a street sign stands for North, but by then Carol had a little practice in accepting the fullness of serendipity. And so she let herself be delighted and filled with the comfort that life sometimes gives us if we'll let it.

Marian is divorced now. She works for a printing company and is still pursuing her interest in spiritual matters. She doesn't talk compulsively anymore, and she's gained much of her weight back.

"Seemingly my life has been destroyed, but I am more at peace than I've ever been," she said. She believes that she would not have survived if the anger and fighting in her marriage had continued to escalate.

All the spirit help in preparing for divorce didn't help her much. Her husband won one financial battle after another, she told me, but her new sense of meaning held. She reframed her defeats as spiritual lessons and tried to learn from them. Greg told her, "What you resist, you perpetuate; what you fear, you manifest." That pretty much explained what happened to her, she said.

"I feared being financially insecure, and I wanted power," she told me. "So I manifested someone who seemed to have those things, but it was an illusion."

She has continued her search for spiritual growth, but she no longer consults mediums. "I believe you put out more than you realize you're putting out when you talk to the mediums," she said. "As I became calmer, the mediums became less accurate. I have friends who are mediums. When I talk to them I talk less about events than about the spiritual process." It's their optimism and hope that she values.

My own life has also been changed.

Patricia's story of two spirit mediums at my shoulder showed me that I didn't have to treat life as a battle I was always about to lose. The more I tried floating through the day, drifting toward what I wanted to do and away from what I didn't, the easier work became.

That experience set me up to consider what Shelley's friend Lynn said about listening to myself and doing what I wanted. Such license attracted and at the same time repelled me. I didn't trust it, but I did try it, and I surprised myself. Life didn't change that much in outward ways. I didn't start shoplifting or kicking dogs. What changed was how I felt. I began to know my own mind in a way I never had. I became noticeably freer and stronger in myself. I even did a few altruistic things that I wouldn't have done before—just because I wanted to.

The spirits I saw at Spiritual Insight Training also affected me. I couldn't forget the woman whose ex-mother-in-law appeared in my mind to say that her former daughter-in-law was still at the table. I didn't want to give that message, but I did. If I hadn't, would anyone else have given it? Maybe not. Maybe I was the only person there who heard the message of acceptance that the ex-daughter-in-law wanted so much to receive. Was it a true vision or something else? I don't know. But it helped her. It may have even healed her. So that was good.

Maybe all living things are linked together, and maybe we all have something to give one another. Who knows how we get it? Maybe the spirits exist. Maybe we invent them to justify knowledge that we draw from some all-knowing, all-wise core within us, from telepathy or from the Cosmic Consciousness. Maybe it doesn't matter.

The spirits haven't visited me since those October days in class, but when my friends are talking about something that's important to them I sometimes know what they mean so deeply that it is as though mere words couldn't have conveyed so much. I haven't used my medium's voice, that fast-talking fount of authority, since Lily Dale, thank God, but I tell people what I think more than I once did. It seems as though I ought to. Maybe no one else knows what I know, and maybe they need it.

I worry about the egotism of that idea. So I tell what I think is right. The listener judges whether it's true or useful. Maybe the mediums and their clients work on the same system. The Lily Dale visitors I interviewed at the five-dollar Monday night readings seemed to follow those rules. They paid their money to hear the mediums, took whatever was said, and then threw out what they didn't agree with.

Maybe Shelley was right when she said Lily Dale is the closest thing we have to the Temple of Eleusis. I wanted the temple to deliver clear answers that were always right, but even the best oracles can't do that. The mediums and their clients work together. They may or may not bring in spirit helpers. I'm not sure it matters whether we agree on that. What does matter is that human beings make meaning out of their experiences. They pull purpose and direction out of their lives. Maybe that universal human tendency is based on delusion; maybe it's based on a deeper wisdom than our conscious minds understand. Maybe other people tap into those unconscious streams to help. Maybe a host of spirits and extrasensory perceptions help too.

After Lily Dale, incidents of synchronicity happened to me so often that I stopped thinking of them as surprising and began to greet them as evidence of how the world works. I began to realize that there were types of magic around me all the time. What varied was my ability to notice.

People told me so many stories of their own ghostly experiences and spirit messages that I no longer even tried to doubt them. Who knows how many people have experiences that aren't considered possible in our culture? They deny them or forget them or save them for the few occasions when it seems all right to mention them. Millions of people just don't say anything. Maybe every human being has touched into some kind of sixth sense.

I learned long ago that spiritual growth is about walking into mystery. It's about confronting the paradox at the heart of every answer. Are the mediums right? Yes. Are the mediums wrong? Yes. After Chapman didn't show up in the psychomanteum, Shelley recommitted herself to living with doubt. She began to say that everything was explainable except 2 percent, and even that fraction wasn't necessarily transcendent. It just held out the possibility. Living between belief and disbelief was a comfortable place to her. Maybe that tension gives us the best place for understanding the true nature of reality, the best place for new surprises and discoveries, even the best place for spiritual growth.

I visited Lily Dale the next summer, and when the mediums talked I understood more of what they meant. I felt pretty much at home until Tom Cratsley told me that he and a class had visited the Stump late one night and seen some amazing transfigurations. I asked for details.

They'd seen people morphing into animals. Fairies had appeared with wings beating.

"Did everyone see this?" I asked.

"Yes," he said. "I think so. It was the most amazing thing."

There it was. That old Lily Dale bounce. One minute I could believe, and then someone would push me too far. I would hit the eye-rolling threshold and stop. As far as Lily Dale was concerned, I was in for a penny but not in for a pound. Then I met Karen.

Karen believes angels are available to help humans. Like millions of other Americans, she concentrates much of the angel power available to her on parking places and other matters of traffic control. Driving toward the mall, she tells the Archangel Michael that she's about to need a spot, and he supplies one. She always gets a place right by the door, she said.

Once, when Karen was to meet her friends for lunch, she lingered too long over her computer and was only roused when her husband mentioned that she had twenty minutes to make the date. Still in her nightclothes, Karen considered going unwashed and scruffy. Instead, she asked the Archangel to stretch time. She showered, washed her hair, dried it, put on makeup, and drove to the restaurant without meeting a single car. Her parking place was ready. She left the car in no particular hurry, pulled open the restaurant door, and looked at her watch. It was noon on the dot. She was the first one there.

Time stretching was a new miracle for me. I'd never heard of that, but I had heard of parking place magic. It may be the most common miracle in America, which is most likely the reason it makes me grimace.

It doesn't bother me that the highest angel in heaven had been turned into a parking lot attendant—Park-angel Michael, to steal a quip from medium Martie Hughes. I've had plenty of born-agains tell me that Jesus himself finds them parking spots. Why should a mere archangel balk? But Karen was more sure of herself than anyone I'd ever talked to. She invited me to test celestial traffic control by asking for angel help as I drove back to Lily Dale. The Archangel would clear the street for me. Just ask, she said, and you're likely to see people turning off in front of your car, right and left.

I didn't do it. I couldn't stop thinking about those hapless souls who would be peacefully driving toward their destinations and then, just after I said my prayer, would find themselves wrenching the wheel toward the nearest exit with absolutely no intention of going there and no reason to want to. Is that how it works?

Perhaps I have too much leftover Baptist guilt. I think spirits ought to do only grand things—a supposition that Lily Dale and now Karen were challenging mightily.

When I told Karen's story to Lynn, she seemed delighted, but I shook my head.

"Do you believe all that? Do you think angels really do find people parking places?" I asked.

"I don't see why not," she said. "They don't do it for me, but I don't drive."

As Patricia Price is fond of saying, "All is in divine order."

But I couldn't accept it. "Lynn, why would the spirits do such trivial things when so many serious problems need fixing? Don't they have better sense than that?"

"Spirit does want to do things for us," Lynn said. "Parking places are simple, everyday things that convince people there's an alternate reality. Once they know that they can grow. And they will."

With that, the last part of the Lily Dale puzzle fell into place. This was what the mediums had tried to tell me, but I couldn't understand. Most people come to the Dale to ask about love or money. They summon the forces of heaven to find them parking places, bend spoons, or make a table dance. What's spiritual about that? I'd asked again and again.

Now Lynn had explained. This is the everyday stuff of life. If the mediums deal well with earthly, mundane questions, they may connect people with a force beyond them, or at least help them know there is such a force. Once Spirit reaches people it can move them, maybe slowly, maybe only a little way, but it can move them.

Did I believe it? Sometimes yes. Sometimes no. But I'd like to.

On my last summer day in Lily Dale, Shelley's husband, Frank, carried my suitcase down the porch stairs and stood waiting to shut the car door. He told me to be careful and made sure the door was securely closed, as though without his care I might somehow fall out of the car before reaching my destination.

Shelley and Lynn went for a somewhat more elaborate send-off. They stood watching, high above me on the wide white porch behind the spindle railing. At first they waved. Then Shelley shouted, "Angel wings. We have to do angel wings."

Both women began lifting and lowering their arms as though they were big feathered wings slowly, lazily lifting into the air.

"Angels have charge over you," they chorused. "Angels, angels, angels go with you."

A Partial Cast of Characters

SPIRIT SEEKERS

PAT NAULTY—a Virginia Beach English professor whose teenage son killed himself playing Russian roulette. She came to Lily Dale hoping for nothing more than rest and a little entertainment, but the mediums had more to give her—much more.

CAROL LUCAS—a retired English teacher and recent widow who tried desperately to save her husband, Noel, from an early death. Her grief was raw on the summer weekend she came to Lily Dale, hoping to make contact with the only love of her life.

MARIAN BOSWELL—a happy woman, beautiful and content, married to Jack, the perfect husband. On her first visit to Lily Dale, a stranger gave Marian an ominous warning, but she took it as a compliment.

SHELLEY TAKEI—a psychologist who summers at Lily Dale and who founded the Lower Archy of the Pink Sisterhood of the Metafuzzies and the Blissninnies. The group's motto is, "We don't know jack shit, but we care." For more than twenty years, Shelley had failed to unravel the secrets of Lily Dale's mediums. "Either they're crazy or I'm stupid," she often said. Her husband, Frank, is a retired philosophy professor.

LYNN MAHAFFEY—a Catholic mother of five who reads runes, heals a backache with prayer, and spiritually mentors many of the women who make Shelley's house a summer retreat. Every day, Lynn rides her bicycle five miles as she says intercessory prayers for the world.

NEW CHOICES WOMEN

When they first came to Lily Dale, these welfare mothers couldn't afford restaurant dining, so they brought supplies purchased with food stamps. Ten years later they were living spirit-filled lives—and I don't mean the kind of spirit usually encountered in a Christian church.

DARCY KIEHL—she suffered through forty-eight car accidents and an industrial accident that cost her her job, her marriage, and her house. Lily Dale taught her that she was a winner all the way.

DAWN GANSS—all she asked of Lily Dale was that it not make her cry. This was not a request the universe honored.

JOYCE PARKER—a former meatpacker and single mother. Joyce was desperate to bust out of all the small-town conventions holding her back. Lily Dale helped.

DORIS GOODMAN—a former Kmart deli cook who had won honors in graduate school. Nobody in Lily Dale told Doris how she was expected to act, and that scared her half to death.

MEDIUMS

MARTIE HUGHES—has never seen a spirit with her physical eyes and hopes she never does, but what she told Carol Lucas changed the widow's life.

SHERRY LEE CALKINS—self-reported astral traveler and eldest sister in a family that has lived in Lily Dale for five generations. Sherry Lee resides in the Divine Wisdom Retreat Center and teaches classes on how to spot angels in our midst.

GRETCHEN CLARK LAZARONY—Sherry Lee's younger sister. She gave me a message that was eerily true. With Sherry Lee, she helped Shelley try to summon their late brother, Chapman, from the Beyond.

PATRICIA PRICE—nobody in Lily Dale has a better reputation for being spiritually minded and mediumistically adept. Past-life readings are just part of her repertoire.

ANNE GEHMAN—a Washington, D.C., medium and summertime resident of Lily Dale who says she helped catch serial murderer Ted Bundy. Anne is said to counsel some of the capital's most powerful people. She can also bend spoons and make tables dance.

GREG KEHN—a medium rumored to be so good that he can tell you which spark plug is misfiring in your car's engine.

LAUREN THIBODEAU—a Ph.D. in counseling helps Lauren, who began receiving spirit messages while a teenager.

JAQUELINE LUNGER—who owns a t-shirt that proclaims: "Small medium at large."

Suggested Reading on Spiritualism and Psychic Phenomena

Braude, Ann. *Radical Spirits: Spiritualism and Women's Rights in Nineteenth-Century America.*

Christopher, Milbourne. *ESP, Seers & Psychics: What the Occult Really Is.*

Eisenbud, Jule. *Parapyschology and the Unconscious.*

Eysenck, Hans J., and Sargent, Carl. *Explaining the Unexplained Mysteries of the Paranormal.*

Gardner, Martin. *The New Age: Notes of a Fringe Watcher*

Hansel, C.E.M. *ESP and Parapsychology: A Critical Re-evaluation.*

Hardinge, Emma. *Modern American Spiritualism,* Vols. 1 and 2.

Houdini, Harry. *Miracle Mongers and Their Methods: A Complete Expose.*

Jahn, Robert G., and Dunne, Brenda J. *Margins of Reality: The Role of Consciousness in the Physical World.*

Koestler, Arthur. *The Roots of Coincidence: An Excursion into Parapsychology.*

Kurtz, Paul. *A Skeptic's Handbook of Parapsychology.*

Lawton, George. *The Drama of Life after Death: A Study of the Spiritualist Religion.*

McDermott, John J. *The Writings of William James: A Comprehensive Edition.*

Mishlove, Jeffrey. *The Roots of Consciousness: Psychic Liberation Through History, Science, and Experience.*

Moody, Raymond, M.D. *Reunions: Visionary Encounters with Departed Loved Ones.*

Moore, R. Laurence. *In Search of White Crows: Spiritualism, Parapsychology, and American Culture.*

Murphy, Gardner. *Challenge of Psychical Research: A Primer of Parapsychology.*

Sinclair, Upton. *Mental Radio: Does It Work and How?*

BIOGRAPHIES

Baldwin, Neil. *Edison: Inventing the Century.*

Barzun, Jacques. *A Stroll with William James.*

Britten, Emma Hardinge. *Autobiography of Emma Hardinge Britten.*

Goldsmith, Barbara. *Other Powers: The Age of Suffrage, Spiritualism, and the Scandalous Victoria Woodhull.*

Houdini, Harry. *Houdini: A Magician Among the Spirits.*

Lewis, R.W.B. *The Jameses: A Family Narrative.*

Lurie, Alison. *Familiar Spirits: A Memoir of James Merrill and David Jackson.*

Pike, James A., with Diane Kennedy. *The Other Side: An Account of My Experiences with Psychic Phenomena.*

Silverman, Kenneth. *Houdini: The Career of Erich Weiss.*

Sinclair, Upton. *The Autobiography of Upton Sinclair.*

Singer, June. *Boundaries of the Soul: The Practice of Jung's Psychology.*

Spraggett, Allen. *Arthur Ford: The Man Who Talked with the Dead.*

LILY DALE AND ITS MEDIUMS

Carrington, Hereward. "Experiences at Lily Dale," *Journal of the American Society for Psychical Research,* vol. II, no. 7 (July 1908).

Hayward, Ernest S., O.B.E., and Hayward, Cecelia F. *Psychic Experiences Throughout the World.*

Lewis, Sinclair. "Spiritualist Vaudeville," *Metropolitan Magazine,* February 1918.

Nickell, Joe. "Spirit Painting: Part I—The Campbell Brothers and Part II—The Bangs Sisters," *Skeptical Inquirer,* Investigative Files, March 2000.

Proceedings of the American Society for Psychical Research, vol. II, 1908.

Richard, Michel P., and Albert Adato. "The Medium and Her Message: A Study of Spiritualism at Lily Dale," *Review of Religious Research,* vol. 22, no. 2 (December 1980).

Sherman, Harold. *You Can Communicate with the Unseen World.*

Acknowledgments

Thank you to all the residents, mediums, and visitors of Lily Dale, who are identified by their actual names except in a few sensitive cases. You were generous with your time and your stories. Special thanks to Joyce LaJudice, who answered many questions and shared many resources and photos with me. Also, Donna Riegel and Jack Ericson for their invaluable assistance. Hilda Wilkinson fortified me with hot tea, many sandwiches, and much wisdom. Thanks to her also for sharing photographs.

To Shelley and Frank Takei, who took me in when I was cold and felt friendless, you made everything come together. Martie Hughes, thanks for using your talent so many times to reassure me.

Thank you to my family and friends, who listened to years of Lily Dale stories. Special thanks to my father-in-law, Charles Seib, for kindness and expertise, for honesty, and for having the bravery to say, "This is not good enough." To my sister, Jamie Langston, who also knew when to say, "This is good," and when to say, "You can do better," thank you.

I am also in debt to many friends who discussed this book for many hours. Sharon Grigsby and Dee Lyons are among them. Sophia Dembling, Donna Johnson, Kirk Wilson, Diane Reischel, and Darla Walker read the manuscript and helped spot places it needed help. They encouraged me with much lavish praise and laughter at the right places.

Thanks to my wonderful editors, Liz Perle, who knew what this book needed from our first conversation to the last, and Gideon Weil, who helped bring it all home. Thanks also to their assistant, Anne Connolly, who kept me afloat with good counsel and fine humor.

To my agent Janet Wilkins Manus, thank you for knowing that of all my ideas this was the one to go for. Your enthusiasm never flagged. To my agent Jandy Nelson, thank you for everything, just everything. You are joyful and brilliant.

And to my husband, Philip, gratitude can't ever be enough. Your faith, your support, your money. I needed them all. And thank you for never once wincing at all the dinner parties when someone asked, "What are you working on?" and the answer generated yet another long night of tales from the beyond.

Plus:

Lily Dale

Plus: Insights, Interviews, and More

What Would *You* Ask?

Countless numbers come to Lily Dale to ask their mediums what will happen in their future. Below are the questions most frequently asked, in three different areas. The most popular questions are, predictably, about love. They follow the cycle of life and eternal hope.

1. Is there a man in my future?
2. Does he love me?
3. Will we marry?
4. How many children will we have?
5. Is he cheating?
6. Will he leave?
7. Should I dump him?
8. Can I get him back?
9. Has he hidden money from me?
10. Will I marry again?

Money is also of great interest.

1. Will I get any?
2. Can you find what I lost?
3. Will I be lucky at the slots?

Eternal destiny is not always the most pressing concern, except for the recently bereaved. Two questions are common.

1. Is he here now?
2. Is he happy?

What Have *You* Learned?

Here are a dozen questions to see how much you know about Lily Dale's Spiritualism. Answers are scattered throughout the book. If you can't remember them, check the next page for reminders.

1. What messages do Lily Dale mediums say they have the most trouble with?
2. What do Lily Dale mediums say can cause their predictions to be wrong?
3. What messages do Lily Dale mediums most want to give?
4. What messages do Lily Dale mediums say they won't give?
5. Why do Lily Dale mediums begin sessions with a prayer?
6. Why do Lily Dale mediums discourage using a Ouija board?
7. What famous actress followed her favorite medium to Lily Dale?
8. Who was called the scourge of Spiritualism?
9. What did Susan B. Anthony say when a Lily Dale medium brought through her aunt?
10. Why do spirits fail to warn people who are about to make a bad decision?
11. What did Lily Dale mediums do when they heard that Harry Houdini was in town?
12. What do Lily Dale mediums say about evil spirits?

Answers

1. They often don't know when their predictions will come to pass.
2. They say it's your own free will.
3. They love those that prove the afterlife exists.
4. They won't say that death is in the future.
5. They pray to draw good spirits and protect themselves from tricksters.
6. It draws low level spirits.
7. That was Mae West.
8. Harry Houdini was called that.
9. "I didn't like you when you were alive and I don't want to talk to you now."
10. Life is for learning lessons and bad decisions are part of that.
11. They hid and locked their doors.
12. They're not evil, just confused and lost.

How to Hold Your Own Séance

(and other ways to invigorate your book club)

Book clubs can get "the spirit" themselves. Here are three ways:

1. Instead of merely discussing *Lily Dale: The Town that Talks to the Dead,* liven up the evening by inviting members of your club to tell their own stories of spirit encounters. You'll be surprised at how many will surface—often ones people don't remember until their memories are prodded. No one has to sign on as a believer of spirit messages to share experiences they've had. Don't be surprised if most of your friends begin their stories by saying, "I don't know what this means." Or "I don't tell this to many people." If people are too shy, give them the option of writing their stories before they come to the meeting and have someone assigned to read them.

2. Go a step further by inviting a local medium to give short individual readings. Many will agree to do so for a modest price. At Lily Dale hundreds of people line up each week for ten-dollar readings that last five or ten minutes.

Typically the medium sits in a circle with the participants and goes around the circle giving messages individually. Or a medium might stand in front of the group and direct specific messages at various people in the room. Any Spiritualist medium will be able to do this kind of public reading. All Lily Dale worship services include messages from a medium for people in the congregation, and every day during the summer session public messages are given at Inspiration Stump and the outdoor sanctuary. Messages that are part of Spiritualist worship never have a fee, but mediums who come to a book club may charge for their time.

3. If your group is more intrepid, you might decide to have your own séance.

Lily Dale mediums believe everyone has the ability to communicate with spirits, just as everyone has the ability to play the piano. It's just that some people can play chopsticks, while others can play Mozart. Practice and talent both count. The first step is to try.

Group mediumship is most often done within a circle. A circle of kitchen chairs can be placed close enough together that people can hold hands, or if your séance is in a living room, the circle can be made up of people sitting on sofas and easy chairs.

It's not necessary to dim the lights. Lily Dale mediums often work in well-lighted rooms. But if you hope to see spirits, vapors, or other physical phenomena, candlelight can help your chances. It can also set the scene more dramatically, and since you're doing this, why not go for the atmosphere? To "spook" up the experience, the circle members hoping to see one another shape-shift into other people or animals sometimes put red paper over flashlights and have group members hold the lights under their chins as messages come.

Begin with a prayer for good spirits to come and bad spirits to stay away. Lily Dale mediums believe in God and often invoke him, her, or it. Some mediums open the session with a prayer and end with one so that their awareness is opened to otherworldly beings and then closed so that ordinary life can resume without all sorts of spirited interruptions.

Energy is important in spirit work. So circles often begin with a few easy songs to get a group's vibrations high and in sync. Campfire and nursery songs are good because so many people know them. Hymns are all right too. *Row, Row, Row Your Boat* and *My Bonnie Lies Over the Ocean* seem to be Lily Dale favorites. Rounds are also popular.

Participants then usually sit quietly until the messages start to come. If one of you has given messages before or has a psychic gift of any kind, that person might start by giving the first message. The responsibility can then go around the circle, with each person giving a message to whomever they feel spirit is leading them to choose, or the group can merely sit quietly while anyone who feels she has a message for another person can give it—and others are free to remain silent. Sometimes it's better to put a little pressure on the group by going around the circle, because people giving their first messages won't always know when they have one. If they feel put on the spot, they'll say whatever comes to their mind. And that's the secret of it.

Lily Dale mediums say messages sometimes come as thoughts expressed verbally, but often they come as images that appear in their minds. Mediums might smell a fragrance, hear music, or even see a figure in the room. People giving their first messages are likely to think they don't have anything worth saying. The group should be told to say anything, even when it seems like it doesn't mean anything.

Messages are rarely for the whole group but are more likely to be directed to one person. How do you know who the message is for? Often people who aren't experienced at giving messages will feel drawn to a certain person. That's the first step. Once they focus on that person, the message will come.

Some circles specify a set task. The goal is to demonstrate that whatever comes could not be known by the "medium" unless she or he was actually in touch with another intelligence. Describing something from someone's childhood might be an option, or circle members might try to visualize a person who has passed on, or a message that such a spirit wants to impart. Among Spiritualists who believe in past lives, messages sometimes concern whom people have been at other times and what has happened to them in lives they lived before this one. If the medium is stuck, the person being spoken to might ask a specific question.

Spirit messages are the most common form of mediumship, but groups can also try other types of mediumship. One kind of message comes from objects. In this kind of psychic work, the medium holds a personal possession and gives whatever comes into her mind to the owner of the object. A ring or other piece of jewelry is often used, but book clubbers could also bring objects that have a particular meaning and see if anyone can pick it up.

A third kind of work is called physical mediumship. It's the most difficult and rare kind. In this endeavor, the group might try to bend spoons by concentrating on them. Spoons can be held at either end with the medium exerting only slight pressure. They can be stroked as the medium concentrates. Or the medium can hold the spoons upright so that the stems protrude from her or his closed fist. In this kind of mediumship, the spoon handles are said to twist into curlycue shapes. Forks will also work. Their tines will bend in different directions, according to mediums who say they've done such work.

Table tipping, a type of physical mediumship that was wildly popular in the 1800s, can be done two ways. People can sit around a small table with their hands laid flat, fingers spread. Hands may be positioned so that each person's little fingers are touching someone else's, but fingers don't have to touch. In this kind of mediumship, the table may be implored to rise at one end so that it can tap out the answers to questions. Usually the questions have yes or no answers, and the table taps once for yes and twice for no.

The second kind of table tipping seeks to make the table dance about the room and/or ultimately rise off the floor. If the table is expected to move, séance members usually stand around it with their hands placed lightly on the table, sometimes with only their finger tips touching the surface. If the table begins to move, people try to keep their hands on it while it rocks. A four-legged table can be used, but a pedestal table often produces the best result.

At a table séance people often sing loudly, pray aloud, and implore the table to cooperate. Keeping energy high is key.

One last suggestion. If you believe you've attracted an evil spirit, don't panic. Many Lily Dale mediums believe evil spirits are rare to nonexistent. Any spirit that doesn't seem friendly is probably just confused and lost, they say. You might direct it toward the proverbial light. Or, some mediums say, the spirit might have died suddenly and not be aware that it is actually dead. A gentle reminder of the difference between their state and yours can be enough to cause them to move on. But if none of that seems appropriate and the spirit seems truly menacing, as one long-time medium said, "Just treat them like any other uninvited guest. Tell them to get out." They will, she assured me.

An Interview with Christine Wicker

1. If the book became a major motion picture, what would the ending look like?

It's August. I am in my rental car about to leave Lily Dale. One fifty-ish woman in a black blouse with draping sleeves and another woman in her eighties wearing a blue housedress that matches her eyes stand on the long white porch of a Victorian house festooned with ropes of tiny clear Christmas lights. Stone angels guard the porch entrance. The younger woman yells, "Angel wings. We have to do angel wings." At which point they both straighten their arms and raise them to shoulder level in the position that any third-rate novelist or halfway decent movie fan with the slightest symbolic ability would know is the crucifixion position. But instead of holding their arms still and letting their necks go limp as they ought to, the women begin waving their arms up and down singing in high, clear voices: "Angels have charge over you. Angels, angels, angels go with you." I smile, give them the queen wave, and drive away.

2. Name the four people—living or dead—you would like most to invite to a dinner party at your house. What would you cook?

Jesus, Muhammad, Buddha, and Hitler. I'm fascinated by men who believe they are on earth to bring about the highest and the best. I'd ask them how they think it turned out. Buddha might think he was resting easy, but two of the first things he felt nonattachment for were his wife and child. I'd ask him about that.

I'd serve Jesus bread and wine, of course. I'd give Mohammed a burger, fries, and a Coke. Hitler would have matzo ball soup. And Buddha would get whatever leftovers were in the fridge. He'd like whatever fate brought him.

I'm not sure this is the optimal group for easy camaraderie. But it's my party and I'd like it.

3. Are you a cat person or a dog person?

I'm a dog person. I adore being fawned over whether it's by women, men, or dogs. But don't much care for having my face licked.

4. Of the seven deadly sins (pride, envy, gluttony, lust, anger, greed, and sloth) which one is the hardest for you to resist?

Sloth, of course. I could stay in bed all day. I'm the queen of procrastination, which is actually the only time I do any work. Procrastinating on my current book, I sharpened all the knives in my neighborhood, shined every brass handle, doorknob, and pot in the house, and dug thirteen large bushes out of my yard with a spade. That was just the first month. No effort is too great in defense of sloth.

5. What are you reading right now?

Philip Roth's *The Plot Against America*. In 2004, all the smart people were reading it and telling each other how great it was. I grimaced, sighed, and shrugged whenever they asked if I'd read it. Even the question bored me. I can't bring myself to read any book or watch any television or see any movie that everyone says is great. I don't know why. I've always been that way. I was sixteen before I could pick up a Barbie. I'm just now watching Seinfeld. It's an inconvenient way to be, especially with comedies. He who laughs last, laughs alone.

6. What is your favorite book of all time?

Too hard. I cannot do favorite, most, or least questions. I always warn television interviewers not to ask me one. The entire interview will grind to a halt while I gaze into the ether and ask, "My very favorite? You mean of all time? My very, very favorite?" Once at a neighborhood housewares party the hostess, a darling little cook who was only hoping to make a little spare money without a lot of hassle, started her pitch by asking me what one implement in my kitchen I couldn't live without.

"One?" I asked." One? It has to be one? Ohhhh. I don't know. Implement? It has to be an implement? Ohhhh. Let me think. Live without? Something I can't live without?" This went on and on until the darling cook lost her temper. "Anything. Just say anything," she shouted. But I couldn't. I couldn't.

She had asked what I couldn't live without. I can live without almost anything in my kitchen, of course. I mean how important are kitchen implements? Appliances, maybe. But then again, maybe not even appliances. . . .

Can we skip this one and I'll get back to you?

7. Coffee or tea?

Coffee. That was quick wasn't it?

8. What was the vision, inspiration, or event that first caused you to start writing this story?

I came to Lily Dale while I was a religion reporter for *The Dallas Morning News*. The village charmed me right away. I was especially taken by a story told by the cafeteria cook, who told me Lily Dale was such a gentle place that even the squirrels weren't afraid of the cats. That was what journalists call a story too good to check out.

9. What do you consider your first real piece of writing?

The next one I do.

The first writing I ever did was inspired by a maiden lady poetess in Summerville, South Carolina, named Miss Hayes. She told everyone that I was born to be a writer, and I've never felt more like one than when I was sitting at her kitchen table laboring away with a pencil in my fist and a piece of lined notebook paper in front of me.

Since then I've been, like most writers, always chasing a vision. On the best of days it just barely escapes me and most of the time it leaves me gasping in the dust.

10. What is your favorite memory?

My most favorite? Of all my memories? The most? Okay. Okay. I'm going to walk the dog and when I come back, I'll answer.

I'm back. I'm ready.

I couldn't do it. Here's one that's among my favorites: the day my husband asked me to marry him. He was a disciplined forty-two-year-old bachelor whose house had no clutter and whose day was planned in strict fifteen-minute segments. I knew he loved me but I didn't have much hope that he would be able to deal with a messy procrastinator whose greatest goal is to sit around all day drinking sweet iced tea in the backyard.

On the afternoon he came to my house with the ring, I'd either just done the laundry and dumped it on the living room sofa or more likely, I hadn't done the laundry and dumped it on the living room sofa. He came in and asked me to sit down. I pushed some clothes to the side and sat. He never even looked at them, just got down on his knees and said, "Will you marry me?"

11. If you could live in another time and place, when and where would that be?

I wouldn't want to be without conveniences. Toilets, central air, running water, showers. So that narrows it. The 1920s, I think. No central air, but I'd go north for the summers so that would okay. I'd be a flapper in my early twenties, wild and confident. But I guess I wouldn't live too long because I wouldn't want to be around in the 1930s or during the war and the 1950s were too uptight. The 1960s are remembered as great times, but I was alive then and in the South. Everyone was scared. They thought the country was coming apart.

Now that I think about it, this time right now might be the best time and place of all.

There's a thought I've never had before. Most days I wake up and the newspaper has so much awfulness that I can't face reading it all. And still, I can't think of an extended stretch of time that's been better for more people over a wider scale. So this is it. My best time and place, bad as it is.

12. Who is your oldest friend?

You mean one who is still my friend? Right. Okay. Barbara Burke. She's a beautiful Italian American woman who was my first roommate after college. She's so gorgeous and sexy that every man who sees her is immediately smitten. I had a boyfriend while we were roommates. I've always counted it to my great credit that I would hang around such a beautiful woman. Most women are too smart.

Maybe that's not to my credit. When I had to move home, my boyfriend moved in with her. They were just friends, of course.

Later, her husband was a Secret Service agent for the first President Bush and Bill Clinton. While Clinton was president, Barbara's husband gave us a tour of the White House. We were in the Oval Office when Clinton came striding in. He was bigger, more handsome, and a whole lot sexier than he is on TV. I got a good look at him, but I'm not sure he saw me. He was getting a good look at Barbara.

13. What do *you* consider the absolute most important question to ask someone when you want to find out their deepest and most heartfelt identity?

How do you feel about your mother?

CHRISTINE WICKER,

a religion reporter for the *Dallas Morning News* for seventeen years, has won numerous awards for her journalism. She now lives in Wisconsin with her husband and is the first reporter to write a book on Lily Dale, a town that refused to cooperate with journalists until a few years ago.